The 100-Year Wealth Management Plan

Howard M. Weiss

BOOK IDEA SUBMISSIONS

If you are a C-Level executive or senior lawyer interested in submitting a book idea or manuscript to the Aspatore editorial board, please email jason@aspatore.com. Aspatore is especially looking for highly specific book ideas that would have a direct financial impact on behalf of a reader. Completed books can range from 20 to 2,000 pages – the topic and "need to read" aspect of the material are most important, not the length. Include your book idea, biography, and any additional pertinent information.

Published by Aspatore, Inc.

For corrections, company/title updates, comments or any other inquiries, please e-mail info@aspatore.com.

First Printing, 2004

10 9 8 7 6 5 4 3 2 1

Copyright © 2004 by Aspatore, Inc. All rights reserved. Printed in the United States of America. No part of this publication may be reproduced or distributed in any form or by any means, or stored in a database or retrieval system, except as permitted under Sections 107 or 108 of the United States Copyright Act, without prior written permission of the publisher.

ISBN 1-59622-089-9 Library of Congress Control Number: 2004115070

Material in this book is for educational purposes only. This book is sold with the understanding that neither any of the authors or the publisher is engaged in rendering legal, accounting, investment, or any other professional service. Neither the publisher nor the authors assume any liability for any errors or omissions or for how this book or its contents are used or interpreted or for any consequences resulting directly or indirectly from the use of this book. For legal advice, please consult your personal lawyer.

This book is printed on acid free paper.

The views expressed by the individuals in this book do not necessarily reflect the views shared by the companies they are employed by (or the companies mentioned in this book).

If you are interested in purchasing bulk copies for your team/company with your company logo and adding content to the beginning of the book, or licensing the content in this book (for publications, web sites, educational materials), or for sponsorship, promotions or advertising opportunities, please email store@aspatore.com or call toll free 1-866-Aspatore.

About ASPATORE BOOKS – Publishers of C-Level Business Intelligence

www.Aspatore.com

Aspatore Books is the largest and most exclusive publisher of C-Level executives (CEO, CFO, CTO, CMO, Partner) from the world's most respected companies. Aspatore annually publishes a select group of C-Level executives from the Global 1,000, top 250 professional services firms, law firms (Partners & Chairs), and other leading companies of all sizes. C-Level Business Intelligence ™, as conceptualized and developed by Aspatore Books, provides professionals of all levels with proven business intelligence from industry insiders – direct and unfiltered insight from those who know it best – as opposed to third-party accounts offered by unknown authors and analysts. Aspatore Books is committed to publishing a highly innovative line of business books, and redefining such resources as indispensable tools for all professionals.

The 100-Year Wealth Management Plan

Contents

1	Fifty Questions	9
2	An Introduction to Family Wealth Governance	15
3	Establishing a Family Office	29
4	Selecting the Right Professional Advisors	52
5	Creating an Investment Policy	69
6	Implementing Your Investment Strategy	199
7	Investing for Charitable Entities	236
8	Wealth Transfer Techniques	245
9	Establishing Charitable Structures	277
10	The Role of Insurance	293
11	Concentrated Equity Strategies	311

12	FINANCIAL GOVERNANCE	330
13	ESTABLISHING A TECHNOLOGY PLAN	342
14	THE FAMILY'S 100-YEAR PLAN	346
	APPENDICES	375
	ABOUT THE AUTHOR	473

1

Fifty Questions

Perhaps you just sold the company your grandfather started 100 years ago. Maybe you are a 66-year-old CEO of a public company and have just announced plans to retire next year. On the other hand, you might have just taken over leadership of your family's financial estate following your father's recent death, realizing its great responsibilities since your father always managed the family's investments himself. Whether you are one of these three people or just the head of a wealthy family, you face the daunting task of steering the family's financial ship. How will you do it? We try to show you in the pages of this book, but first, you might want to ask the following fifty questions.

Family Culture and Governance

1. What do we really want to do with our family's money? How much do we invest in financial assets, in the community and in the family itself?
2. Do we wish to establish a culture of entrepreneurship and should the family fund new business ventures of its members?

3. Should we also provide family funds to help its members pursue interests beyond business such as setting up a summer camp for children or a day care center?
4. Do we need a family office and if so, who should run it? What services should it provide to the family members? How much are we willing to spend on it?
5. Do I want our children to be in business together? Should we, their parents, be making that decision for them?
6. How do we effectively invest in family education?
7. Should we have regular family meetings and what are the agendas?

Investing

1. Do I manage our investment portfolio myself, train our children to do so or hire professionals?
2. What type of professional advisors do I need and want? Should we have an overall investment consultant who would recommend and then monitor individual investment managers?
3. How should we select money managers and when do we fire them?
4. What asset classes should we invest in and in what percentages?
5. Should we own hedge funds and if so, how do we go about investing in them?
6. How do we put together the "right team" of managers? How do we blend the various manager styles within each asset class?
7. Should we own tangible assets including real estate, timber, or oil and gas?
8. How do we balance the competing forces of profit taking, portfolio rebalancing and taxes?

9. How do we look at and fully understand the "risk" inherent in the financial markets? Should we have a "safety" portfolio of high- grade municipal bonds and how much should that be?
10. What is the level of assured income we need?
11. How can I manage a large bond portfolio? What are the alternatives in the marketplace and what are the comparative costs?
12. How much should we invest in illiquid assets such as private equity?
13. How do I figure out how much our overall investment program is costing? How do we manage these costs and, more importantly, how do we know whether we are getting our money's worth?
14. Our family's wealth is still concentrated in a single public company. Should we still hold on to this large concentration and what strategies should we employ to manage this risk and even diversify away from it? Is today a good time to sell or hedge the stock?
15. I have substantial stock options, representing an overwhelming share of our family's wealth. When and how should I exercise these options? Can I efficiently manage the taxability between capital gains and current income?
16. Why shouldn't we just invest our financial equities in index funds? What are the differences between index mutual funds and exchange traded funds? Which should I use?

Wealth Transfer

1. If my spouse and I were to die today, what tax bill would our children face? What can we do to minimize it?
2. Should our assets be titled any differently today?
3. Without giving our children and grandchildren direct control over the funds today, what wealth transfer vehicles would be

most efficient for us to employ to transfer parts of our estate to the next generations?
4. I am willing to establish a perpetual fund to benefit future generations. How do I establish this? Also, what are the most efficient ways to utilize our generation skipping transfer tax exemption and how do we keep future estate taxes to a minimum?
5. I heard a lot about family limited partnerships and limited liability companies, but also heard that the IRS is attacking these. I do not like to live on the edge of IRS regulations, so would you advise me to use the FLP format? If, so, how would I structure it considering the makeup of our family assets?
6. We do not want to subject our children to enormous probate expenses. We heard that it can be advantageous to place considerable assets into a revocable trust. Is this true and what are the advantages and drawbacks of this strategy?

Philanthropy

1. We have decided to establish a charitable legacy. How can we establish charitable structures in a tax efficient way?
2. What are the alternatives to setting up a private family foundation and what are the advantages and disadvantages of each?
3. If we establish a private foundation, what resources are available to assist us in managing the grantmaking function? Can I employ family members and what expenses can a family foundation legitimately absorb?

Fiduciary Administration

1. I understand that some state jurisdictions are friendlier for trusts than others. Given our family situation, should we establish our trusts in states other than our "home" state?

2. Which jurisdictions offer asset protection? Are the trusts well protected against divorce and creditors?
3. Should I consider offshore trusts? Are there any meaningful tax advantages?
4. Who should be our trustees? What are the real advantages and disadvantages of a corporate co-trustee? How many trustees should we have? What about succession?

Reporting and Technology

1. We have investments ranging from stocks and bonds to hedge funds, private equity and real estate. How do I keep track of everything and what tools are available to provide us with a consolidated reporting format?
2. How do I establish effective benchmarks for our managers so that the family truly knows how our portfolios are performing? What reporting formats would be informative yet not overwhelming?
3. How do I monitor and evaluate the risk level of the portfolios? What are the effective risk measures we should be using?
4. What are the different family office technology and reporting systems available in the market today?
5. How much money should a family of our wealth spend on reporting and technology, keeping in mind that we do not want overkill?

Insurance and Risk Management

1. Should I have an overall insurance advisor to help us figure out what insurance our family needs and to then evaluate the different products to meet those needs? Or, should we just deal with local insurance agents in life, health and property?

2. Will our heirs have an adequate estate after they pay estate taxes? Do we need a more extensive insurance program to preserve the current value of our estate? How will my insurance needs change over time?
3. What specific life insurance products fit our needs today and which ones will we likely need in the future?
4. Should I be concerned about disability and long-term care risks? How should we insure against these risks?
5. How do I evaluate the features of individual insurance policies?

Banking and Credit

1. When is it efficient to employ leverage in managing an investment portfolio? For example, should I borrow against our municipal bond portfolio to invest in hedge funds?
2. What is the state of the art in banking services today?
3. Leaving investment advisory services aside, what do I look for when choosing a private banker?
4. How does one best manage or leverage a banking relationship?

In the next thirteen chapters of this book, we will hopefully provide answers to these fifty questions and set in motion a family governance plan and legacy that could last for a hundred years and beyond.

2

An Introduction to Family Wealth Governance

Society recognizes "wealth" in many different ways. First, an individual is deemed to be wealthy by his or her material possessions such as mansions, yachts, cars and even private planes. Second, wealth is easily measured in terms of business and financial assets such as family companies, land and investment real estate. Many people would stop here, believing that wealth is measured merely in financial terms. However, enlightened families have realized that their family wealth is also measured by its "intellect," or contribution to the greater society. Families that have employed their wealth to produce physicians, musicians, professors, lawyers and social workers are perhaps the wealthiest of all.

A family invests its money along three different paths. The first and most obvious are *investments in assets*, including financial (stocks, bonds, hedge funds, etc.), business and real property. Also highly visible are a family's *investments in community*, through direct charitable giving, charitable trusts, the local community foundation or a private family foundation. Less visible but of growing importance today are what we call *investments in family*, which uses wealth to support family members in their business and personal endeavors. The objective here is to not only build family financial wealth, but to continually expand its "intellectual capital" by encouraging its members to contribute to each other and to the greater community.

Even wealthy families can face great challenges in trying to preserve and grow their wealth over the generations. Essentially, there are at least three factors that can inhibit their ability to do so. First, there is the tax collector. At the highest marginal tax rate of 55 percent, the estate tax has been the most onerous in the tax code. While the current Bush tax plan envisions an elimination of the estate tax, it is unlikely that Congress will allow its complete phase-out considering the ballooning federal budget deficits at the time of this writing. Second, wealthy families, like the rest of society, are not immune from ill-fated investments. Poor business investments or concentrated equity holdings that collapsed have checkered the landscape over the years. Third, there is the phenomenon of demographics. As succeeding generations expand and multiply, there are more people sharing the original family fortune. Consequently, the overseers must not only grow the assets, but also ultimately find new ways to create wealth.

Preserving and growing wealth over the generations requires proficiency in three areas. The first area lies in how you title the assets. Keeping wealth away from the ravages of taxation requires very skillful estate and tax planning. Accordingly, we saw the emergence of such structures in grantor retained annuity trusts, family limited partnerships, charitable trusts and dynasty trusts. The next area involves how you allocate your wealth among the wide range of asset classes in the marketplace today. Investment experts have long professed that asset allocation provides nearly 90 percent of a portfolio's return. Finally, you must be skillful in how you select individual investments. This entails not only the actual selection of specific securities, real estate or private equity, but also the identification and hiring of investment advisors.

Considering the above backdrop, how then have families managed the complex set of material, financial and intellectual assets over the generations? Historically, families used trust structures as the preferred vehicle to preserve assets and minimize generational transfer taxes. With trust structures, came "trustees" and in many cases, these trustees were institutional trust companies. Over the years, corporate trustees performed admirably in preserving the fortunes entrusted to them. At times, they were criticized for being too conservative and consequently lost market share. However, today, many trust companies have changed their conservative posture and offer access to a wider range of asset classes and investment products. Nevertheless, the concept of having a trustee or trust company at the center of a family's wealth management began to show strains with the enormous liquidation of family business wealth during the 1980's. The critical reason for losing this grip is that while trust companies were arguably very effective in preserving assets and even in helping families administer philanthropic structures, they were not well equipped to oversee the *investments in family* that we referred to above. By their nature, trusts can be restrictive and trustees need to be careful in following the terms of trust instruments. Moreover, children tend to view the provisions of trusts as creations of not only their parents but of the family attorney and corporate fiduciary. As a result, there became a need for a new governing structure to handle the emerging needs of the modern wealthy class even though the concept of using trusts was and still is very valid. Answering this call was the "family office." Before discussing what a family office is and what it does, it is useful to first review the evolution of this concept and structure.

Evolution of the Family Office

One might say that family offices had their origin with the Europeans. Centuries of warfare in continental Europe prompted wealthy aristocrats to safely hide their assets in private financial offices, generally in Switzerland, where they had the added attraction of numbered bank accounts along with universal recognition of that country's political neutrality. More specifically, perhaps the first real semblance of modern day family governance lied with the Rothschilds. In his widely acclaimed book, *Family Wealth: Keeping it in the Family*, James Hughes, Jr., describes the system of family governance established by Meyer Amschel Rothchild, founder of the House of Rothchild.

Essentially, Meyer sent each of his five sons to the five principal financial centers in Europe during the mid-eighteenth century–London, Paris, Frankfort, Vienna and Naples. Their mission was to establish banking businesses in each center. To finance their ventures, Meyer did not just give them the money; instead, he set up a "family bank" whereby he lent each child the funds and required repayment with interest. This way, the family bank would be able to recycle capital in the future. Throughout the next 250 years, the Rothchild family achieved great success despite the setbacks brought on by wars, particularly the Holocaust. They have also been extraordinary philanthropists. However, more than anything, the Rothchilds have shown us the importance of organized family governance.

The genesis of family offices in the United States lies with the industrialists of the late 1800's and particularly with the Rockefellers. After creating and leading the Standard Oil Company to the top of the petroleum industry, John D. Rockefeller, Sr. established a family office in 1882. Its purpose was to provide financial counseling for the family and its emerging foundation. His only son, John D. Rockefeller, Jr., then became the real force behind the development and expansion of both the family office and the Rockefeller Foundation. He was a strong believer in all three aspects of family investing and the results speak for themselves. On the asset management side, the Rockefeller Family Office later evolved into a multi-family office, bringing in other families and managing their wealth alongside the Rockefeller family's wealth. This firm later became Rockefeller & Co., a leading wealth advisory organization, serving high net worth individuals and institutions globally. In the philanthropic field, the Rockefeller Foundation is among the most prestigious in the world, having provided the funding to establish such venerable institutions as the University of Chicago. Equally important, the family has employed its wealth to enable family members to pursue careers and achieve great leadership roles in government, international banking and philanthropy.

Alongside the Rockefellers, another great industrialist pioneered the concept of the family office, taking it a step further to ultimately become what is now one of the largest multi-family office organizations. In 1861, Henry Phipps invested with his boyhood friend, Andrew Carnegie, in an iron works operation in Pittsburgh. This operation later became known as the Carnegie Steel Company and in 1901, they sold it to J.P. Morgan. The company then became known as U.S. Steel. A few years later, in 1907, Henry Phipps established a family office to handle the investing for the $50 million he received from the sale of Carnegie Steel. He named this family office "The Bessemer Trust Company," after the Bessemer Process, which was the first industrial process for mass producing steel from molten pig iron. The process was named after Henry Bessemer who took out a patent on the process in 1855. This process was instrumental in helping Carnegie and Phipps build their great fortunes. The Bessemer Trust Company exclusively managed the assets for the Phipps heirs until 1974, when it began to take in non-family clients. Today it manages over $40 billion for over 1800 clients. Bessemer serves as an example of how a single- family office can grow into a multi-family office trust company.

Another "captain of industry" and contemporary of Rockefeller and Phipps, John Pitcairn, also contributed to the creation and growth of the family office form of governance. Pitcairn was a co-founder of the Pittsburgh Plate Glass Company and like many of his time, strongly believed in preserving family fortunes through good financial stewardship. He passed his philosophies on to his three sons who established Pitcairn Trust in 1923. The company followed the pattern of Bessemer where it managed the family monies for a number of years and then opened their doors to outside clients. Today, Pitcairn manages $2.4 billion for around 350 clients. Of these clients, 90 are family members. The company is still solely owned by the Pitcairn Family.

After these early industrialists, the family office industry remained somewhat dormant for nearly 60 years. America fought two world wars and survived a ravaging depression before a new economic era began following the return of our soldiers from the Second World War. For the next 40 years or so, an emerging class of family business owners led America through a golden age of economic growth and prosperity. Individual entrepreneurs started new businesses or substantially expanded businesses that their parents and grandparents started before them. These business owners constantly reinvested their earnings back into the family business and looked at their companies as their total investment portfolio. Investing in the securities markets was of secondary importance to most.

However, the landscape began to change one August day in 1982. By mid-August of that year, the Dow Jones Industrial Average sank below 800 and on August 16th, closed at 792.43. The next day, while we were still in the midst of the highest interest rate period in history and while economic prospects were still grim, the stock market, on extraordinary strong volume in excess of 900,000 shares, soared nearly 39 points and we began a new chapter in our financial history. After living through years of languishing stock prices, corporate leaders soon realized that the inherent value of certain underlying company assets far exceeded the market prices placed on them by Wall Street. This realization ushered in the greatest period of corporate mergers, acquisitions and leveraged buy-outs. Corporate managers believed it was far more efficient to buy a company on Wall Street than to build new plants, create new products or enter new markets directly. The new wave of mergers began in the oil industry but rapidly spread to other sectors as well. Moreover, these activities moved from Wall Street to Main Street as many family businesses became targets of acquisition. Families that always believed their company would be passed down from generation to generation suddenly found themselves with "offers they could not refuse."

Accordingly, during the 1980's, we began to witness the liquidation of enormous wealth from the businesses that families built over the prior half-century or more. Family operating businesses became wealth management firms or investment companies overnight. For many families, this was the first time they had any appreciable liquid wealth and, for the most part, were not structured to handle it. It had been many decades since we last witnessed the unleashing of such great financial wealth. Nevertheless, this new wealthy class soon began to find the answers about managing and governing wealth from their predecessors of nearly a hundred years before. Like the Rockefellers, Phipps and Mellons before them, many in the class of the 1980's looked to the "family office" as a way to govern their wealth. As a result, we saw the re-emergence of the family office. Furthermore, over the ensuing years of the 80's and early 90's, the family office actually evolved into a true industry within the financial services arena.

Just as we were witnessing the enormous liquidation of family business wealth, a new form of economic revolution was taking hold. This revolution, centered around the internet, has forever changed the way we communicate. In a certain respect, an entirely new economy has emerged around it. New corporate powerhouses such as Microsoft, Intel, Oracle and Cisco now dot the landscape. All of this spawned a new class of multi-millionaires who were suddenly faced with the challenges brought on by the realization of substantial wealth. At the same time, the soaring stock market enabled corporations to radically scale up the pay of their executives. Employing a pay-for-performance philosophy, corporate boards began to base most of an executive's pay on stock options. Accordingly, the better the company performed and the higher its stock price, the more compensation its executives received. As a result, still another wealthy class began to emerge. The new economy wealthy class differed from its predecessors in several important ways. It is instructive to look at these differences before proceeding:

- The new economy millionaires made their money much faster than the prior generation. In some cases, they made it in as little as three to five years. With the old economy, it took business owners several decades to realize their wealth.
- Many in the new economy are young and have young children or no children. In old economy families, they generally have adult children who may have also been participants in the business. As a result, the ownership structures are generally more complex as the stock has been distributed to the children and even grandchildren.
- Old economy families tend to favor real estate as an alternative investment, while the new economy families favor private equity and venture capital since they may have started that way.
- The old economy families are usually concerned with safety nets for future generations, reflecting in many cases the parents growing up in poor neighborhoods. In some cases, they even lived through the depression. Some new economy millionaires believe they can make the money all over again since they made it once and made it quickly.

- The philosophy toward philanthropy is also different between the two groups. The old economy families believe in giving back to the communities where they lived and worked. They tend to support the local hospitals, homeless shelters, universities and museums. The new economy philanthropist approaches giving like an entrepreneur. They are not interested in just throwing money at a problem or just supporting an institution. Instead, they look for organizations that offer attractive solutions. They want to "invest" in programs that can be models which can then be replicated around the country.
- Finally, there is one overarching difference between these groups. The new economy wealthy class did not experience a bear market until 2000, while the old economy families lived through good and bad times. Some of the new economy millionaires were ill prepared for the ravaging bear market which zeroed in on the technology and telecommunications sectors. The old economy millionaires more than likely had significant municipal bond portfolios and real estate to get them through the past few years.

The new economy wealthy class also needed to deal with not just investing their money, but governing their wealth. For many, the solution again lied in some form of family office. The family offices of these new economy entrepreneurs very much reflect the business attitudes and lifestyle of this group.

Who Needs a Family Office?

While we may give the family office concept a great deal of coverage in this book, it is by no means the only form of family wealth governance. Moreover, it is not for everyone. Families with substantial wealth may find this form of governance unnecessary or ill-advised. Let's first look at who a family office is best designed for:

- Families that have wealth that is likely to last for multiple generations. If your wealth is going to run out in the next fifty years or so, it is not worth the expense of establishing a formal family office. You should just transfer the money to the next generation.
- Families that have a need for complex ownership structures and have multiple ownership levels. Many families have or had businesses and needed to downstream the ownership to successive generations in order to mitigate the future impact of transfer taxes. Additionally, others have established family limited partnerships as vehicles to manage investments and gift assets to the next generations. Still others have established such wealth transfer structures as grantor retained annuity trusts and even certain charitable trusts as efficient ways to move family assets to children and grandchildren. As a result, the family may have in place a number of involved structures, and in many cases, has not equipped the next generation with the tools and skills to oversee them. Accordingly, family offices can oversee the creation and, more importantly, the administration of these structures.
- Families that wish to invest in common vehicles and are willing to make financial decisions through group consensus.
- Families that want to have a structure for efficiently managing the costs of multiple providers. In other words, they wish to achieve the benefits of group purchasing.
- Families that have a strong interest in philanthropy and wish to implement their charitable giving as a family unit.
- Families that want to have a mechanism for educating and training the next generation on financial and investment matters so that they are ready to take over the supervision of the family's wealth when their time comes.

On the other hand, family offices are not suitable for the converse of the above. For example, families that have simple ownership structures and few children probably do not need a family office and can manage their wealth entirely through traditional financial institutions. Also, family groups that wish to go their separate ways and not invest in common and not conduct philanthropic activities together will not want a formal family office. Finally, some family patriarchs and matriarchs do not wish to impose a formal structure on their heirs forever. Accordingly, these people will tend to just divide up the family fortune among their children and expect them to do the same.

When Do You Set Up the Family Office?

If the family office form of governance is right for you, when do you establish one? While there is no hard and fast rule as to when these should be established, here are some common times during an individual's life cycle:

- The most common time is after a major liquidity event such as the sale of a family company. Here, the family wealth moves from being tied up in an operating company to being a quasi investment firm. Financial services that may have been provided by the company now need to be acquired directly by the family members. Examples could include: health, property and liability insurance; retirement fund management; tax reporting and; banking services.
- Similarly, a family office might be established when the company does an initial public offering and the family wishes to separate its personal affairs from that of the now public company.
- Corporate CEOs and other senior executives will establish family offices upon retirement or shortly before, especially if they are in the process of monetizing their stock holdings. With the recent

corporate office abuses, we could, in fact, begin to see more executives separate their personal affairs from the executive office suite.
- Some families, who previously saw no urgent need for a formal governance structure, may begin to establish one as the founding patriarch and matriarch age. This is especially the case where none of the children are in a position to manage the family's investment portfolios and coordinate its tax, insurance and wealth transfer programs.
- Families that have large trust complexes and partnership structures may ultimately want a family office or similar entity to oversee the management of their wealth.

A Journey through the Book

We are now ready to embark on the journey of managing wealth for today's ultra high net worth individuals and families. Before summarizing the basic contents of each chapter, let's review the primary mission of this book. First, I attempt to provide the reader with ideas for governing family wealth, whether that is in the form of a family office or some other structure. Second, I will provide the reader with a series of templates to assist in establishing investment policies, risk management structures, concentrated equity strategies, wealth transfer techniques and performance monitoring procedures. Third, I will introduce the reader to the range of products and resources available in the marketplace to assist them in managing their wealth. At the same time, it is important to emphasize what this book is not. First, I will not be providing specific legal and tax advice. For this, you need to consult your own attorney and CPA, as this advice needs to be very specific to your situation. Second, I will also refrain from providing specific investment recommendations, as you need to obtain that from your own investment advisor who will determine the proper course of action based on your risk tolerance and objectives. Third, I will not recommend any specific financial services firm for any product or service, as you need to again obtain that advice from your respective advisors.

Regarding the book itself, we begin in chapter three with a discussion on how to set up and operate a new family office once you have decided upon that form of wealth management governance. In chapter four, we review the process for managing your advisors, including lawyers, accountants, insurance agents, investment managers and a range of others.

We then begin a multi-chapter discussion on some of the key functionalities of family wealth management, whether or not they are conducted within a formal family office. In chapters five and six, we cover extensively the process of formulating and implementing a comprehensive family investment policy. We particularly focus on how to design a formal investment policy statement that effectively serves as the overall governing instrument for implementing the family's investment program.

Additionally, we thoroughly cover asset allocation, investment manager selection and performance monitoring. Investing today is more than allocating assets into traditional financial markets. There is a growing trend to allocate some wealth into real assets such as investment real estate, timber, farms and ranchland, and oil & gas properties. In addition, investors have enthusiastically committed monies to hedge funds. As a result, we will cover why these asset classes are attractive along with ways to invest in them.

As many wealthy families also have charitable foundations, we will briefly apply some of these investment techniques to foundations in chapter seven. Wealth transfer is the topic of chapters eight and nine. In chapter eight, we explore the range of estate planning techniques that many wealthy individuals and families employ, including the ways family limited partnerships and limited liability companies are used.

We then examine the range of charitable options in chapter nine, looking at the types of charitable trusts as well as alternatives to formal private family foundations. We elected to look at the topic of insurance and personal risk management in chapter ten, even though we will refer to various insurance techniques throughout the book. Insurance is a critical part of a family's wealth management plan and does not work in isolation from its other components; however, from an oversight and governance standpoint, it can be instructive to look at this topic as one discipline.

Another risk component in a family's portfolio is concentrated equity holdings, particularly of public or even private companies that the family does not control and operate. In chapter eleven, we look at the various methods for managing and diversifying away from this risk. We also discuss some of the basic aspects of managing corporate stock options. Titling and governing the assets is the topic of chapter twelve as we explore the alternative trust and fiduciary structures that families put into place to mitigate the impact of wealth transfer and certain state taxes as well as to efficiently carry out the wishes of the original grantors. In this chapter, we will specifically discuss the selection and role of trustees along with the various aspects of governing family trusts. Investors that have complex trust and partnership structures, coupled with multiple money managers, require the right reporting systems.

Reporting is proving to be one of the great challenges for family offices and we will suggest, in chapter thirteen, a process for managing your way through it. Concluding the book is a capstone chapter on what we term "The 100 Year Plan." Here we try to tie everything together to provide the reader with a process for formulating his and her family's vision and mission. We also suggest some ideas for establishing and building a family culture and ultimately, its legacy.

3
Establishing a Family Office

You have decided to set up your own family office. So how do you go about doing it and what do you want it to look like? Do you want it to arrange travel for family members, invest money, prepare income tax returns, pay bills, buy insurance, manage the family foundation, obtain credit cards or teach the next generation about wealth management? Or, do you want it to do all of these things? Arguably, the most important time for a family office is when you start it. It is critical to define the mission of the office and its initial range of services. A bad beginning could very well sink the family office altogether.

Our discussion will focus on seven major points:

1. Alternative structures
2. Family office types
3. The lifecycle of a family office
4. Staffing
5. Universal roles of family offices
6. Best practices
7. Cost and tax structures

Alternative Structures

You will generally begin by considering the global structure you wish to have–there are three major alternatives. The first is a *stand-alone* family office. As the name implies, here you establish a family office that just serves your own family, which of course could include parents, children and grandchildren. It can also include two or more families where the patriarchs and matriarchs are siblings. Advantages of this format are confidentiality, control and buying power. However, compared to other structures, this format is more expensive since you need to hire your own staff and provide for all of your overhead including office space, computers, etc. Also, your family needs to get along well together and have a somewhat common investing outlook. Finally, you have the issue of succession should your family office executive leave. There are an estimated 3,500 recognized stand-alone family offices in the U.S., with perhaps thousands more that are very private and therefore not visible for counting among these numbers.

A second alternative is the *multi-family office*. There are actually several definitions for a multi-family office but for the purposes of our discussion, we are defining it as a family office that serves more than one core family group. Moreover, at least one and generally several of these families are not descendents of or related to the original founding family. An advantage of joining a multi-family office is that you can share overhead expenses and participate in the buying power of a larger group. Additionally, multi-family offices can command the attention of top investment advisors so you can gain access to managers that may have higher account minimums than you are able to meet alone. The drawbacks of this structure could be your compatibility with the managing family, less direct control than if you had your own structure and a limited investment menu in some cases. There are an estimated 50 multi-family offices in the country but the industry is growing.

The third alternative is the *institutional* approach. Here you engage an institution to serve as your family office. This institution could be a private bank/trust company, brokerage firm, law or accounting firm or a stand-alone company specializing in family office services. A key advantage of this format is that you do not need to have a formal structure along with its overhead. You can also take advantage of a wide array of investment products and fiduciary services should you engage a large private bank/brokerage complex. In fact, many of these firms now offer a more "open architecture" where you have access to a wide array of third-party managers and products, including those of competitor firms. With an institution, you also gain the benefit of their fiduciary liability and with a large institution, you have the added advantage of their "deep pockets." Large institutions generally stand behind their products and services and will readily reimburse you for their errors and omissions. On the other hand, some point to the disadvantages of staff turnover, biased advice and less control when you employ a large institution to serve as your family office.

What structure is right for you? As you might expect, this depends upon the dynamics of your family as well as the size and complexity of your assets. I should also point out that these structures are not necessarily mutually exclusive. For example, most stand-alone offices will engage institutions to provide a range of services to them in the form of investment management, trust administration and custody. Even multi-family offices will use large financial institutions for many of those same services.

Family Office Types

Once you decide upon the structure for your family office, you then need to determine what functionalities it will perform. However, if you decide on a stand-alone family office, there is an important intermediary step, which is to determine the specific type of family office you wish to have. To assist in this evaluation, we display in exhibit 3-A the six common types of family offices. The source for this exhibit is an article written by Sara Hamilton, founder of the Family Office Exchange, in the August 1977 issue of *Trusts & Estates* magazine. Many family offices take on one of these forms while others take on a hybrid of two or more. Nevertheless, it is instructive to approach the design of a family office from these distinct perspectives and we will consider each, in turn.

EXHIBIT 3–A

FAMILY OFFICE TYPES

Compliance	Investments	Philanthropy
• Tax reporting • Insurance • Record keeping	• Direct investing • Investment manager • Investment consultant • Business investing • Managing concentrations	• Large foundation • Pooling of gifts • Targeted giving

FAMILY OFFICE TYPES

Financial	Private Trust Company	Multi-Client Office
• Investment advisory and execution • Integrated wealth planning • Financial reporting • Financial education	• Control • Perpetuate family • Consolidate assets	• Need for revenue • Cost sharing • Business ventures

Compliance

A basic and very common form of family office is the compliance format. Here the focus is on making sure the family members adhere to all tax rules and file timely returns. Additionally, the office makes sure that effective insurance coverage exists for family members whether that entails life, property & liability, health care or long-term care. Also part of the compliance-oriented office is a strong reporting structure where family members receive comprehensive and timely reports on investment activities. In this format, the individual in charge is generally a CPA type who is well versed in tax planning and risk management. In many cases, the tax preparation work is actually performed in house. The investment functions are generally outsourced.

Investments

As the name implies, the focus of this type of family office is the management of assets. Families that establish this format seek to achieve the economies of pooling the family's assets as well as the centralized coordination and monitoring of the portfolios. Families that have significant equity concentrations will also find this format attractive especially if they are engaged in diversification strategies. The person running this type of family office is most likely an investment-trained family member or hired professional. An interesting point, however, is that family offices of this type will not necessarily manage all of its assets in house. They frequently hire external managers and advisors. Many investment-oriented family offices will also outsource the tax preparation and reporting activities.

Investment-oriented family offices also display different styles, with at least the following four as common ones:

Direct Investing

This is the type of office that does handle its own investing directly. They will frequently have internal analysts/portfolio managers and maintain a series of brokerage relationships to handle the securities trading. This is not a very common structure today but some families handle this very effectively.

Investment Manager

Under this format, the family office staff directs the asset allocation and sets strategies for each of the asset classes. It also decides on the types of investment vehicles such as mutual funds, separate accounts, exchange traded funds, etc. Then, the staff hires individual investment managers or purchases mutual funds where appropriate.

Investment Consultant

Here you actually bring in an advisor to do many of the oversight functions, including asset allocation and asset class strategies, investment manager selection and performance monitoring. In some cases, a family may have multiple consultants, particularly where they engage bank/brokerage advisors who offer comprehensive consulting, manager, trading and reporting platforms.

Direct Business Investing

Where a family is involved in buying direct ownership in real estate, private companies and other investments such as oil & gas properties, they may predominately staff their family office with experts in those fields. The family office therefore takes on the look of a real estate investment or private equity firm. Another activity could be hedge fund investing. Some families invest heavily in hedge funds and may actually run their own fund of funds for family members. Such operations may even grow to later include outside investors. In many situations, this family office type does not invest a substantial portion of its assets in the traditional stocks and bonds and consequently looks more like an operating business.

Philanthropy

Some wealth creators take the bold step of putting a substantial portion of their assets into a charitable foundation. At the same time, family members may be employed by the foundation or become directors of it. Accordingly, within some family offices, the foundation itself becomes the dominant structure and is the center of activity. The foundation may also hire professional program and financial staff. The foundation may also dominate the investment activities and family members may even invest in some of the same strategies employed by their foundation.

Financial

Wealthy families willing to invest significant resources in a family office may opt for a completely integrated financial model. Here the family office may have an internal chief investment officer along with tax, accounting and estate planning expertise. They may also have a technology expert to integrate all of the reporting systems. This family office type is also used as an entity to train the next generation of family leaders and effectively serves as a center for family education.

Private Trust Company

Some families have large, complex multi-generational trusts with difficult-to-manage assets. Embetted within these trust structures could be layers of partnerships. There could also be very significant single stock concentrations. This generally causes consternation for independent, non-family trustees such as bank trust departments and even certain law firms. Conflicts are sometimes inevitable between beneficiaries and trustees over control of the investment decisions. As a result, some families have established their own private trust companies. Aside from giving the family added control over the decision-making, private trust companies can perpetuate the family name and provide future generations with a place to consolidate and govern their assets. We will discuss the private trust company concept in greater detail in chapter twelve.

Multi-Client Office

Some of the family office types lend themselves for expansion beyond its founding family. For example, family offices that purchase real estate or buy private companies can readily bring in other partners. Families that operate their own hedge fund programs frequently bring in other investing partners. As a result, these offices evolve into investment firms that are called "multi-family offices." At the same time, they begin to provide these new investors/partners with some of the other investment and administrative services it provides to the host family. Families that elect this structure will do so for a few reasons. They may want the additional capital to make their deals work. In other cases, they may want additional revenue to offset some of the costs to operate their office. Some families may just look at this structure as an opportune business venture.

The Lifecycle of a Family Office

When considering the range of options when establishing your family office, you should step back for a moment and reflect on the expected life cycle of a typical family office. Exhibit 3-B summarizes these life cycle stages. While each family has its unique characteristics and the longevity of any family office certainly depends on the extent of the family's wealth, there are some common trends worth considering:

EXHIBIT 3–B
FAMILY OFFICE LIFECYLE

First Generation	Second to Third Generation
• Integrated with family operating business • Use of company personnel	• Independent entity • Philanthropic structures • Wealth transfer to children / grandchildren

FAMILY OFFICE LIFECYLE

Fourth to Fifth Generation	Fifth to Seventh Generation
• Active philanthropy • Extended generational planning • Formalized investment program	• Income stress • Business investments • Solicit additional families • Private trust companies

First Generation

As expected, most family offices originate within the family operating business. In many cases, the family financial office remains within the company until the founder retires or the business is sold. Frequently, company personnel, particularly the controller or CFO, handle many of the family office functions for the shareholder family. As most of the family's wealth is still tied up in the company, the family office function is generally very light at this stage.

Second to Third Generation

At this stage, the family office is separated from an operating business, either because the family sold the business or the founder retired and wants to separate the family business from the company's business. The family office is now an independent entity. You begin to see a more formalized investment policy with money managers in place. Significant wealth is being transferred to the next generation if it had not already taken place before the business was sold. Philanthropic structures are being formed. Some families will begin to embark on its next business venture at this time, whether it is real estate or private equity investing.

Fourth to Fifth Generation

By this time, successful financial families have very formalized investment programs in place ranging from a broadly diversified money manager structure to extensive real estate, private equity and hedge fund programs. They have efficiently transferred wealth to the next generations and consequently mitigated the impact of inheritance taxes. An active family foundation is in place. On the other hand, there are other families that have not begun to plant the seeds for new wealth creation and are more consumers than investors. These families will begin to face the real possibility of going from "shirt sleeves to shirt sleeves"; in other words, they may run out of money.

Fifth to Seventh Generation

Even successful family offices may begin to feel the stress between family demographics and wealth creation by the fifth generation. By this time, families have expanded to a level that begins to tax the ability of its wealth to generate adequate income to support everyone in the lifestyle they have become accustomed to. Accordingly, it becomes imperative that the family find ways to recreate wealth all over again. Engaging in successful business ventures becomes a priority along the way. Some family offices begin to think about converting into multi-family offices, bringing in new families to help defray costs or generate revenue.

Establishing a Family Office

Long range planning and foresight are so critical for families and family offices that want to survive and prosper into the future. Failing to plan properly will most certainly result in going from "shirt sleeves to shirt sleeves in three generations."

Staffing

Who runs a family office? As with other aspects of family offices, there is no set pattern. Families choose from a range of people to operate their offices. Consider some of the following:

- The person who made the money is always an option. In many cases, the patriarch or matriarch will sit at the head of the table until they grow older and elect to turn over the reigns to their children or someone else.
- Some families have brought along one or more of their children to assume leadership positions in overseeing the family wealth. In such cases, one of the children is in a position to run the family office.
- It is sometimes tricky if more than one child is ready or wants to assume this leadership role. The parents need to then choose, potentially creating future family conflict.
- Frequently, a trusted advisor is tapped to run a family office. Examples include a long time family attorney or CPA who may wish to retire from practice and become a family office director.
- Alternatively, the family may hire a law firm or accounting firm that may offer family office management services.
- Ex-bankers sometimes lead family offices, particularly where the focus may be investment management, private equity or real estate. Private bankers or investment bankers are generally capable of overseeing money managers and

investment bankers can frequently handle private equity and venture capital investing. Real estate lenders are sometimes at the helm where the family is focused on building a real estate business.

- A very common director is the ex-CFO of the company, whether it was a family operating business or a public corporation. Many CEOs and family business owners, who have trusted their chief financial person for many years while running the company, are quite comfortable to have them oversee their personal financial fortune later on. Moreover, in many cases, the CEO or founder's family knows the CFO very well and is also willing to trust that person with oversight of their wealth.
- On the other hand, it is not uncommon for a family to tap a "trusted friend" from childhood or college. An interesting facet of family offices is that the most important attribute of the person leading it is how much the family knows and trusts you. Many believe that a person with good business sense can learn the basics while looking out for the best interests of the family.
- Finally, some families do go outside their sphere of contacts and search for an experienced family office executive. You will more frequently find this practice among some (but not all) of the larger, sophisticated offices. Even when this occurs, there is usually a family member or a close trusted advisor working in the family office.

Universal Roles of Family Offices

In the chapters that follow, we will cover, in depth, the roles of family offices, but in this introductory chapter, we will summarize some of their major oversight duties. Exhibits 3-C and 3-D provide basic organization templates of the various functions commonly performed in family offices. We will consider each major category in turn.

EXHIBIT 3–C

ROLES OF THE FAMILY OFFICE

Asset management	Tax management & wealth transfer	Financial administration
• Investment policies and guidelines • Concentrated single stock strategies • Real estate management • Private business oversight	• Leading edge estate planning • Tax compliance & reporting • Tax efficient investment management • Philanthropic objectives and structures	• Trust & partnership structures • Technology, reporting & integration • Expense management & bill paying • Family meetings & education

Banking & credit	Insurance & risk management
• Investment banking • Business and lifestyle credit • Deposits & transactions • Efficient use of leverage	• Life insurance strategies • Property & casualty analysis • Health & disability • Long term care

Asset Management

Central to any family office is some form of investment oversight. A primary role is to insure that formal investment policies are established and preferably, in the form of a written investment policy statement.

They are then responsible for effectively implementing the program, including the oversight of investment managers and advisors. Where the family has its wealth concentrated in a single stock, the family office is usually tasked with developing diversification strategies to manage that risk. Family offices may also manage real estate and private business assets. These business assets could range from farms and ranchland to timber, oil & gas properties and even small operating businesses.

Tax Management & Wealth Transfer

Preserving wealth today requires highly efficient tax planning and management. Some family offices are set up exclusively for this purpose. Families look to its staff, along with external legal and tax counsel, to provide leading edge (but safe) estate planning advice and to insure that all tax reporting is accurate and timely. This also includes implementing appropriate charitable vehicles. In recent years, families have also tasked their offices to develop better tax efficient investment management, seeking advisors who can deliver better after-tax returns.

Financial Administration

Families who go through the time and expense of establishing a formal family office expect to have their financial affairs managed far more efficiently than if they continued to manage them by themselves. First, a centralized family financial office can oversee the administration of trusts and partnership structures, working daily with trustees and business partners. In particular, they are there to work through any problems and disagreements that take place between beneficiaries and trustees as well as between partners. Second, families with many individuals and complex financial structures, require specialized reporting that may only be provided through advanced technology platforms. It therefore takes a family office staff versed in accounting and computer skills to create those platforms. Third, some use their family offices as the "whipping boy" to keep provider costs as low as possible. Fourth, family offices can be effective in coordinating communication among members, including the design of and preparations for family meetings.

Banking & Credit

An important and sometimes involved function is the acquisition of various banking services for family members. Family office staff will become engaged at several levels. All family members generally need checking accounts and credit cards and some will want custom mortgages. Others may purchase boats or even planes and therefore require specially structured credit facilities. Family office staff provides a comfortable service to its members when it can do their negotiating with the bank for all of these credit and banking needs, taking advantage of relationship pricing. At the higher end, family office staff can advise individuals on the efficient use of leverage for financing investments, including interest rate swaps during the right interest rate climate. Finally, family offices can arrange investment banking facilities when the family wants to sell an operating business or if it wants to do a secondary offering for a large concentrated holding.

Insurance and Risk Management

Purchasing insurance can also be an involved process for wealthy families and a knowledgeable family office can provide measurable benefits to its members through effective analysis, coordination and negotiation. Family office staff can oversee the evaluation of family life insurance needs and recommend the most effective products for providing them. It can also look at various ways insurance can be used to build wealth and determine if any are appropriate. It can likely save the family meaningful money on property & casualty insurance through negotiating on behalf of all family members as a package. For some members, health, disability and long-term care insurance may be prudent and again, the family office can be tasked with obtaining these.

Exhibit 3–D
Financial Organization Template

Banking & Transactions
- Checking accounts
- Cash management
- Debit cards / transfers
- Use of credit

Staff
- Payroll
- Tax reporting
- Banking services
- Bill paying

Business & Lifestyle Credit
- Leveraging portfolio
- Business investments
- Aircraft & yacht financing
- Fine art lending

Insurance
- Life
- House, autos, collectibles
- Liability
- Health and long term care

Advanced Life Insurance
- Private placement life insurance
- Premium financing
- Foreign variable universal life

Insurance Providers
- Direct underwriters
- Brokers
- Consultants
- Family office insurers

Investment Policy
- Risk profile
- Concentrated equity strategies
- Asset allocation
- Manager search, & implementation

Equity Concentrations
- Financial derivative solutions
- Exchange funds
- Estate planning techniques
- Charitable structures

Cash Management
- Mutual funds
- Trading desk
- Separate account management
- Pooled fund

Financial Organization Template

Alternative Investments
- Allocation commitment
- Real estate
- Private equity
- Hedge funds
- Natural resources

Hedge Funds
- Strategy
- Direct investing
- Sector investing
- Fund of funds
- Due diligence

Private Equity
- Strategy
- Direct investing
- Individual funds
- Fund of funds
- Secondary market

Wealth Transfer
- Personal estate plan
- Family partnerships
- Offshore trusts
- Life insurance trusts
- Retirement funds

Charitable Structures
- Charitable annuities
- Charitable trusts
- Donor advised funds
- Private foundation
- Supporting organization

Philanthropy
- Fields of interest / issues
- Monetary commitment
- Structures
- Governance
- Grantmaking policies

Real Property Management
- Real estate
- Timber
- Farm & ranchland
- Oil & gas
- Tax free exchanges

Administration
- Bill paying
- Distribution policies
- Unitized payments
- Fees
- Opening & closing

Taxes
- Arrange tax preparation
- Tax positioning in portfolio
- Tax efficient investing
- Wealth transfer / charitable impact

Financial Organization Template

Trust Management	International	Reporting
• Term • Tax situs • Asset protection • Trustee selection • Trust protector	• Foreign non-grantor trust • International Business Corporations • Jurisdictions • Foundations • PIC	• On-line banking • On-line portfolios • Unitized accounting • Transaction auditing • Aggregation

Collectibles	Advisors	Education
• Art • Antique cars • Jewelry • Furniture • Oriental rugs	• Legal • Tax • Investment • Insurance • Business	• Banking products • Financial markets • Risk management • Money management industry • Taxes & wealth transfer

Best Practices

Well functioning family offices display similar patterns, including a combination of the following:

- The family is always able to reach consensus on major issues, even if there are differences in opinion from time to time.
- The family office is able to assemble the best team of strategic advisors with no private agendas or conflicts of interest.
- The director's skills match the financial mission of the office.
- The office outsources the right things, seeking highly capable providers who can handle certain functions more effectively than the family office itself.
- The office balances fees and performance of providers, understanding that "cheaper is not always better."
- The office employs the right level of technology at the right cost. There is no need to overkill.
- The family expends the effort to educate its members and trains the next generation for future leadership.

Cost Structures

Finally, we arrive at the issue of how much it costs to operate a family office and manage someone's wealth. We might first look at the various fees and expenses a family pays to run its financial affairs and then examine some of the considerations when structuring the family office.

The range of fees and expenses include the following:

- Director's compensation
- Staff salaries and bonuses
- Occupancy expenses including rent, telecommunications, utilities, etc.
- Computers and other equipment
- Attorney fees
- CPA expenses including tax preparation
- Insurance premiums
- Banking service charges
- Investment consulting fees
- Investment manager fees
- Trustee fees
- Board of advisor fees

An important best practice is to effectively balance costs, efficiencies and effectiveness. Here are some of the issues and trade-offs you need to consider when putting together a family office:

- What do you outsource and how will you measure its effectiveness?
- What is an appropriate level of overall expenses given the size of the family's wealth?

- How do you manage overall investment management costs? Is the performance justifying the expense? How do you lower the costs?
- While you will never eliminate the need for external legal services, at what point should you have in-house legal counsel to help guide the family office staff on a daily basis?
- Should you prepare your own tax returns or have your CPA do them? At what point do you change? Should you have an experienced tax expert on staff?
- How can you allocate the costs of running the family office among all family members who benefit from it?

Once the costs are in place, some family offices want to have a process and methodology for allocating the expenses to the various family members it serves. There are a several ways to accomplish this, depending upon your operating philosophy as well as tax strategies. Here are some options:

- Utilization of services by each family member
- Asset size
- Ability to pay
- Billable hours
- Estate tax minimization
- Income tax minimization

Tax Deductibility of Costs

Everyone is naturally interested in best positioning expenses to gain the most favorable tax treatment. Certain regulations will provide guidance and we will consider some of those below:

- First, there are the **section 162 expenses.** These are expenses incurred in carrying out a trade or business. Examples are real estate and an operating business. Such expenses are deductible without limitation.
- Next, there are **section 212 expenses.** These involve costs related to the production of investment income and may include financial planning, legal and tax preparation fees. Such expenses are deductible subject to the 2% limitation of the taxpayer's adjusted gross income. They are further subject to the 3% phase out of the itemized deductions if income is above certain thresholds. Furthermore, these expenses are not deductible for AMT purposes.
- There is special consideration for **trust expenses.** These expenses are related to the administration of trusts or estates and would not have been incurred if the assets were not in trust form. These costs are deductible without limitation. Keep in mind that investment management expenses are outside of this.
- Finally, we should speak about direct income that the actual family office receives. Any fees received from family members or external clients are considered as taxable income to the family office. However, contributions of capital to fund the infrastructure of the family office are generally not considered as income. For individual family members, fees paid to the family office as compensation for services, are treated as section 212 expenses on their individual tax returns.

One should again consult with his/her tax advisor before implementing any cost allocation program and structuring expenses for tax purposes, so as to keep clear of any IRS problems.

In concluding this section, it is important to comment on the compensation for the family office director and key staff members, particularly if they are non-family professionals. The Family Office Exchange conducts several studies and writes white papers on the subject of compensation and I invite you to consult their website for more detailed information. At this time, however, we will summarize some of the key elements of family office executive compensation.

- As with any job, you have a base salary along with an annual cash bonus based on achieving certain performance metrics. The performance metrics could include investment results, a profit/loss level, completion of projects, etc.
- Families also need to provide the standard benefit packages including health care, group life insurance, disability and basic retirement programs.
- As a means of attracting and retaining top talent, you may also need to craft some type of long-term incentive plan. This plan has the same impact as corporate stock option or stock grant programs.
- Deferred compensation plans are also an attractive way to hold on to key staff and many family offices will have a program of this type.

You can gain more information on constructing a compensation program by consulting a white paper titled "Summary of Key Plan Elements," written for the Family Office Exchange by Claire Kluever.

Industry Associations

Two independent groups have emerged to support family offices and wealthy individuals and families in managing the complexities of modern day wealth. The first is the *Family Office Exchange*. Established in 1989 by Sara Hamilton, the Family Office Exchange (FOX), serves as a strategic advisor for wealthy families, essentially acting as a type of clearinghouse for industry best practices, leading edge trends, philanthropy and family financial education. Perhaps most importantly, it provides its members with the ability to network with other families. Among the specific services provided by FOX are the following:

1. **Educational Events-** Their centerpiece function is the annual Fall Forum, where they gather family office executives, family members and professional advisors. This is a multi-day conference featuring such topics as hedge fund and private equity investing, family governance, manager selection, risk management and leading edge estate planning. Throughout the year, FOX also holds special interest group teleconferences as well as special sessions targeted to family office directors and other key staff.
2. **Benchmarking Study-** This is a study that compares family offices across a number of statistical benchmarks such as services offered, costs, systems, etc.
3. **Compensation Consulting-** FOX will assist family offices in designing compensation programs for staff. They also publish studies from time to time on compensation and benefit issues.
4. **Family Office Blueprint-** Here FOX helps families design their family offices, establishing service offerings, cost structures and operating goals. They will also provide members with access to executive search firms to assist them in filling key positions.
5. **Buyer's Exchange-** FOX helps its members to access selective products and services, particularly hedge fund data bases, family office insurance and software.

Another important membership organization is the *Institute for Private Investors (IPI)*. Founded by Charlotte Beyer in 1991, IPI provides educational and networking opportunities for its members. It neither sells nor promotes any products or services. Among its feature programs are:

1. **Forums-** IPI holds two educational conferences or forums each year. One is generally held in San Francisco while the other is held in New York.
2. **Special Briefings-** IPI will also hold individual briefings on topical subjects throughout the year.
3. **Private Wealth Management School-** With the Wharton School of the University of Pennsylvania, IPI holds a week-long program on family wealth management. The program is designed for family office executives and family members, particular those of the next generation. The faculty includes Charlotte Beyer along with several leading professors in the Wharton School.
4. **International Destinations-** IPI also plans trips to selected foreign locations to show its members global investment opportunities first hand. Participants will meet with public officials, business leaders, fund managers and entrepreneurs.
5. **Annual IPI Report-** Each year, IPI publishes a report that includes current and past articles of interest across a wide range of topics.

4

Selecting the Right Professional Advisors

One can argue that the most important aspect of family wealth management is hiring the right advisors across all disciplines. We will now turn to that important process. We will first review the range of advisors, categorizing them according to product & service providers, tactical advisors or strategic advisors. We will then focus specifically on governing the investment process, reviewing the alternative types of advisors you can hire to oversee your investment portfolios. Then we will share some templates for conducting RFPs (requests for proposals) when searching for various service providers.

The Basis of Competition

Professional advisors to wealthy families and family offices fall into the three categories mentioned above. Some providers just sell specific products and services. These providers are generally world class and focus on what they can do very well. Other providers offer advisory services as

Selecting the Right Professional Advisors

opposed to products. The advice is again very focused in a specific discipline. They generally recommend products offered by other firms, thus serving as an impartial advisor. A third category is that of a strategic advisor. These advisors are the big picture thinkers who guide families on how to best integrate their wealth management across the disciplines of investing, estate planning, philanthropy and banking. Some firms are capable of playing in all three fields while others focus more narrowly on a specific area where they enjoy a core competency. We will now review some of the specific providers in each general category. We will briefly describe the role of each provider, offer thoughts on how to select them and then discuss how to manage them effectively. In some cases, we will defer the discussion to a later chapter where we discuss the actual discipline in more detail. We summarize these providers in exhibit 4-A.

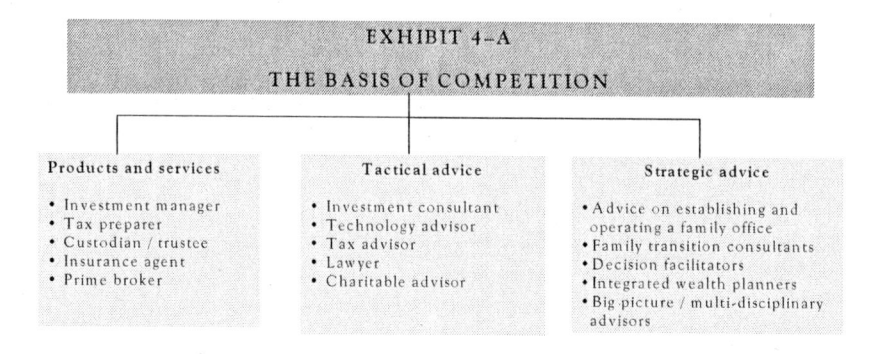

EXHIBIT 4-A
THE BASIS OF COMPETITION

Products and services	Tactical advice	Strategic advice
• Investment manager • Tax preparer • Custodian / trustee • Insurance agent • Prime broker	• Investment consultant • Technology advisor • Tax advisor • Lawyer • Charitable advisor	• Advice on establishing and operating a family office • Family transition consultants • Decision facilitators • Integrated wealth planners • Big picture / multi-disciplinary advisors

Product and Service Providers

Investment Manager

Families generally have many individual investment managers in their line up. These providers usually manage portfolios in specific asset classes such as equities, fixed income, hedge funds, etc. We will discuss the process for hiring, managing and terminating investment managers in chapter five when we cover investment policies.

Tax Preparer

Tax management is one of the key services where family offices and individuals need to seek competent professional help. Some firms provide a full range of tax services including tax preparation, income tax advice and wealth transfer planning. Some firms may be very competent at one of the functions but not necessarily each one. It is therefore not uncommon for you to have an excellent tax preparer compile your annual tax returns but look elsewhere for tax planning advice.

Custodian

For your securities portfolios, you will need a custodian of some nature. The custodian can be either a bank or brokerage firm. The basic role of a custodian is to hold your securities, collect interest and dividends and produce monthly asset and transaction statements. Here are some considerations when selecting a custodian:

- Compare the reports you would receive from each potential custodian. Does any one custodian provide superior reporting?
- Determine if any custodian has a superior web delivery. Most banks and brokerage firms offer online access to your accounts. You should compare each according to ease of use, information detail and functionalities of the site.
- Fees are obviously important. Banks generally charge fees along the line of basis points of assets plus transaction charges. They will also make money inside the money market sweep vehicles used within the portfolio. Brokerage houses generally do not charge much, if anything at all, for custodian services. However,

they do earn fees within the money market sweep vehicles and earn commissions on the trades within each portfolio.
- If you have multiple investment managers and wish to have all of your assets custodied in one place, you need to make sure that potential custodians can accommodate your range of managers. Brokerage firms, while they may charge nothing, may also not be in a position to custody assets that are not traded through the market.
- With large portfolios, some custodians may offer securities lending. By lending out your securities, you earn fees which can offset some of your custody charges.
- Determine if any potential custodian offers aggregation services whereby they could report on assets held at other custodians as well, thus giving you a complete accounting of all of your assets.

Trustee

Trustees can be either individuals or institutions. The individuals could range from family members to attorneys to trusted friends. Institutional trustees could be banks, private trust companies or law firms. We will cover the role of trustees and how to select them when we discuss fiduciary structures in chapter twelve

Insurance Agent

Your insurance needs to cover life, health, disability, long-term care, property & liability and automobile. Your first decision is to determine what type of insurance provider you engage. Do you work with a direct underwriter, broker or consultant? Each model has its advantages and drawbacks. We will cover the selection of an insurance provider in chapter ten where we discuss insurance issues and opportunities facing wealthy families.

Prime Broker

By definition, a prime broker first provides operational services in the form of custody, securities settlement and reporting. Generally, they do not make a lot of money performing these functions. Their revenues mainly come from margin lending and securities lending activities. Their clients could be investment managers, hedge funds or family offices. Exhibit 4-B displays how a prime broker functions. Essentially, they act as clearing brokers. Their clients may maintain multiple brokerage and money manager relationships, but have all of these brokers settle their trades through the designated prime broker. The prime broker then reconciles all of the brokerage positions and prepares a range of reports to their clients. The consolidated reporting platform is one of the distinguishing features of a prime brokerage relationship. Hedge funds are the largest users of prime brokerage services as their business operates on the use of leverage and the ability to borrow securities. They also maintain multiple broker relationships and can benefit from the clearing and consolidated reporting services of a prime broker. Family offices may use a prime broker if it conducts its own money management and trading operation and maintains a large hedge fund portfolio. Prime brokers can be a good source of hedge fund ideas. Prime brokers frequently put on hedge fund conferences for family office and institutional clients. On the other hand, family offices would not use prime brokers when it predominately hires external money managers since pure custody is not a popular activity for prime brokers. The firms that offer prime brokerage services are the largest bank and brokerage firms in the world, as you need significant operational facilities as well as financial capital to provide margin and securities lending.

EXHIBIT 4–B

PRIME BROKER NETWORK

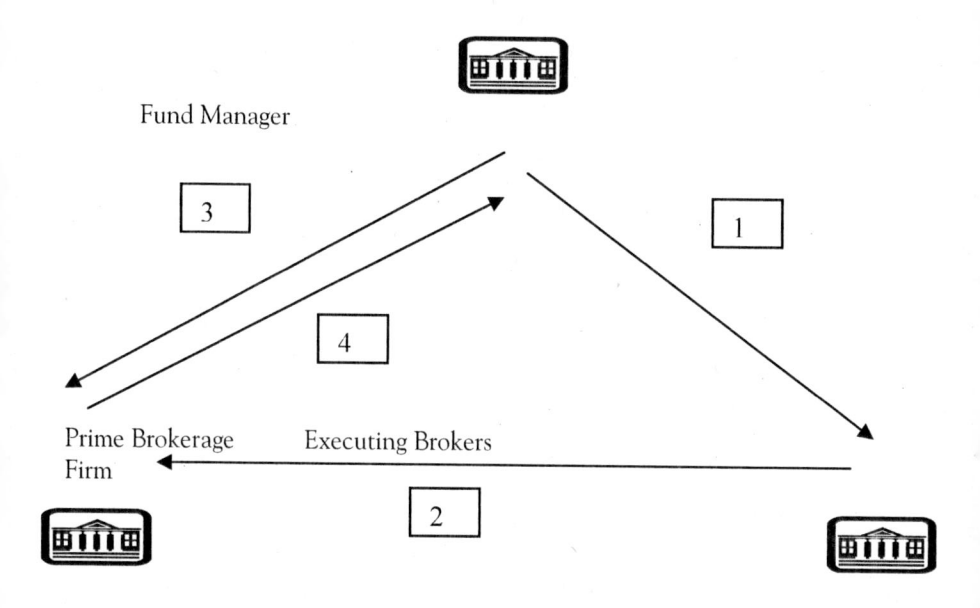

Fund Manager

Prime Brokerage Firm   Executing Brokers

1. Manager executes with multiple brokers

2. Those brokers "give up" the trades to the prime broker

3. Manager provides all trade information to the prime broker

4. Prime broker reconciles positions between client and brokers and consolidates all securities and reports back to fund manager

Private Banker

Private banking has evolved over the past decade to encompass far more than credit and banking services. Private banking today means an integrated wealth management platform including investment management & consulting, wealth transfer planning, trust services, philanthropic planning, derivative strategies, private equity investing and even real property management. With this much extended platform, how then do you evaluate a private bank before selecting one? You need to evaluate both the institution as well as the individuals who will handle your relationship. Despite the enormous size of many banks today, banking is still a personal business. People will still make or break a good relationship. Accordingly, here are some things to consider when selecting a new private bank or in just evaluating your current private bank:

- Does the firm only offer its own proprietary investment products or does it also offer access to best of class third-party investment managers?
- What is the range of asset classes the bank covers?
- Does it offer alternative investment products such as hedge funds, private equity and real estate?
- To what degree has it invested in technology and how does the firm's reporting and website features compare to competitors?
- Is the bank able to meet my credit needs for both investments as well as lifestyle (e.g. yachts, planes)
- If I have a significant block of stock, can the bank execute hedging strategies or does it need to always bring in a third party?
- Does the bank offer trust services and does it have the reputation of being a "friendly" trustee?
- Can the bank offer access to jurisdictions that provide attractive tax and asset protection situs such as Delaware?
- How experienced are the people who would be (or currently are) handling our portfolios?
- How long have they been at the firm and what is the general turnover at the firm?
- How is the banker compensated? Do they get penalized for lost business?

- Does the firm allow its officers to customized services in some cases or does it like everything to be standardized?
- How do its fees compare to competitors?
- Does it offer relationship pricing?

Tactical Advisors

Investment Consultant

Investment consultants essentially advise clients on what managers to choose to handle their assets. Consultants can be independent firms, brokerage houses or banks. These service providers were originally developed to handle pension funds and later foundations and endowments. More recently, they have begun to serve wealthy individuals and family offices. We will cover how you select and manage your consultant in chapter six, when we cover investment policies in greater depth.

Lawyer

Arguably, your core advisor will always be your attorney. In fact, many individuals and families rely on the attorney for advice and counsel on matters beyond legal and tax issues. Let's first look at some of the factors involved when selecting an attorney:

- Needless to say, your attorney should be well versed on current estate planning techniques. Some families may continue to use their attorney who has always handled their real estate and business transactions. While this same attorney may be adept at estate planning in general, it may not always be wise for the family to engage that same person when they need some advanced estate planning.

- An aging patriarch and matriarch should make sure the family's attorney relates well to their children. It is not uncommon for children to change lawyers and law firms once they assume leadership of the family. Many times this takes place because there has been no real relationship between the attorney and the next generation.
- Where you are considering a small firm (e.g. proprietorship or small partnership) versus a large law firm, you will need to balance a couple of competing issues. For example, to a small firm you may be a key client and therefore receive considerable attention. On the other hand, there may not be staff depth in the event your attorney retires. Additionally, if you are with a small firm that specializes in estate planning, you may not have access to other areas of law should you need them, such as real estate or pensions.
- You may also want your attorney to be dealing with similar type clients as yourself. This allows them to share best practices and insures his or her advice is always up to date.

Once you select an attorney, it is also important that you effectively manage that relationship. Here are a few important aspects of efficiently managing your law firm relationship:

- If you are with a prominent attorney with a large firm, you will want to manage costs. Top attorneys charge high fees. Accordingly, where you can have junior partners perform certain functions, you should do so.
- Many investors utilize their attorney to help them select and manage their investment advisors. Attorneys are generally in a good position to assist as they are regularly dealing with the investment community. However, when you place your attorney in a key role, you should make sure that he or she is willing to

consider many alternatives and is not just directing business to a very few. More importantly, you should also make sure that your attorney is free of conflict and does not necessarily recommend managers that regularly provide new business to them.
- Needless to say, you should have your attorney review and even help negotiate contracts with other providers, including money managers, custodians, insurance companies and bankers.

CPA/Tax Advisor

Many of the same factors are involved with CPAs as with attorneys. Of particular importance is whether your tax advisor has many similar clients. This insures that he/she is current on tax issues. You may also want to be dealing with a firm that has staff depth. There are some additional factors that are particular to managing CPAs and tax advisors:

- To what extent does your tax advisor offer creative ideas? You certainly want everything to be well within the limits of tax laws today; nevertheless, you still want creative solutions that will mitigate your overall tax bill.
- However, be careful with new tax avoidance ideas, particularly if your tax advisor asks you to sign a disclaimer or waiver.
- Will you tax advisor also work well with your investment advisors to optimize the tax efficiency of your portfolios? It is important that your advisors coordinate year-end tax gain/loss selling.
- Some public accounting firms offer investment consulting advice. Where this is the case and you are using your tax advisory firm to do this, you should evaluate them the same way that you would other firms in that business, including stand-alone companies, private banks or brokerage firms.

Technology Advisor

Where you are considering a substantial investment in portfolio accounting and general ledger systems, it may be prudent to engage a technology consultant before spending the money. The consultant would evaluate your family's reporting needs and survey the marketplace for alternative products. A good consultant can also help you negotiate the best deal. Consultants are available in different ways. Some public accounting firms offer this service as do general family office consulting firms.

Charitable Advisor

In lieu of hiring a large professional staff to run its grant making function, some private foundation directors will engage a charitable consultant to formulate a program for distributing its grants. The plan would articulate the fields of interest as well as the process for receiving grant requests. It would also highlight the procedure for reviewing and evaluating the various grant requests. There are specialized firms that offer this service. Some of these firms have a national practice while others concentrate their efforts locally.

Strategic Advisors

There is yet a third set of advisors to wealthy families and they are designated as strategic advisors. These advisors are big picture in nature and are skilled in helping wealthy individuals and families "connect the dots," so to speak. While there is no single standard or function that adequately describes strategic advisors, the following activities are common:

- Strategic advisors provide counsel to clients on how to establish formal family offices. They will provide guidance in the areas of mission, type of office, functions performed, staffing, budgets and measurement.
- They can provide broad direction on strategic asset allocation. This may go beyond financial portfolios and include business investments, real estate and private equity.
- They generally provide guidance on family governance issues which could include setting up the investment decision process, foundation directors and trustee designations.
- They advise on integrating wealth transfer, charitable and investment plans. This could entail dynasty trust planning as well.
- Many strategic advisors help the family with preparing the next generation to manage the family wealth. In particular, they will arrange for educational seminars and provide one-on-one counseling.

There is no set type of firm or individual who can assume this role. Sometimes a family will have a small group of strategic advisors from various disciplines. Accordingly, your core strategic advisors could be your private banker, attorney, lawyer or investment consultant. A key attribute of a strategic advisor is that the person needs to be multi-disciplinary in thinking and needs to be objective when advising on the selection of providers. In other words, there can be no hidden or personal agendas.

Chief Investment Officer Model

The key decision point for a wealthy individual or family group is how they will operate or govern their investment program. In exhibit 4-C, we highlight seven alternative approaches along with a summary of the advantages and disadvantages of each. This decision will have a significant influence on how the remaining investment providers are selected, managed and terminated, if necessary. Throughout the book, we will be commenting on each of these approaches in more detail. At this point, we will just provide a definition of each approach.

EXHIBIT 4-C

CHIEF INVESTMENT OFFICER
ALTERNATIVE MODELS

MODEL	KEY ADVANTAGES	DRAWBACKS
1. Hire Independent Person	• Virtual impartiality • Does not represent a product or firm • Will search alternatives among competing firms	• May not have access to wide range of resources • Succession
2. Investment Consulting Firm- Independent and Fee Based	• A business solely focused on providing asset allocation, manager search and performance monitoring. • Does not sell products or manage portfolios; only gives advice. • Can usually work out pricing deals with managers. • Provides due diligence on managers.	• Some firms have favorites or biases and their manager lists may remain static. • Depending on the firm, it may be difficult to expand their platform due to limited capital and other resources.

3. Brokerage/ Bank Consulting Platform	• Generally an "open architecture" combining proprietary with third-party management. Can be all third-party management. • A comprehensive package of asset allocation, manager selection, custody & reporting, and trading for one overall price. • Deep distribution networks can attract top managers.	• Not inexpensive for smaller portfolios, but can be very cost effective for larger ones. • Relationship advisors are generally incented on revenue generation (not necessarily bad, but you need to know that).
4. Corporate Trustee	• Institutional succession & continuity • Fiduciary liability protection.	• Staff turnover • Subject to company risk polices and procedures.
5. Trust Protector	• When you have a team of professionals covering investments, legal and tax, this model can provide effective oversight. • In a "trust protector" you have someone evaluating the trustees and investment	• Not always a rich, hands on investment model. • More of a coordinator.

	professionals with the responsibility to recommend hiring and firing. • The Protector can sometimes change provisions of the Trusts without going to court.	
6. Senior Banking/ Investment Advisor	• Experience • Can share best practices of other families • Has access to and backing of a large organization.	• Individual may face the need to recommend reducing funds committed to his / her organization.
7. Advisory Committee	• Can complement any of the above strategies. • Provides diversity of opinions and ideas. • Can cover if individual leaves or firm is fired.	• Requires populating and managing.

1. **Hire Independent Person-** Under this arrangement, you would hire a chief investment officer who would then select individual money managers or hire investment consultants. This person would be on your payroll.
2. **Investment Consulting Firm-** Here you would hire an independent firm whose business is asset allocation, manager search and performance monitoring. This business model assumes the provider has no proprietary products. Under this arrangement, you would likely have to hire a custodian to provide securities safekeeping and trade settlement.
3. **Brokerage/Bank Consulting Platform-** Some of the larger commercial banking and brokerage organizations provide

investment consulting services coupled with custody, trading and reporting. It is sometimes referred to as a "wrap" account where there is one fee for the entire spectrum of services. Some firms will also offer proprietary investment products as part of the program.

4. **Corporate Trustee-** In situations where a significant amount of the family's assets is in trusts, the Corporate Trustee could be designated as the chief investment officer as long as the family members have appropriate confidence in the trustee and the individual handling the relationship.

5. **Trust Protector-** This arrangement could also be appropriate where there are a number of family trusts involved. However, instead of giving the corporate trustee supreme power over the trusts, you have a "Trust Protector" who ultimately calls the shots. The trust protector concept originated in the British legal system, where the protector can hire and fire trustees and change certain provisions of trusts without going to court. The trust protector does not conduct any of the day-to-day fiduciary, investment or administrative functions as they remain with the trustee.

6. **Senior Banking/Investment Advisor-** In some cases, you may have a great deal of confidence in your retired private banker or investment advisor and wish to engage that person in a chief investment officer role. This will only work if the advisor's former firm does not control a great deal of the portfolio and you are working under an appropriate compensation arrangement. Otherwise, there could be a potential conflict of interest.

7. **Advisory Committee-** Some families choose to establish an advisory board to oversee its investments and to ratify major investment decisions. These boards can include family members, professional advisors, trusted business associates and even friends.

Requests for Proposals

Once you decide upon the types of advisors you want to employ, you then need to go about the process of selecting them. Some families like to establish a formal review and selection procedure, which sometimes involves preparing what are known as "requests for proposals." These are essentially questionnaires that deal with a prospective firm's technical capabilities, management structure, staff experience, investment performance and client profile. A sample set of requests for proposals is contained in Appendix I. Included are sample templates for investment consultants, investment managers, custodians and trustees.

We have completed the introductory part of this book and are now ready to begin a multi-chapter discussion of the various functionalities of managing family wealth, whether it is performed within a family office or not.

5
Creating an Investment Policy

Overseeing the management of substantial wealth is a daunting task. For some, it can be as daunting as making the fortune in the first place. As such, it is important that one adopt and follow a deliberate process. That process should, of course, reflect the unique circumstances of the family while at the same time be consistent with sound investment principles.

To assist in traveling through this journey, we constructed a chart in exhibit 5-A called "The Investment Management Process." This chart depicts the various stages in setting up and implementing an investment program. We will cover this topic in two chapters. In this chapter, we will go through the journey of first establishing an investment strategy and overall plan. This entails the process depicted in the first four boxes. Then in chapter six, we will discuss the execution and monitoring of the plan. This covers the process depicted in the last two boxes.

EXHIBIT 5-A
WEALTH MANAGEMENT PROCESS

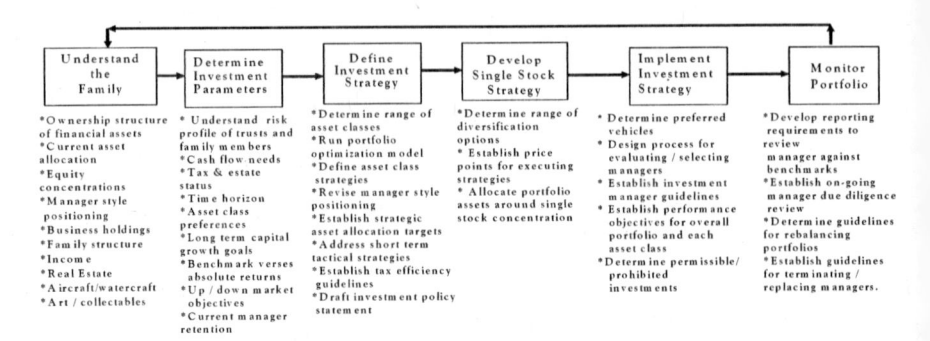

Understand the Family	Determine Investment Parameters	Define Investment Strategy	Develop Single Stock Strategy	Implement Investment Strategy	Monitor Portfolio
*Ownership structure of financial assets *Current asset allocation *Equity concentrations *Manager style positioning *Business holdings *Family structure *Income *Real Estate *Aircraft/watercraft *Art / collectables	*Understand risk profile of trusts and family members *Cash flow needs *Tax & estate status *Time horizon *Asset class preferences *Long term capital growth goals *Benchmark verses absolute returns *Up / down market objectives *Current manager retention	*Determine range of asset classes *Run portfolio optimization model *Define asset class strategies *Revise manager style positioning *Establish strategic asset allocation targets *Address short term tactical strategies *Establish tax efficiency guidelines *Draft investment policy statement	*Determine range of diversification options * Establish price points for executing strategies * Allocate portfolio assets around single stock concentration	* Determine preferred vehicles * Design process for evaluating / selecting managers * Establish investment manager guidelines * Establish performance objectives for overall portfolio and each asset class *Determine permissible/ prohibited investments	*Develop reporting requirements to review manager against benchmarks *Establish on-going manager due diligence review *Determine guidelines for rebalancing portfolios *Establish guidelines for terminating / replacing managers

Understanding the Family

Before getting into the investment strategy points, one needs to thoroughly review and understand the family's current asset structure along with its plans for dealing with some of those assets in the future. Here are some of the important aspects of a family's wealth structure:

Ownership Structure

As we indicated in an earlier chapter, the way you title assets is critical if you are to effectively manage transfer taxes. Some of the important aspects of a family's ownership structure are:

- What assets are held individually and what are held jointly?
- How much generational wealth transfer planning has taken place?
- What assets are held in family limited partnerships or limited liability companies? How are those entities structured?
- Are there any Grantor Retained Annuity Trusts and when do they expire?
- What do the patriarch and/or matriarch's estate plans look like?

Asset Allocation

You would naturally want to see the current asset allocation. Additionally, you should find out how the asset allocation evolved to its current state. You will also want to see where the gaps are and determine whether these gaps should remain.

Equity Concentrations

Many investors have large single stock positions. These may have originated from the sale of a family business to a public company, which in turn paid for the purchase in stock or in cash and stock. To the extent that you have significant equity concentrations, you will want to explore the following:

- What diversification efforts took place in the past? How much has been sold and redeployed from the original position.
- How did you sell or reduce your position? How much was gifted or transferred to the next generation? Did you engage in any derivative transactions or transfer the stock to an exchange fund? How much was contributed to charity via charitable trusts, donor advised funds or a private foundation?
- How has the stock performed over the past one, three and five years or since you owned it?
- What is your outlook for the stock over the near, intermediate and long term?
- How much of the stock are you willing to sell or part with in some way on an annual basis?

Current Portfolio

We now want to examine the attributes of the current portfolio, considering some of the following:

- How well is the portfolio diversified among the various asset classes and manager styles?
- Identify the style gaps.
- What has the performance history been?
- How volatile have the annual returns been? What has been the range of performance?
- How much income is generated by the portfolio?

Business Holdings

Always impacting a family's investment posture are its business holdings. These investments set the tone for the degree of risk the family is willing to take with portfolio assets. For example, business holdings that produce meaningful income better enable a family to take additional risk with its financial assets. On the other hand, if a family has a significant amount of its wealth tied up in business holdings, it is unlikely going to commit further investments to private equity or real estate funds where liquidity may be an issue.

When looking at business holdings, you may wish to examine the following:

- Investments in operating companies and the actual ownership that the family has in those companies.
- Real estate direct investments and real estate partnerships.
- Natural resource partnerships such as oil and gas, copper or silver.

For each of these, you will want to examine the past performance as well as consider the future outlook. Also, is there an exit strategy for any of these investments?

Family Structure

A critical aspect in understanding the family dynamics is to diagram the family structure. When doing so, you should ask the following questions?

1. What are the consumption patterns of the family members?
2. What are their individual sources of income and cash flow? Which trusts support which family members?
3. Do the family portfolios provide adequate income and cash flow to support the family members' consumption needs?
4. What does the family demographic picture look like? Will there be future stress on the family wealth where the family increases at a rate that exceeds its ability to grow its wealth? Does the family need to look at ways to once again create new entrepreneurial wealth?

Real Assets and Collectibles

To round out the picture, you should assess the amount of your family's wealth that is tied up in real assets of some kind. These may include some of the following:

- Real estate including primary residences, vacation homes, etc.
- Yachts and other watercraft
- Planes
- Art collections
- Antique cars
- Jewelry
- Antique furniture

Income

Finally, you should assess the income and cash flow from all sources including:

- Salary and wages of family members
- Trusts
- Private portfolios
- Operating businesses
- Real estate direct investments
- Real estate partnerships
- Retirement funds
- Annuities and insurance policies
- Other investments such as oil and gas partnerships, etc.

Determine Investment Parameters

Objectives

At the outset of establishing investment parameters, you will first articulate a set of goals and objectives. In today's investment world, objectives are much more than just beating the market or hitting an artificial number. Instead, objectives today can be multi-faceted and set the tone for the portfolios that you will later construct in an effort to achieve them. Consider the range of portfolio objectives you might establish:

- You may need to set an **absolute return** goal over a number of years. The absolute number may be tied into the family's spending needs or it may be the number that is needed to offset the expected growth in the family over the upcoming years.

Creating an Investment Policy

- You will likely set **benchmark** goals for specific portfolios. For example, you will want your equity funds to outperform the S & P 500 Index.
- Alternatively, you could set an overall portfolio objective based on a premium over the **risk-free return.**
- Your goals could also be expressed as a premium over **inflation.**
- Goals are frequently expressed as performance **after taxes and after fees.**
- Frequently, you will have **income** objectives.
- In some cases, investors will develop differing goals in different market conditions. For example, you may be willing to **lag in up markets** but want to **outperform in down markets.**

Portfolio Risk

Investors have historically viewed risk in terms of volatility and the statistical term frequently used to describe risk has been the standard deviation. We will cover the strict definition of standard deviation in a moment, but for now, it essentially means the volatility of a portfolio's returns around its expected average or mean return. While overall performance volatility is certainly a critical risk element in the investment world, there are additional important risks as well and we will consider some of those below.

1. **Concentration Risk-** High on the list of risks are those inherent in holding large concentrations in a single stock position. Additionally, you could have significant industry risks in a portfolio.
2. **Style Risk-** Investors frequently have style risk in their portfolios. For example, many investors may be value investors, but when value goes out of favor, their performance will lag the general market.

3. **Benchmark Risk**- Even with strong managers, you may very well face the risk that your portfolios do not reach the performance benchmarks you have established.
4. **Manager Risk**- With investment managers you are dealing with people and you face risks with managers as you would with people in any other profession or business. For example, a money management firm could break up or the principal could become disabled.
5. **Interest Rate Risk**- This risk can impact many of your asset classes but is likely to hit bonds more than most. Rising rates obviously hurt longer term bonds more than shorter term ones but falling rates also have an important effect on your portfolio. Declining rates will impact your reinvestment rates and income levels.
6. **Liquidity Risk**- This is one of the more important risks that individual investors consider. Nothing seems to scare the individual more than the inability to sell or liquidate an investment in a time of need. Real estate, hedge funds and private equity have varying degrees of ill-liquidity.
7. **Credit Risk**- In both the equity as well as fixed income markets, investors will face company-specific risk. These risks manifest themselves in a number of ways. A bad economy will certainly impact cyclical companies but criminal activities can also bankrupt a company as we have witnessed in recent times.
8. **Transparency Risk**- With some investments, such as hedge funds, you have the added risk of not clearly seeing the underlying securities in the portfolios on a daily basis.
9. **Legislative/Tax Risk**- Changes in tax laws can significantly impact the attractiveness of an asset class. As an example, the 1986 Tax Reform Act severely limited the tax deductions one could get from investor real estate.

Creating an Investment Policy

10. **Call Risk**- With bonds you face the risk that the bond will be called by the issuer prior to maturity. It is likely that issuers will call bonds when interest rates are lower than when they first sold the bonds. Accordingly, you as the investor will be forced to reinvest your proceeds at a lower rate.
11. **Prepayment Risk**- With mortgage-backed securities, you will experience a faster payback of principal as rates drop. As a result, you again face the problem of reinvesting proceeds at lower interest rates.
12. **Single Year Loss Risk**- Some investors are not tolerant of an overall portfolio loss in a given single year. There are ways to assess the probability of that happening. Should this be an important factor, you may need to configure your portfolio in ways that mitigate the probability of an overall loss in a given year.

A common way to assess an investor's tolerance for volatility is to consider the returns on the two portfolios below. The overall portfolio market value of each portfolio is the same after seven years. Which one do you prefer?

	Portfolio A	Portfolio B
Year 1	10%	6.79%
Year 2	30	6.79
Year 3	35	6.79
Year 4	(15)	6.79
Year 5	(24)	6.79
Year 6	27	6.79

At the end of the six-year period, the annualized return is 6.79 percent. You can arrive there with a constant return or by highly volatile returns.

Time Horizon

Consistent with your objectives and risk profile is the investment time horizon. A longer time horizon certainly gives you added flexibility when selecting asset classes and securities. With a longer time horizon, you can weather the business cycle and be in a position to better capture the expected long-term return on more volatile asset classes.

Time horizons, however, are sometimes dictated by age, years to retirement, number of children to educate, asset structure and overall wealth.

Legal Parameters

Needless to say, your investment program will be constrained by any legal issues surrounding the structures employed to house the assets. Also, there are some general laws regarding prudence when acting as a fiduciary. A fiduciary could be family members, professional investment managers, investment consultants, attorneys and corporate trustees. Here are some of the common legal issues to consider:

- **Trusts-** As we will cover in later chapters, a trust is governed by its own document or agreement as well as federal and state statutes. A trust agreement covers a range of items including, but not limited to, duration, distributions of income and principal, investment restrictions, trustees, powers of trustees and ultimate disposition of the trust funds. A recent trust legal issue surrounds the Uniform Principal and Income Act, which has been enacted in many states. This act permits trustees to distribute a stated unitized percentage amount to income beneficiaries instead of just the net income. This has become important in light of the current low interest rate environment. Accordingly, the distribution could include income plus some principal amount to reach the stated payout. Generally, the stated payouts range from 4 to 6 %.

- **Charitable Trusts-** Where you have charitable remainder trusts, there are distinct IRS regulations governing the taxability of annual distributions and the types of prohibited investments. For example, you cannot invest in assets that generate unrelated business income. We will cover this topic in a later chapter.
- **State Laws-** Individual states generally govern the management of trusts within its situs. They will frequently cover such rules as the taxability of income distributions, maximum duration, allowable trustees and investment standards. Some states even developed their own lists of permitted investments within trusts under its jurisdiction.
- **Prudent Investor Rule-** Over the years, the courts have become involved in establishing case precedent for evaluating the results of trustees. This case history was built from a series of lawsuits stemming from alleged mismanagement of funds. The landmark case that formed the basis for future judgments and statutes was *Harvard College v. Amory* in 1830. In this case, Harvard College sued Francis Amory for $10,000 to recover a loss of principal from the estate of John McLean. Amory was the trustee of McLean's estate, which was valued at $50,000 at the time of his death. The trust was established to provide income to McLean's widow with the remainder interest passing to Harvard. At the death of Mrs. McLean, the estate dropped to $40,000. The Massachusetts court ruled in favor of the defendant, focusing its decision on the concepts of risk and conduct. The decision spawned the legal standard, which became known as the *Prudent Man Rule*. Here is an excerpt from the case, highlighting this standard:

"All that is required of a trustee to invest is, that he shall conduct himself faithfully and exercise sound discretion. He is to observe how men of prudence, discretion and intelligence manage their own affairs, not in regard to speculation, but in regard to the permanent disposition of their funds, considering the probable income, as well as the probable safety of the capital to be invested."

It is important to note that this standard applied to individual investments. Also, states that did not have specific statutes dealing with permissible investments relied on the prudent man rule for its guidance. The prudent man rule remained the cornerstone for adjudicating disputes and setting investment standards for much of the next 100 years. Additional cases along with statutes governing institutional investing sprung up over this time but it was not until the early 1990's that a watershed change took place.

One of the problems with the prudent man rule was that it focused on each and every investment in isolation. Over the past twenty years or so, new investment vehicles came to the marketplace. While some of these investments, such as hedge funds, may be inherently risky in isolation, they can serve a useful diversification purpose in the overall portfolio. Also, high yield bonds can be good diversification assets. From time to time, these higher risk assets could experience losses on individual securities and it would not necessarily be right to bring legal action against an investment manager for one or a very small number of securities losses so long as the portfolio as a whole is performing well. Accordingly, legal investment standards evolved when the American Law Institute adopted *The Restatement of the Law Third, Trusts: Prudent Investor Rule* in 1992. This restatement is shown in exhibit 5-B, taken from the website of Altruist

Creating an Investment Policy

Financial Advisors, LLC. There are also five basic principles to the rule and they are highlighted as well on exhibit 5-B. The new prudent investor rule then became the basis for *The Uniform Prudent Investor Act,* which was developed by the National Conference of Commissioners on Uniform State Laws in 1994. The American Bar Association then approved the act in 1995 and recommended its enactment in all states. Since that time, the act has been adopted in most states.

A key feature of the *Uniform Prudent Investor Act* was that the standard of prudence was no longer applied to a single investment. Instead, the standard of prudence was to now be applied to the portfolio as a whole and each investment would be judged as to its contribution to or role in the overall portfolio. The Act provides that fiduciaries should weigh the following considerations when making investments:

1. The size of the trust.
2. The nature of the trust and its distribution policies.
3. The liquidity of the trust's investments and its distribution schedule.
4. The role that each investment plays in the overall portfolio strategy.
5. An assets special relationship or value to the trust or its beneficiaries.
6. The extent to which an investment is known to support the distribution needs of the beneficiaries.
7. The other income and resources of the beneficiaries and related trusts.

EXHIBIT 5–B

General Standard of Prudent Investment

The trustee is under a duty to the beneficiaries to invest and manage the funds of the trust as a prudent investor would, in light of the purposes, terms, distribution requirements, and other circumstances of the trust.

- a. This standard requires the exercise of reasonable care, skill, and caution, and is to be applied to investments not in isolation but in the context of the trust portfolio and as a part of an overall investment strategy, which should incorporate risk and return objectives reasonably suitable to the trust.
- b. In making and implementing investment decisions, the trustee has a duty to diversify the investments of the trust unless, under the circumstances, it is prudent not to do so.
- c. In addition, the trustee must:
  1. conform to fundamental fiduciary duties of loyalty (§ 170) and impartiality § 183);
  2. act with prudence in deciding whether and how to delegate authority and in the selection and supervision of agents (§ 171); and
  3. incur only costs that are reasonable in amount and appropriate to the investment responsibilities of the trusteeship (§ 188).
- d. The trustee's duties under this Section are subject to the rule of § 228, dealing primarily with contrary investment provisions of a trust or statute.

The new rule contains five basic principles (the bold phrases below are taken from Restatement of the Law Third, Trusts; Prudent Investor Rule, 1992):

- Sound diversification is fundamental to risk management and is therefore ordinarily required of trustees. Diversification is a basic tenet of risk management, without which investment portfolios would tend to be more volatile than necessary while having similar long-term expected returns.
- Risk and return are so directly related that trustees have a duty to analyze and make conscious decisions concerning the levels of risk appropriate to the purposes, distribution requirements, and other circumstances of the trusts they administer. The point here is that risk is not inherently bad though it is prudent to avoid uncompensated or unsystematic risk when possible (i.e., through diversification). Investment risk should be deliberately taken on only when it is judged likely to contribute to desirable investment performance for the portfolio as a whole. The level and nature of investment risk should be consistent with the trust's need, desire, and ability to tolerate that risk.
- Trustees have a duty to avoid fees, transaction costs and other expenses that are not justified by needs and realistic objectives of the trust's investment program. It is usually both reasonable and appropriate to minimize incurred fees whenever possible, consistent with the investment strategy being implemented.
- The fiduciary duty of impartiality requires a balancing of the elements of return between production of income and the protection of purchasing power. This confirms that a strategy which endeavors to generate current income while preserving principal is likely to result in a reduction of real income to beneficiaries due to inflation. For that income (i.e., through dividends) and for capital appreciation, even if it means income alone is inadequate to meet a beneficiary's cash-flow needs.
- Trustees may have a duty as well as having the authority to delegate as prudent investors would. This delegation is often in the form of investing in mutual funds. Trustees should exercise due care in

selecting mutual funds for investment, concentrating on the most relevant predictors of future performance: fees, diversification, and asset class focus.

Source: Restatement of the Law Third, Trusts; Prudent Investor or Rule, 1992. Website of Altruist Financial Advisors, LLC.

Retention of Current Managers

Before embarking on a widespread investment strategy and plan, you do need to segregate those managers that are essentially "untouchable" for one reason or another. There can be a number of reasons why you will want to retain certain managers. Some may have given you strong performance over the years or they may occupy a niche that you wish to retain. There could also be other non-investment reasons like the manager may be a relative or friend, or you may have an ownership interest in the firm or be on the firm's board of directors.

Define Investment Strategy

Defining an investment strategy is an involved discipline covering the range of asset classes, investment manager styles, tax issues and statistical techniques. Before going into the various aspects of an investment strategy, we will first cover two philosophical underpinnings of an individual's approach to investing.

Overarching Investment Mission

At the outset, it is important for investors to establish a basic mission or philosophy for how they wish to invest. For the sake of simplicity we will break out this mission in two distinct ways. First, you could adopt the philosophy of striving for wealth preservation. Alternatively or secondly, you could adopt a philosophy of striving for long-term capital growth.

Creating an Investment Policy

Certainly, there is a wide area in between these philosophies and adopting one does not preclude you from always taking advantages of new investment opportunities from time to time. Let's look at some of the attributes of each philosophy:

Wealth Preservation

- Focus on not losing money
- Limited capacity to take substantial risks
- Desire to predominately hold highly liquid assets outside of residences
- Meaningful bond portfolio which is essentially a buy and hold portfolio
- Highly diversified portfolios
- Emphasis on annual cash flow
- Tax efficiency

Capital Growth

- Willing to take measured risks to achieve commensurate growth
- Not concerned with investment concentrations
- Employ range of alternative investments
- Tax efficient growth
- Income not a significant factor
- Willing to hold illiquid investments

Establish Investment Posture

As an investor, you are going to exert a certain posture toward the investment markets. We are going to define this posture in three ways. You may be a defensive investor, a moderate investor or an aggressive investor. We will look at each one in turn.

1. **Defensive-** As a defensive oriented investor, you seek, first and foremost, to manage risk and volatility. You are quite willing to sacrifice high performance for relative consistency in returns. You are likely to select managers that display favorable performance in down markets. Additionally, you are likely to seek more income-oriented investments, including high dividend stocks. You will favor value stocks and more value oriented equity managers. Within the alternative investment arena, you may find hedge funds, particularly absolute return funds, very attractive due to their low volatility and low correlation to domestic equity markets.

2. **Moderate-** As a moderate investor, you favor wide diversification across the asset classes and are willing to assume market risk on your investments. However, you demand that your managers perform in line with their respective market benchmarks. You generally do not like to experience wide deviations in your portfolio compared to the overall market. Consistency is therefore judged in how tightly your managers and portfolios perform compared to their industry benchmarks. You want short-term as well as long-term consistency in comparative performance.

3. **Aggressive-** As an aggressive investor, you are willing to assume short-term performance volatility in an attempt to achieve strong long-term performance. Performance versus a market benchmark is measured over longer rolling periods as opposed to quarterly or even annual periods. You will also be comfortable with more directional, higher volatility hedge funds as well as private equity and real estate investments.

Determine Range of Asset Classes

In formulating an investment strategy, we are going to start at 30,000 feet and work our way down to ground level. First, we will lay the groundwork for devising an asset allocation structure. As an investor, you will want to understand the full range of asset classes available for investment. In exhibit 5-C, we highlight the major asset classes by cash equivalents, fixed income, equities and alternative investments. Briefly, let us consider the role that each major class plays in an overall portfolio.

EXHIBIT 5–C

Range of Major Asset Classes

Cash Equivalents	Fixed Income	Equities	Alternatives
• U.S. Treasury Bills • Federal Agencies • Municipal notes • Commercial paper	• U.S. Treasuries • Federal agencies • Mortgage-backed bonds • Municipal bonds • Corporate bonds • International bonds • High yield bonds	• Domestic stocks • Convertible securities • International equities • Options & futures	• Real estate • Hedge funds • Private equity • Natural resources • Collectibles

- **Cash equivalents** represent the liquidity in your portfolio. You would maintain liquidity to cover living expenses as well as commitments for business investments. Additionally, you might hold liquid funds if you want dry powder for investment opportunities that may come up in the future, or if you do not like the current market environment and therefore wish to be defensive.
- **Fixed income**, as the name implies, provides you with your income needs. It can also serve as the safety portfolio, offsetting some of the risk of your equity and real estate investments. However, bonds carry interest rate as well as credit risk, so they do not always represent a "free lunch."
- **Equities** represent the growth part of your portfolio and generally require more attention than the cash or bond segments.
- **Alternatives** provide a portfolio with assets whose performances are not highly correlated with the traditional asset categories. Many of these investments are less liquid than the traditional classes and possess their own unique characteristics that investors find appealing.

We now turn to identifying those asset classes you wish to include in your portfolio as well as those you might wish to exclude. In reaching this determination, you need to consider a number of factors. To assist in this process, we suggest a five-stage model. This model will get you to your asset allocation structure.

1. **Real Versus Financial Assets-** In this first stage, the investor considers the attractiveness of holding real verses financial assets. Real assets, particularly real estate properties and timber, have shown steady appreciation over long-term periods. Wealthy families have always believed in holding a meaningful portion of their assets in real, tangible investments. Real assets generally

include real estate, farm & ranchland, natural resources, art and other collectibles.

2. **Traditional Versus Alternative Investments-** Again at the global level, you should determine the overall commitment you are willing to make to alternative investments. This will have a definite bearing on not only the diversification of your portfolio, but the performance and volatility of it as well.

3. **Income and Cash Flow-** Especially during periods of low interest rates, investments that throw off income and cash flow are especially attractive. Fixed income asset classes are not the only sources of income. High dividend stocks as well as convertible securities can be good sources of income as well as capital appreciation. Real estate, of course, is also a source of cash flow. Your required level of income will dictate your allocation to these classes.

4. **Risk and Return-** For all of the asset classes, you want to assess their comparative return and risk profiles. The graph in exhibit 5-D shows how the various asset classes line up along the return/risk continuum. This is not the end of the story, however. As we will see later, a portfolio's overall risk is not derived by just adding up the risk of its individual components.

EXHIBIT 5–D

RISK AND RETURN

Rate of Return

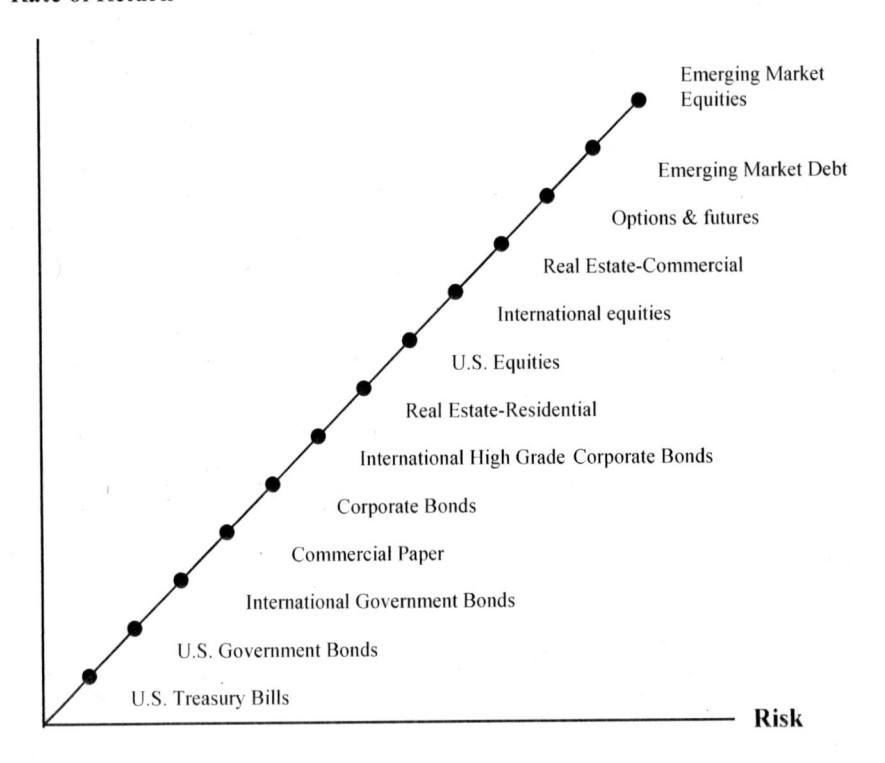

- Emerging Market Equities
- Emerging Market Debt
- Options & futures
- Real Estate-Commercial
- International equities
- U.S. Equities
- Real Estate-Residential
- International High Grade Corporate Bonds
- Corporate Bonds
- Commercial Paper
- International Government Bonds
- U.S. Government Bonds
- U.S. Treasury Bills

Risk

5. **Portfolio Optimization-** The last stage in setting asset allocation targets lies in running a type of optimization model. Most investment and financial advisors maintain some form of computerized model, which will indicate the most efficient combination of asset classes for a particular investor profile. We will cover this topic next.

Portfolio Optimization

Portfolio optimization, sometimes called mean variance optimization, is rooted in modern portfolio theory, which is the basis of all risk/return literature. The idea behind portfolio optimization is to allocate assets among various asset classes with the objective of optimizing your overall portfolio return for a given level of risk. The result is to build what is commonly called the "efficient frontier." By definition, the efficient frontier shows the set of portfolios (asset allocation structures) that have the maximum expected return for every given level of risk or the minimum level of risk for every level of return. Exhibit 5-E shows an example of an efficient frontier. It may be instructive to discuss how this concept works. Looking at portfolio or point "C" on exhibit 5-E, this portfolio is not optimal, as it does not lie on the efficient frontier curve. Compare this portfolio to those of "A" and "B." Compared to portfolio C, portfolio B has a higher return at the same level of risk. Alternatively, portfolio A has the same return as portfolio C but at a lower level of risk. We should also describe the areas under and over the efficient frontier curve. The area under the curve represents portfolios that can be improved while the area over the line represents portfolios that are virtually nonexistent. Mechanically, the efficient portfolios are derived through the automated portfolio optimization programs that your investment advisor maintains.

EXHIBIT 5–E

THE EFFICIENT FRONTIER

Expected Return

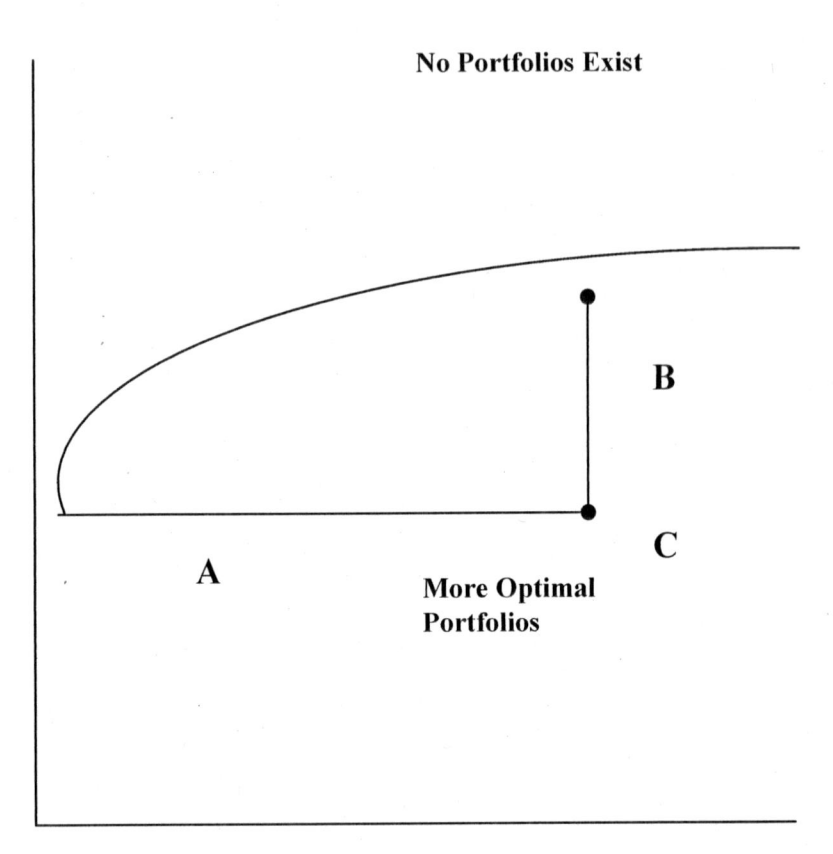

No Portfolios Exist

B

A

C

More Optimal Portfolios

Standard Deviation (Risk)

To better understand the output of these models, you need to first consider its inputs. There are three essential inputs to an optimization model:

1. **Expected Return-** For each asset class, you will need to insert an expected rate of return. These returns are generally based on historical returns, but some advisors will modify the historical results to take into account current information. Then, for the portfolio as a whole, the expected rate of return is the weighted average of the expected rates of return for the individual asset classes. The weights correspond to percentage of the portfolio that each asset class holds. Here is the actual statistical formula:

$$E(R_{port}) = \sum W_i E(R_i)$$

   where:

   R_{port} = the expected return on the entire portfolio
   W_i = the percent of the portfolio in asset class i
   $E(R_i)$ = the expected rate of return for asset class i

2. **Standard Deviation-** For each portfolio, there is also a statistical measure of the variation of returns from its expected return. This is termed the variance or standard deviation of returns. The standard deviation is just the square root of the variance. Statistically, the formula for the variance is as follows:

$$\text{Variance} = \sum [R_i - E(R_i)]^2 P_i$$

   Where:

   R_i = the return on an individual asset class i in a sample year
   $E(R_i)$ = the expected return for asset class i
   P_i = the probability of the observed return of asset I

The standard deviation is the common measure of portfolio variability or risk. Statistically, the standard deviation is interpreted as follows:

- The variability of portfolio returns is measured from its expected return as described above. The returns of a portfolio are generally assumed to follow a normal, bell shaped distribution as demonstrated in exhibit 5-F
- The standard deviation provides you with probability statements about the dispersion of returns.
- For example, one standard deviation contains approximately 68 percent of the outlines and two standard deviations contain 95 percent of the outcomes.
- We then translate these numbers into portfolios. For example, a given portfolio may project an expected return of 9 percent with a standard deviation of 7 percent. In this case, you may expect that 68 percent of its outcomes would range from 2 percent to 16 percent. You derive this range by adding and subtracting one standard deviation from the expected return. You naturally would like to see the standard deviation as low as possible for each expected return or conversely, would like the highest expected return for each level of standard deviation. This is the essence of the efficient frontier.

EXHIBIT 5–F

Distribution of Returns

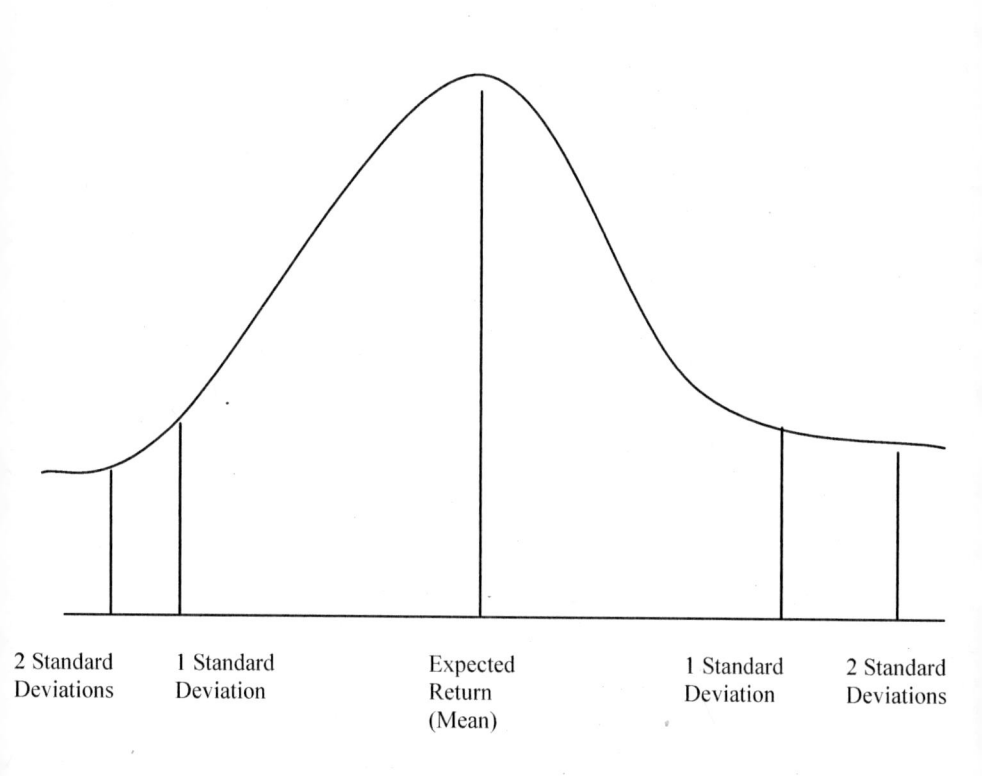

| 2 Standard Deviations | 1 Standard Deviation | Expected Return (Mean) | 1 Standard Deviation | 2 Standard Deviations |

Correlation- The concept of correlation is the extent to which two asset classes move together over time. It is important to a portfolio optimizer because it is quite possible to reduce the risk or variability of returns in a portfolio by combining assets that tend to move in opposite directions. The correlation between two assets is measured by their correlation coefficient. We will not go into its statistical formula, but here is an interpretation of what the statistic means. It will range between minus 1 and plus 1:

- A correlation coefficient of +1 indicates that the returns on the two asset classes always move together in the same direction. They are considered to be perfectly correlated. Each asset class contributes directly to the portfolio's volatility.
- A correlation coefficient of –1 indicates that the returns on the two asset classes move in the exact opposite direction. They are therefore considered to be perfectly negatively correlated. Having each in the portfolio will actually reduce overall portfolio risk since one may be up when the other is down.
- A correlation coefficient of zero indicates that there is no relationship between the returns of the two asset classes.

Another statistical measure is the Sharpe Ratio, which is defined as the return per unit of risk. The formula is derived as follows:

$$\frac{[\text{ expected return }] - [\text{ risk free return }]}{\text{standard deviation}}$$

This ratio allows you to easily compare multiple portfolio alternatives. The higher the ratio, the better.

Creating an Investment Policy

The next phase of portfolio optimization is to derive the inputs for the model. There are essentially four input categories that drive an optimization model. The first three are those we discussed earlier–expected return, standard deviation and cross correlations. In addition to those, an investor should guide the model as to the minimum and maximum constraints on each asset class. A final input is the expected yield on each asset class. Consider these guidelines when establishing the model inputs:

- While the expected returns will be based to a great extent on historical results, your advisor should adjust them for known data deficiencies, economic trends and market expectations. This way, they will be somewhat forward looking.
- The standard deviation should be built in a similar fashion whereby your advisor adjusts historical results for known deficiencies and market expectations.
- The relationships among the asset classes must remain internally consistent. For example, there needs to be enough of a risk and return premium between stocks and bonds and then between both and private equity.
- Minimum and maximum constraints on each asset class are important so that the result is something you can implement. Left unchecked, an optimization model is likely to display, investing most of your funds in hedge funds.

Exhibit 5-G is a framework that demonstrates how these inputs can be organized. The numbers in these tables are just estimates derived from several sources and are displayed only as a sample template. The next step is to have your advisor run the optimization model and interpret its output. The output is expressed in terms of the overall portfolio's expected return and standard deviation. You and your advisor then decide whether this anticipated outcome is acceptable or whether you wish to run alternative scenarios. Let's consider a hypothetical example. Assume the portfolio optimizer displays the following asset allocation output:

Asset Class	%
Large cap core equity	20
Mid cap core equity	10
Small cap value equity	10
Small cap growth equity	5
International	15
Municipal bonds	15
Hedge funds-low volatility	5
Hedge funds-high volatility	10
Real estate	5
Private equity	5
Total	100

Let's next assume that the portfolio's expected return is 9.83 percent with a standard deviation of 12.1 percent. You reflect on these expected numbers and come back to your advisor with a willingness to accept a slightly lower return if he/she is able to reduce the volatility factor to under 11 percent. Your advisor believes this is realistic and shows you a few ways to accomplish that. One way may be to reduce international and small cap equity by 5 percent each and invest an additional 10 percent into bonds. You could also reduce the high volatility hedge funds and redeploy the monies into the low volatility hedge funds. Remember, you impact the overall portfolio risk by the way the asset classes mix together in the portfolio, as we discussed above in our definition of correlation.

EXHIBIT 5–G

MODEL INPUTS & CONSTRAINTS

Asset Class	Expected Return	Standard Deviation	Expected Yield	Minimum Constraint	Maximum Constraint
Equities Large Cap Value	9.5	15.0	1.8	10	25
Large Cap Growth	10.1	18.2	1.1	10	25
Mid Cap Core	10.5	18.3	1.2	5	15
Small Cap Value	11.2	17.6	0.8	3	10
Small Cap Growth	12.2	24.2	0.5	3	10
International Core	10.8	20.0	1.4	10	20
Fixed Income Municipal Inv. Grade	4.3	4.9	4.0	20	50
High Yield Bonds	8.6	9.4	8.0	5	15
Alternatives Real Estate	7.2	5.5	6.5	0	10
Natural Resources	7.5	13.5	1.2	0	10
Hedge Funds – Absolute Return	11.0	9.5	1.0	3	10
Hedge Funds – Directional	15.0	20.6	1.0	3	10
Private Equity	15.5	24.5	0.3	0	10

EXHIBIT 5–G1

CORRELATION COEFFICIENTS

	Large Cap Value	Large Cap Growth	Mid Cap Core	Small Cap Value	Small Cap Growth
Large Cap Value	1.00	0.78	0.86	0.70	0.59
Large Cap Growth	0.78	1.00	0.82	0.57	0.71
Mid Cap Core	0.86	0.82	1.00	0.85	0.87
Small Cap Value	0.70	0.57	0.85	1.00	0.77
Small Cap Growth	0.59	0.71	0.87	0.77	1.00
International Core	0.55	0.56	0.53	0.38	0.45
Municipal Investment Grade	0.34	0.27	0.29	0.22	0.10
High Yield Bonds	0.44	0.42	0.52	0.56	0.48
Real Estate	0.03	0.01	<0.04>	<0.7>	<0.06>
Natural Resources	0.25	0.20	0.27	0.13	0.18
Hedge Funds – Absolute Return	0.50	0.53	0.70	0.66	0.75
Hedge Funds – Directional	0.40	0.46	0.57	0.62	0.70
Private Equity	0.55	0.72	0.84	0.71	0.96

EXHIBIT 5–G2

CORRELATION COEFFICIENTS

	International Core	Municipal Invest. Grade	High Yield Bond	Real Estate	Natural Resources	Hedge Funds – Absolute Returns	Hedge Funds – Directional	Private Equity
Large Cap Value	0.55	0.34	0.44	0.03	0.25	0.50	0.40	0.55
Large Cap Growth	0.56	0.27	0.42	0.01	0.20	0.53	0.46	0.72
Mid Cap Core	0.53	0.29	0.52	<0.04>	0.27	0.70	0.57	0.84
Small Cap Value	0.38	0.22	0.56	<0.07>	0.13	0.66	0.62	0.71
Small Cap Growth	0.45	0.10	0.48	<0.06>	0.18	0.75	0.70	0.96
International Core	1.00	0.22	0.32	0.01	0.20	0.45	0.40	0.47
Municipal Investment Grade	0.22	1.00	0.36	<0.12>	0.13	0.27	<0.03>	0.15
High Yield Bonds	0.32	0.36	1.00	<0.16>	0.10	0.62	0.47	0.45
Real Estate	0.01	<0.12>	<0.16>	1.00	<0.02>	<0.20>	<0.17>	<0.07>
Natural Resources	0.20	0.13	0.10	<0.02>	1.00	0.15	0.10	0.16
Hedge Funds – Absolute Returns	0.45	0.27	0.62	<0.20>	0.15	1.00	0.92	0.70
Hedge Funds – Directional	0.40	<0.03>	0.47	<0.17>	0.10	0.92	1.00	0.68
Private Equity	0.47	0.15	0.45	<0.07>	0.16	0.70	0.68	1.00

We close our discussion of portfolio optimization by stressing the importance of asset allocation. As we know, pictures are better than words, so look at exhibit 5-H. From chemistry class, you may remember the periodic table of the elements. This is the periodic table of asset class returns, shown over a 15-year period. Well-known and highly used market indices are proxies for each asset class. You will glean a few important points from this table. First, no asset class stays on top forever. Conversely, no asset class stays on the bottom either. The second point is that the only way to beat the game or to prevent you from losing it is to stay diversified. Another interesting way to visualize the asset index rankings is to categorize each year's returns according to the top, median and low positions. Then, look at the range from the top to bottom performing class. This further highlights the risk of trying to aggressively time the markets and being wrong. See exhibit I for this analysis.

EXHIBIT 5–H

ASSET CLASS RETURNS

1989	1990	1991	1992	1993	1994	1995
Large Cap Growth 36.40%	Fixed Income 8.96%	Small Cap Growth 51.19%	Small Cap Value 29.14%	Int'l Stocks 32.94%	Int'l Stocks 8.06%	Large Cap Growth 38.13%
S&P 500 31.69%	Large Cap Growth 0.20%	Small cap 46.04%	Small Cap 18.41%	Small Cap Value 23.77%	Large Cap Growth 3.14%	S&P 500 37.58%
Mid Cap 26.27%	S&P 500 -3.11%	Small Cap Value 41.70%	Mid Cap 16.34%	Small Cap 18.88%	S&P 500 1.32%	Large Cap Value 36.99%
Large Cap Value 26.13%	Large Cap Value -6.85%	Mid Cap 41.51%	Large Cap Value 10.52%	Large Cap Value 18.61%	Large Cap Value -0.64%	Mid Cap 34.45%
Small Cap Growth 20.17%	Mid Cap -11.50	Large Cap Growth 38.37%	Small Cap Growth 7.77%	Mid Cap 14.30%	Small Cap Value -1.54%	Small Cap Growth 31.04%
Small Cap 16.26%	Small Cap Growth -17.41	S&P 500 30.47%	S&P 500 7.62%	Small Cap Growth 13.37%	Small Cap -1.82%	Small Cap 28.45%
Fixed Income 14.53%	Small Cap -19.48	Large Cap Value 22.56%	Fixed Income 7.40%	S&P 500 10.08%	Mid Cap -2.09%	Small Cap Value 25.75%

Creating an Investment Policy

Small Cap Value 12.43%	Small Cap Value -21.77	Fixed Income 16.00%	Large Cap Growth 5.06%	Fixed Income 9.75%	Small Cap Growth -2.43%	Fixed Income 18.46%
Int'l Stocks 10.80%	Int'l Stocks -23.19	Int'l Stocks 12.49%	Int'l Stocks -11.85%	Large Cap Growth 1.68%	Fixed Income -2.92%	Int'l Stocks 11.55%

1996	1997	1998	1999	2000	2001	2002	2003
Large Cap Growth 23.97%	Large Cap Growth 36.52%	Large Cap Growth 42.16%	Small Cap Growth 43.09%	Small Cap Value 22.83%	Small Cap Value 14.02%	Fixed Income 10.27%	Small Cap Growth 48.53%
S&P 500 22.96%	S&P 500 33.36%	S&P 500 28.58%	Large Cap Growth 28.25%	Fixed Income 11.63%	Fixed Income 8.44%	Small Cap Value -11.43%	Small Cap 47.25%
Large Cap Value 22.00%	Small Cap Value 31.78%	Int'l Stocks 20.33%	Int'l Stocks 27.30%	Mid Cap 8.25%	Small Cap 2.49%	Int'l Stocks -15.66%	Small Cap Value 46.02%
Small Cap Value 21.37%	Large Cap Value 29.98%	Large cap Value 14.69%	Small Cap 21.26%	Large Cap Value 6.08%	Mid Cap -5.62%	Mid Cap -16.18%	Mid Cap 40.08%
Mid Cap 19.00%	Mid Cap 29.01%	Mid Cap 10.09%	S&P 500 21.04%	Small Cap -3.02%	Small Cap Growth -9.23%	Small Cap -20.48%	Int'l Stocks 39.17%
Small Cap 16.49%	Small Cap 22.36%	Fixed Income 8.70%	Mid Cap 18.23%	S&P 500 -9.10%	Large Cap Value -11.71%	Large Cap Value -20.85%	Large Cap Value 31.80%
Small Cap Growth 11.26%	Small Cap Growth 12.95%	Small Gap Growth 1.23%	Large Cap Value 12.72%	Int'l Stocks -13.96%	S&P 500 -11.88%	S&P 500 -22.10%	S&P 500 28.69%
Int'l Stocks 6.36%	Fixed Income 9.64%	Small Cap -2.55%	Fixed Income -0.82%	Large Cap Growth -22.07%	Large Cap Growth -12.73%	Large Cap Growth -23.59%	Large Cap Growth 25.67%

Fixed Income	Int'l Stocks	Small Cap Value	Small Cap Value	Small Cap Growth	Int'l Stocks	Small Cap Growth	Fixed Income
3.64%	2.06%	-6.45%	-1.49%	-22.43%	-21.21%	-30.26%	4.11%

EXHIBIT 5 – I

ANNUAL ASSET CLASS RANKINGS

Year	Top Rank	Median Rank	Bottom Rank	Differential Top - Bottom
1989	Large Cap Growth 36.40%	Small Cap Growth 20.17%	International 10.80%	25.60%
1990	Fixed Income 8.96%	Mid Cap -11.50%	International -23.19	32.15
1991	Small Cap Growth 51.19	Large Cap Growth 38.37	International 12.49	38.70
1992	Small Cap Value 29.14	Small Cap Growth 7.77	International -11.85	40.99
1993	International 32.94%	Mid Cap 14.30	Large Cap Growth 1.68	31.26
1994	International 8.06	Small Cap Value -1.54	Fixed Income -2.92	10.98
1995	Large Cap Growth 38.13	Small Cap Growth 31.04	International 11.55	26.58
1996	Large Cap Growth 23.97	Mid Cap 19.00	Fixed Income 3.64	20.33
1997	Large Cap Growth 36.52	Mid Cap 29.01	International 2.06	34.46
1998	Large Cap Growth 42.16	Mid Cap 10.09	Small Cap Value - 6.45	48.61
1999	Small Cap Growth 43.09	S & P 500 21.04	Small Cap Growth -1.49	44.58
2000	Small Cap Value 22.83	Small Cap -3.02	Small Cap Growth -22.43	45.26
2001	Small Cap Value 14.02	Small Cap Growth -9.23	International -21.21	35.23

| 2002 | Fixed Income 10.27 | Small Cap -20.48 | Small Cap Growth -30.26 | 40.53 |
| 2003 | Small Cap Gr. 48.53 | International 39.17 | Fixed Income 4.11 | 44.42 |

Alternatives to Portfolio Optimization

The traditional form of portfolio optimization has come under criticism in recent years. At the heart of this criticism is the charge that the inputs reflect past history more than anything else. It assumes that historical returns are normal and can be expected to play out as they have in past cycles. Also, the model assumes that the standard deviation and correlation are normalized and will repeat. Critics also point out that the model does not readily allow for changes in capital market assumptions.

Accordingly, two other techniques have emerged to challenge the traditional portfolio or mean variance optimization model. We will consider each in turn.

Monte Carlo Simulation

Monte Carlo simulation involves the use of a computer to generate a large number of sample outcomes based on varying inputs. In the investment world, it can produce a number of future scenarios based on a variety of input assumptions such as interest rates, inflation, etc. The result is a distribution of outcomes along with the probabilities that you will achieve certain results within a specified time period. To illustrate this technique in a very general sense, consider the following range of portfolio returns:

Confidence Range	Return
Upper 5%	15.5%
Upper 25%	12.6%
Expected 50%	10.4%
Lower 25%	4.3%
Lower 5%	1.6%

You would interpret this output as follows:

- Based on the range of outcomes, you would expect that 5 percent of the results will exceed 15.5 percent or you have a 5 percent probability of outperforming a level of 15.5 percent
- Moving along, you would expect 25 percent of the results to exceed 12.6 percent or you have a 25 percent probability of outperforming 12.6 percent
- You may also say that you have a 50 percent probability of performing between 4.3 percent and 12.6 percent.
- Then, on the negative side, you have a 5 percent probability of under-performing a 1.6 percent return.

Value at Risk

With the proliferation of financial instruments over the past decade, a more comprehensive analytical tool was needed to evaluate portfolio risk and return. One such tool to emerge has been the concept of "value at risk." Simply described, value at risk is the dollar that the portfolio can lose from market movements within a specified period of time and at a given confidence level. For example, one may explain a portfolio's value at risk as follows: There is a 95 percent probability that the portfolio will lose less than $500,000 due to market movements over the next year.

Alternatively, there is only a 5 percent probability that the portfolio will lose more than $500,000 over the next year.

Without going into an elaborate discussion of the actual statistics behind it, value at risk essentially involves a mapping process for all of the instruments of the portfolio. The inputs required for each instrument are the same as for normal portfolio optimization return or cash flow, standard deviation and correlation. There are also many proprietary models in the marketplace, but there are essentially three common methods employed:

- **Parametric,** which uses the standard deviation as its key statistical measure and assumes a somewhat normal distribution of return.
- **Historical,** which uses real past data and will therefore be non-normal in its distribution of returns.
- **Monte Carlo,** as described above, runs a significant number of trials, resulting in a range of returns along with the probabilities of achieving them.

Each of these methods will likely produce different results. It is therefore only important that when comparing alternatives, you employ the same method. To demonstrate one of these methods, consider the parametric value at risk calculation below. This is perhaps the simplest formula, incorporating the mean and standard deviation.

$$\text{Value at Risk} = \frac{P \times [(\chi - 1.65\sigma)]}{\sqrt{N}}$$

P = Value of the portfolio
χ = Expected return of portfolio
σ = Standard deviation of portfolio

N = Years in the measurement period
1.65 = The number of standard deviations to give you a 95% probability or confidence level in the outcomes.

Let's apply a short example to illustrate how this formula would work. Assume the following parameters:

Portfolio size = $15 million

Asset allocation is $7 million in equities with an expected rate of return of 12 percent; $5 million in bonds with an expected return of 6 percent; and $3 million in hedge funds with an expected return of 10 percent.

The portfolio's standard deviation is 14 percent.

The investment time horizon is one year.

We will be trying to determine the maximum loss we might incur in any one-year period. We want to be 95 percent confident in this number.

Our first step is to calculate the mean or expected return. We do this accordingly:

$$\chi = (.47 \times .12) + (.33 \times .06) + (.20 \times .10) = .0962$$

We next apply this to the formula:

$$\frac{\$15,000,000 \times [.0962 - 1.65(.14)]}{\sqrt{1}} = \$2,022,000$$

This translates into a 95 percent probability that your portfolio will not suffer a loss in any year that is greater than $2,022,000. Alternatively, there is only a 5 percent chance that your portfolio will suffer a loss that is greater than $2,022,000 in a given year.

The value at risk measure has become popular because it enables investors to employ a uniform measurement across all risk types and asset classes. It is also based on observed market relationships and historical correlations. The concept itself is easily understood and government regulators have adopted it in some quarters to evaluate the risk in the portfolios of financial institutions. On the other hand, like other measurement tools, value at risk has its limitations. It is not necessarily the worst case situation, as there is still a small percentage probability not covered. Also, it is not a cumulative measurement. For example, your value at risk loss could be $2,000,000 in a given 12-month period, but you could have two or three consecutive periods of significant losses, even if not at this level. The measurement is also based more on historical relationships and not driven by future market scenarios. In summary, the value at risk is an excellent tool but generally needs to be used alongside others in order to manage complex portfolios.

Establish Asset Allocation Structure

After running whatever portfolio optimization model or combination of models you and your advisor prefer, you are then ready to establish precise asset allocation targets. Most advisors will speak of asset allocation in terms of strategic versus tactical. Strategic asset allocation is long term and represents those asset classes you wish to remain in through the entire investment cycle. You will generally establish a target allocation for each asset category, along with a minimum and maximum range for each. A sample format is displayed on exhibit 5-J.

EXHIBIT 5-J

ASSET CLASS RANGES (%)

	Minimum	Target	Maximum
CASH	1	2	5
FIXED INCOME			
Investment Grade Bonds	20	25	35
High Yield Bonds	3	5	10
EQUITIES			
Large Cap Value	5	10	15
Large Cap Growth	5	10	15
Mid Cap Core	3	5	10
Small Cap Value	2	5	8
Small Cap Growth	2	5	8
International	5	10	15
ALTERNATIVES			
Real Estate	0	5	10
Natural Resources	0	3	6
Hedge Funds-Absolute Return	3	5	15
Hedge Funds-Directional	3	5	15
Private Equity	0	5	10
TOTAL		100	

Tactical asset allocation, on the other hand, is more short term in nature and may include the following actions:

- Adding an asset class to the portfolio based on current market conditions or where we are in the business cycle. For example, as a recession seems to be bottoming out, some investors find high

yield bonds to be attractive because they expect credit conditions are going to improve. As a result, they will add that asset class to the portfolio if they do not already have it. Convertible securities could play a similar role in the portfolio, as investors may not yet be ready to increase their commitment to equities. With convertibles, they can achieve the benefit of a higher yield while still being in position to benefit from an increase in the underlying stock.
- If the market seems to be overheating, you may want to decrease your equity commitment temporarily and redeploy the funds to bonds or hedge funds.
- International monetary conditions may suggest asset allocation shifts. For example, investors will tend to move funds into international equities as the dollar weakens against world currencies or as overseas markets strengthen verses the U.S.

Tactical asset allocation can be risky and many investment advisors discourage it on a widespread basis. However, there is room for both strategic as well as tactical asset allocation to work in a given portfolio. We will speak more about how they can interact well when we discuss portfolio rebalancing in the next chapter.

Define Asset Class Strategies

The process continues with one of the most important elements in formulating an investment strategy today. While the decision as to allocating assets among stocks, bond and cash is still the critical high level one, investors have found that the process has become much deeper today with the proliferation of investment alternatives. Here we will discuss the various ways to invest within each asset class, including the alternative investment categories.

Equities

Over the years, investors have learned that many professional equity managers have their good and bad years. While their performances in some of those years can be attributed to good or bad stock picking, most money managers are also subject to specific conditions in the economy and securities markets. This is particularly the case where a manager follows a specific or narrow style of investing. For example, your manager may be a "value" investor who has performed brilliantly over the years. Then, as happened in the late-1990, value investing began to lag behind other styles of investing. The performances of some great value managers began to cause deep concern among some of their clients. As you would expect, the managers advised their clients that their style was just out of favor at the current time. The smart clients would have stayed with their good value managers, because value investing recovered in 2000, outpacing growth investing again. At the same time, many investors then became concerned with their growth managers who, like their value counterparts a few years earlier, were suffering from poor performance and began advising clients their style was just out of favor. All of this points to the fact that investors need to be cognizant of shifting styles and the only effective way to balance out the risks is to diversify to some extent among the various styles. As exhibit 5 –I demonstrated, there can be considerable gaps between the top and bottom performing styles in any given year.

We will now look at the various ways to craft an equity investment strategy. To help guide us through the process, consider the chart depicted in exhibit 5-K. This delineates the range of equity asset classes as well as the manager styles and sub-styles. This is an important starting point, so we will briefly define the sections of this chart. After doing so, we will suggest ways to organize an equity portfolio around its asset classes.

EXHIBIT 5–K

EQUITY ASSET CLASS STYLES

Major Asset Classes	Manager Styles	Sub Styles
• Large Cap • Mid Cap • Small Cap • Multi-Cap • Global • International – Developed • Emerging Markets • Convertibles	• Value • Core • Growth • Index / Quantitative	**Value** • Deep Value • Traditional Value • Relative Value
	Index / Quantitative • Benchmark Driven • Tax Enhanced	**Core** • Core w/Value Tilt • Style Neutral • Core w/ Growth Tilt **Growth** • Growth at Reasonable Prices • Traditional Growth • Aggressive Growth

Major Asset Classes

1. **Capitalization-** The first cut in defining equity classes lies in their capitalization. The marketplace segments equities into four categories. *Large Cap* stocks are generally defined as companies with market capitalizations of over $10 billion. These firms are,

as the name implies, the large corporations with significant products and market shares. *Mid Cap* stocks are generally defined as those firms with market capitalization between $1 billion and $10 billion. *Small Cap* stocks are those companies with a market capitalization below $1 billion. Today, many investment advisors manage distinct portfolios according to capitalization. They categorize themselves as large, mid or small cap managers. Some, however, do not like to just stay within a single capitalization box, so there is a category of manager called *Multi Cap or All Cap* in order to capture their style. The capitalization of your portfolio can have a significant bearing on performance as we showed earlier. Therefore, diversifying by capitalization class can be critical in managing not only your return, but your risk as well.

2. **International-** This sector includes three distinct classes where investments are predominately outside of the United States. The first is *International-Developed*, which includes companies in the developed world outside the U.S. The second class is *Emerging Markets*, which includes the less developed world and the third is *Global*, which includes the entire world, even investments in the United States. This asset class has an added dimension in that is subject to currency fluctuations in addition to normal business and market risks.

3. **Convertible Securities-** These investments are either preferred stock or bonds where the holder has a right to exchange it into common stock according to a pre-determined formula. In essence, they are hybrid securities consisting of a bond or preferred stock on the one hand and a call option to purchase the underlying stock on the other hand. The best way to describe these securities is to look at an example. We will look at a convertible bond. Consider a convertible bond with a par value of $1,000. The terms of the offering are that you can convert the bond into 20 shares of common stock. This means that the *conversion ratio* is 20 and the *conversion price* is $50. The bond's

Creating an Investment Policy

conversion value is the value you receive if you were to convert the bond into stock today. For example, if the stock were selling at $60 per share, its conversion value would be $1,200. You arrive at this by multiplying the conversion ratio of 20 by the value of the stock. In this case, the bond would be selling at a price of at least $1,200 or there would be an arbitrage opportunity to buy the bond at less than $1,200, convert it to common and then sell the stock. Observing this relationship, you can conclude that when stock prices are high, the convertible security will reflect its conversion value. On the other hand, when stock prices are low, the convertible bond will sell at its straight bond value since it is out of the money. Consider the above illustration where the stock is selling at $45 instead of $60. The conversion value would then be $900. If interest rates were at the same level as when the bonds were issued, there would be no value to convert as the bond would be selling at around par.

Manager Styles

Over the past decade, equity investing has become somewhat of a contest between "value" and "growth" investors. Many investment managers define themselves as either value or growth shops. We will look at these as well as a couple of other manager styles that now define the investment industry.

1. **Value-** These investors focus primarily on the price they are paying for a stock. In other words, they are interested in the price component of the price/earnings ratio. They also believe that the company's stock price does not fully reflect its underlying asset value or future earnings potential. More specifically, value investors will tend to favor low price/earnings and price to book ratio stocks. They will also gravitate toward higher yield stocks and generally have investments in cyclical companies.

2. **Growth-** These investors focus more on the earnings side of the P/E ratio. They are looking at the economic story behind the company. They expect companies to exhibit superior growth, well above the average company in the market as well as against its peer group. Specifically, they will tend to invest in higher P/E stocks. Their portfolios will usually include technology and health care companies but may also include consumer stocks with steady earnings growth.
3. **Core-** These investors will select stocks from both the value as well as the growth camps. They tend to have broadly diversified portfolios across all major sectors of the market.
4. **Index/Quantitative-** Passive or index managers strive to design portfolios that can replicate the performance of a specific index. Key features of these portfolios are low turnover, low taxes, lower fees and low tracking error to the benchmark. There are essentially three different ways to construct an index portfolio. First, you can try to replicate it exactly, such as buying the entire 500 stocks in the S&P 500 Index. This may not be the most efficient model as you may incur substantial transaction costs to constantly rebalance the portfolio and to reinvest the dividends. A second option is to construct the portfolio through statistical sampling. Here you would try to arrange a representative sampling of the index. For example, you may only buy 200 to 250 of the 500 stocks in the S&P 500 index. You would try to select those stocks that, in combination, would come close to approximating the index. The only risk here is that your selection may lag the benchmark in certain periods. A third option is to design your portfolio through a computerized process called quadratic optimization. This program uses as inputs the historical changes in stock prices and the correlations among those stocks. The idea is to achieve an output that minimizes the tracking error of the portfolio against the benchmark. The risk with this

technique is that you are relying on past information, and as we know, the past does not guarantee the future.

Manager Sub-Styles

As the investment markets have become more and more complex, we learned that not all value managers are alike, nor are all growth managers the same. Each of these styles, as well as the central core and index styles, can be more finely segmented. We will look at each major style in turn.

Value

1. **Deep Value-** At the far end of the value spectrum are the deep value investors. As a deep value investor, a manager will search for stocks trading at a substantial discount to their historical value and to the stock market in general. Low price earnings and price to book ratios will characterize this style of investing. Deep value investors will regularly buy out of favor companies with the expectation that they will improve as economic conditions change in the future. These investors are what you would term "contrarian" investors. From a performance standpoint, they will be erratic compared to the general value benchmarks. When they outperform, it will be by a significant margin; on the other hand, when their style is out of favor, they may lag the value benchmarks by a meaningful margin.
2. **Traditional Value-** These are the middle of the road value investors. They emphasize companies that have low valuations compared to their own history and to their industry. You expect that the stock prices will increase as their P/Es expand. The performance of these managers will approximate the general value indices.
3. **Relative Value-** As we move toward the end of the value spectrum, investors begin to look at the relationship between a

company's earnings and its stock price. Here, the investment manager seeks stocks that represent good valuations where the company's earnings are growing faster than its price indicates. Its price earnings ratio is accordingly, not where you believe it should be and you will expect to realize some appreciation due to additional P/E expansion.

Core

1. **Core with Value Tilt-** With the core styles, you invest in a combination of growth and value names. The degree to which you select value verses growth will more finely define the particular sub-style. With this style, you have more value names in your portfolio but are willing to include growth stocks that appear to be reasonably valued.
2. **Style Neutral-** With this style, you pretty much balance the allocation to value and growth stocks. There is generally no bias either way.
3. **Core with Growth Tilt-** This is the counter to the earlier Core with Value Tilt sub-style. In this instance, you will have both value and growth names again, but will favor the growth side. You will also have a portfolio that starts to reflect higher price earnings and price to book ratios.

Index/Quantitative

1. **Benchmark Driven-** With indexing, you can adopt one of two strategies. First, you can strive to perform in line with a specified benchmark such as the S&P 500 or the Russell 2000. The performance would be gross of fees and before taxes.
2. **Tax Enhanced-** A second way to manage an index portfolio is to focus on after-tax and after-fees. The manager is constantly searching for ways to take tax losses and balance gains against

losses. Also, the manager tries to limit turnover so as to limit not only capital gains but transaction costs as well. Many quantitative investment managers will promote themselves as tax enhanced index managers.

Growth

1. **Growth at Reasonable Prices-** Moving now into the growth style sector, the emphasis is on the earnings side of the P/E ratio. Accordingly, with a GARP style, investors look for companies with demonstrated earning growth. Moreover, their stock prices are not yet very expensive. However, you expect their stock prices to increase due more to earnings growth as opposed to an expansion in their price earning multiplier.
2. **Traditional Growth-** Here you believe the P/E ratios are pretty much reflected for the individual stocks. You also expect that the share prices will continue to increase as earning expand. However, you do not expect significant further expansions in the P/E multiplier.
3. **Aggressive Growth-** We are now in the far end of the growth style sector. As an aggressive growth investor, you expect a company's earning will not only grow in the future, but will show accelerating growth. Accordingly, you are willing to pay up for this anticipated growth. Stocks in this category will reflect high price earnings ratios as investors believe earnings will rapidly catch up to their lofty P/E ratios.

Equity Strategies

How do we now put all of this together? Before discussing some optional equity strategies, let's rearrange exhibit 5-K in a different manner. In exhibit 5-L we present an investment style matrix, combining asset classes and manager styles in a continuum. This better enables us to visualize the alternatives.

EXHIBIT 5-L

INVESTMENT MANAGER MATRIX

Manager Style

	Value	Core	Growth
Large Cap			
Mid Cap			
Small Cap			
International			

1. **Index-** As the name implies, you could theoretically index your way through the various asset classes and manager styles. In the next chapter, we will discuss how you could implement this approach either using traditional index funds or exchange traded funds. Investors favor this approach because of its low cost and its low tracking error to a benchmark.
2. **Core/Satellite-** A variation of the index approach is the "core-satellite" strategy. Here the investor indexes the large

cap core sector of the portfolio but employs active management for the other asset classes and management styles. The reasoning here is that large cap managers have historically had a difficult time beating the S&P 500 index, while other style managers have fared better. The large cap market is also much more efficient than the mid cap, small cap and international markets. These managers have a better chance of adding "alpha" than do their large cap counterparts.

3. **Barbell-** As the name implies, with this strategy, you employ both ends of the spectrum. You would construct a portfolio by combining deep value with aggressive growth managers. Your expectation is that each manager will outperform his/her peers and that over time, this will enable you to achieve superior results. Moreover, you will generally have one manager style performing well at any time.

4. **Centrist-** So as to stay close to your core benchmark, you may want to just carve out the middle. You can achieve this in a couple of ways. First, you can combine the three styles within the core sub-style with the expectation that you can select superior managers in each area. You may also achieve this by combining the relative value and GARP styles. As a third option, you may even be able to combine the traditional value and traditional growth styles, again with the expectation that if your managers outperform their style benchmarks, you will have a very good chance of outperforming the general market.

5. **Value Tilt-** Some investors may prefer to have a diversified portfolio of asset classes and manager styles but with a value tilt. There are, of course, several ways to accomplish this. One way is to combine the core value and style neutral managers with one or a couple of the value style managers. Another way is to maintain broad exposure in all of the style boxes but overweight the value areas. You may also decide to

just invest in the value styles for certain capitalization areas. For instance, while you may broadly diversify the large cap and international areas, you may concentrate your mid and small cap portfolios in the value sectors.
6. **Growth Tilt-** Conversely, some investors will want to tilt the portfolios toward growth. You would approach this construction in the same way that we discussed value in the section above.
7. **All Cap-** Some investment managers choose not to be confined to just one of the boxes. Instead, they may offer what is termed an "all cap" portfolio within a major discipline. For example, you will see managers who are all cap value managers or all cap growth managers. These managers will therefore not be restricted by capitalization sectors and will invest in large, mid and small cap stocks, using their skills to determine the most advantageous allocation at any point in time. While this style requires some degree of market forecasting, there are investment managers who have successfully operated in this space.
8. **Options and Hedging-** A discussion of equity strategies would not be complete without mentioning the deployment of derivatives to not only enhance the returns but to manage the risks of your overall portfolio. It is beyond the scope of this book to go into the topic of derivatives in great detail, but we will briefly mention some of the common strategies below. We will also cover this topic in somewhat greater detail in the chapter dealing with concentrated equity strategies.
    - *Call options* are one of the basic derivative techniques. A call option is the right to purchase a security at a specified price before a stated expiration date. For this right, the holder of the call option pays the seller a premium. An example will better illustrate this concept. Assume that Procter &

Gamble stock is selling for $85 in November. You are able to buy a February call option on P&G for a premium of $5 at a strike price of $90. This means that you are able to buy the stock at anytime until the third Friday in February (options expire on the third Friday of the expiration month) at a price of $90. This call option is obviously valuable only if P&G is selling above $90 and you can profit on the transaction only if the stock sells at a price in excess of $95. For example, assume that the stock is selling at $98 in January. Should you exercise your call, you can purchase the stock at $90 and sell it at $98, for a gain of $8. From this gain, you then subtract the $5 premium you originally paid for the option, so you are left with a net profit of $3. On the other hand, if P&G is selling for $80 in January, there would be no value in exercising the option. If the stock does not reach the exercise price, the call option expires and is worthless. At any exercise price between $90 and $95, there will be some incremental revenue in exercising before expiration, but once again, the stock needs to go above $95 for you to realize a net profit. For the investor, there are a number of ways call options can be used. If you do not currently own the stock, buying a call may be attractive if you expect the stock to significantly increase over the near term or want to bet that it will. Your risk is just losing the premium you paid for the call option. If you own the stock, selling call options may be attractive as an additional source of income, particularly where you believe the stock is fully valued and you do not care if it gets called away. Also, if you believe the stock is not likely to go up or down much in the short run, writing a call can be attractive. A more active strategy is to hire a manager that employs a covered call writing strategy. This entails buying a stock and then selling calls on it. In some cases, the manager may not want the stock to be called away so he/she may actually repurchase the current call and then write a new one (option overwriting).

- Somewhat of a mirror image to a call option, the **put option** gives its holder the right to sell the underlying security at a given exercise price. Suppose you purchased a put option on Intel, which currently sells for $28. You pay a premium of $3 for a February put at an exercise price of $26. We can again look at various scenarios. If the stock were to be selling at $22 before expiration, you could either sell your put or buy the stock at $22 and exercise the put option at $26, for a gain of $4 per share. From this, you have to take away the $3 premium you paid for the put option. On the other hand, if the stock were selling at $35, the put option would be out of the money and could likely expire worthless. A common strategy where investors want guaranteed downside protection is to engage in **protective put transactions**. Here you purchase a stock along with a put. At expiration, you purchase another put unless it was favorable to exercise it during the term. A protective put is sometimes compared to a stop-loss order where your stock is sold when it breaks through a certain price point. With a put, you are not obligated to exercise it when the price point is reached, where you are obligated to sell the stock in a stop-loss transaction. The only real disadvantage of a put is that you pay a premium to acquire it while there is no up-front cost to engage in a stop-loss order.

- There are other types of individual option strategies. One is a **straddle**. You create a straddle when you buy a call and a put on a stock with the same strike price and the same expiration date. Here is an example:

  Buy an IBM Feb 110 Call @ 10
  Buy an IBM Feb 110 Put @ 7

  Current market price is 108

  When you buy a straddle, you believe that the stock will move in price but you are uncertain of its direction. You benefit either way. Should the price increase, you can buy the stock at an attractive price. On the other hand, should it decrease, you can exercise your put at an attractive level. As the stock becomes more volatile, you have greater opportunity for profit. One way to visualize the profit on calls, puts and straddles is to examine the figures in exhibit 5-M.

  In each case, the area between the solid and dotted lines represents the premium paid for the options. As the figures indicate, you make money on a purchased call as the stock price goes up. Conversely, on a put, you profit as the stock price decreases. Then, with a straddle, you can make money either way so long as there is a degree of volatility. You only lose when the stock price stays steady.

EXHIBIT 5–M

OPTION PROFITS

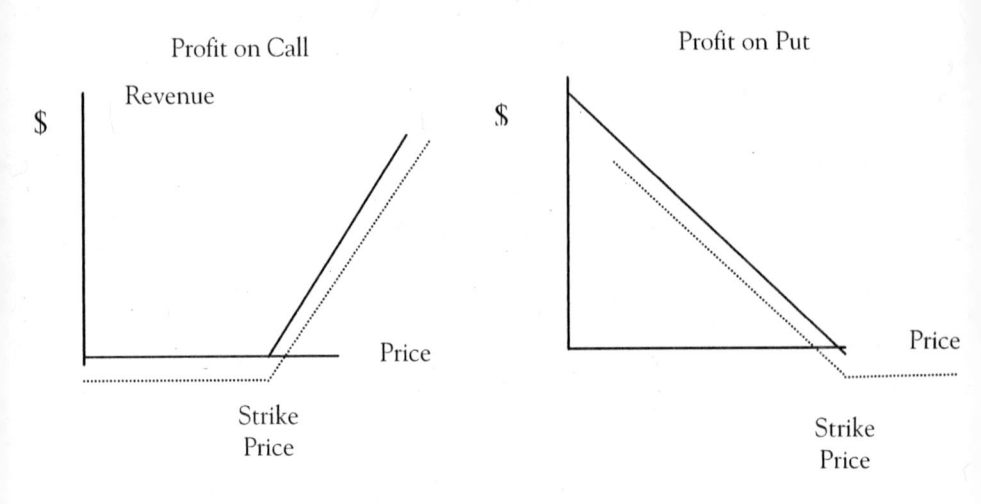

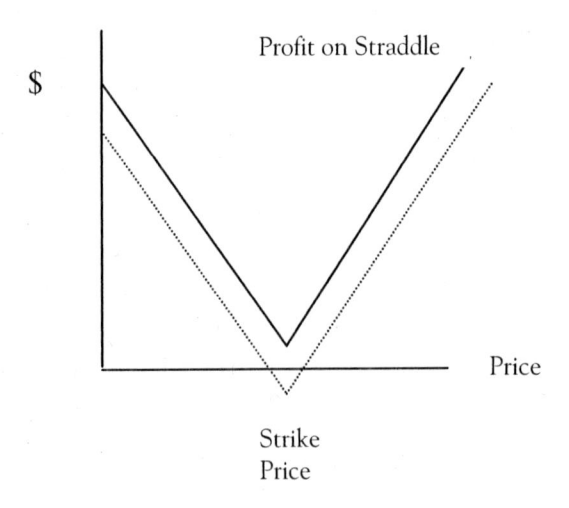

Source: Investments by Bodie, Kane & Marcus

- Another variation is a *spread option.* A spread option is the purchase and sale of the same class of options (e.g., calls or puts) but with different expiration months or strike prices. A *price* or *vertical* spread is when the expiration months are the same but the strike prices are different. An example is as follows:

Buy a PG Feb 80 Call @ 6 ½
Sell a PG Feb 85 Call @ 4 ¼

A **calendar** or **horizontal** spread is when the exercise prices are the same but the expiration months are different. Consider this example:

Buy a PG Feb 80 Call @ 5
Sell a PG Nov 80 Call @ 3

When engaging in these transactions, the investor will want to determine the potential profit, loss and break-even points. Exhibit 5-N can assist us in following the numbers to determine the maximum profit or loss on these transactions. As the table indicates, there are two sources of income and expense. First, you have the net premium paid or received. In the case of a debit spread, you will be paying out more in premiums than you receive. In the example presented, you are paying $4.50 per share for the Feb 50 call option. This gives you the right to buy GM stock at an exercise price of $50 until February. You then sell the GM Feb 55 call option and receive $3 per share. Your net outlay is $1.50. This represents your maximum loss. With a debit spread, you can only profit if the stock price moves and the options are exercised. In this case, you would realize a gain that is equal to the difference in strike prices. For example, should the price of GM go to 60, you would likely be forced to sell the stock to the holder of the 55 call. However, you would offset that by exercising your purchase rights on the 50 call. This gives you a $5 profit. Your net gain on the overall transaction is therefore $3.50. With a credit spread, the process works somewhat in reverse. In this case, you receive a net premium of $5. You would therefore hope that the calls remain unexercised so that you can realize the entire gain. However, should the stock price increase to 60 again, it is likely the calls will be exercised. In this case, you would suffer a loss on the exercise of $10 as you will need to sell the stock to the holder of the 50 call option but would be forced to buy the offsetting position at 60.

EXHIBIT 5–N

PROFIT ON OPTION SPREADS

DEBIT SPREADS	CREDIT SPREADS
Buy a GM Feb 50 Call @ 4½ **Sell a GM Feb 55 Call @ 3**	Buy a GM Oct 60 Call at 2 ½ **Sell a GM Oct 50 Call at 7½**
Net outflow of 1 ½ (Payment of 4 ½ premium verses sale of 3) Exercise price spread of 5 Maximum profit of 3 ½ (Price spread of 5 verses net cost of 1 ½)	Net inflow of 5 (payment of 2 ½ verses receipt of 7 ½) Exercise price spread of 10 Maximum loss of 5 (Price spread of 10 verses receipt of 5 from net premiums)

Spread options lend themselves to specific strategies. These strategies bet on the direction of the stock and accordingly are termed "bull" or "bear" spreads. Exhibit 5-O provides an illustration of the four spread strategies and we will briefly describe each. There are two **bull spread** strategies. The first is a **bull call spread strategy**. In this case, the option you purchase has a lower strike price than the option you sell. Here you want the price of the stock to increase as you will benefit most if the price increases and the calls are exercised. The second bull strategy is a **bull put spread**. Again, the option you purchase has a lower strike price than the option you sell. If the stock price increases, the puts go unexercised, so you are able to pocket the net credit premium. There are also two **bear spread** strategies. The first is a **bear call spread**. With bear spread strategies, the option you purchase has a higher strike price than the one you sell. You therefore want the price of the underlying security to decrease. With a bear call spread, you will be able to pocket the net credit premium if the stock increases and the calls go unexercised. Finally, when you engage in a bear put strategy, you realize an overall profit as the stock declines and the options are exercised. The spread exceeds the net debit premium that you paid. To summarize these bull and bear strategies, you can identify them by comparing the exercise or strike price. Where the strike price on the option purchased is lower than on the option sold, you are engaged in a bull spread strategy. Conversely, where the strike price on the option purchased is higher than on the option sold, you are engaged in a bear spread strategy.

EXHIBIT 5-O

OPTION SPREAD STRATEGIES

BULL SPREADS   BEAR SPREADS

Bull Call Spread	Bull Put Spread	Bear Call Spread	Bear Put Spread
Buy GE Oct 30 Call @ 5 ½ Sell GE Apr 37 Call @ 2	Buy GE Feb 30 Put @ 3 Sell GE Oct 38 Put @ 8	Buy IBM Oct 100 Call @ 2 ½ Sell IBM Apr 90 Call @ 7 ½	Buy GE Feb 36 Put @ 6 Sell GE Oct 28 Put @ 2
Net debit premium of 3 ½ Exercise spread of 7 Maximum profit of 3 ½ Benefit if stock increases, and calls exercised	Net credit premium of 5 Exercise spread of 8 Maximum loss of 3 Benefit if stock price increases and options remain unexercised	Net credit premium of 5 Exercise spread of 10 Maximum loss of 5 Benefit if stock price decreases and calls remain unexercised	Net debit premium of 4 Exercise spread of 8 Maximum profit of 4 Benefit if price decreases and put options exercised

- Up to this point, we have been discussing options on individual stocks. However, sometimes an investor will want to hedge against an overall decline in the market. It is possible to accomplish this through **stock index futures** or **index options.** Here you engage in an option or futures contract that is based on an underlying stock market index like the S&P 500 or the S&P 100. There is no physical exchange of securities. Instead, the value of the index option fluctuates until maturity. Your profit depends on the movement in the value of the index itself. Also, if you purchased a call option on the S&P 500, you will profit if the market rises and the value of the index increases above the exercise price. If you purchased a put option, you realize a profit as the index falls below the strike price. By employing put options on the broad market indexes, you can hedge your portfolio against falling markets.

- Before leaving the topic of options, it is important to note one of the riskiest options strategies. This involves selling *"naked" call options*. An example will best illustrate this. Assume you sell a call option on General Electric at a strike price of $33 for a premium of $3.50. If the stock increases to $50 and you do not own the shares long, you will need to go into the market and purchase GE at $50. However, you are obligated to then sell it for $33. Extrapolating this beyond the $50, you can see that your potential loss is unlimited. Accordingly, this strategy is extremely risky.

9. **Short Selling-** Completing the range of equity class strategies, we will speak briefly about another risky strategy. By definition, short selling involves selling a stock that you do not own. You arrange to sell a particular stock at the current price but borrow that stock from your broker before selling it. You will therefore be required to purchase the stock at a later date in order to cover the short position. You obviously anticipate that the stock will go down so you can purchase it at a lower price and earn a profit. However, should the stock price rise significantly, you will be in trouble. As a result, short selling is highly regulated by brokerage firm and federal banking policies. An example will illustrate how this works in practice. Assume that you want to sell short 2000 shares of Merck at $50 per share. Your broker gets you the shares to sell and then credits your account at the brokerage firm for $100,000. The cash proceeds stay at the firm. You will receive some interest on these funds but will have to give any stock dividends to the lender of the stock. The brokerage firm will also have margin requirements as specified by the Federal Reserve Bank. Usually this is 50 percent. This means that you need to have

an additional $50,000 of cash or securities in the custody of the broker, bringing your total account value to $150,000. The $100,000 short position is your future liability. The broker may also have what is called a maintenance margin requirement on short sales. This means that the equity level in your account must be at least equal to this maintenance margin. Many brokers will specify a maintenance margin of 30 percent. You therefore need to know how high the stock can go before you hit the maintenance level. At that point, you have to post additional collateral. The general formula for determining this level is as follows:

$$\frac{\text{Equity}}{\text{Value of Short Shares}}$$

In the example with Merck, the maintenance price at which you would have to post additional collateral is derived as follows:

$$\frac{\$150{,}000 - 2{,}000(\text{price of Merck})}{2{,}000(\text{price of Merck})} = 0.30$$

Applying the formula, the price of Merck can rise to $57.69 until you will receive an additional margin call. On the other hand, your profit on short selling takes place as the price of the stock falls. For example, if Merck were to fall to $40, you could close out your short position and realize a $20,000 profit. Buying the stock at 40 and selling it at the contracted price of 50, gives you 10 points. Applying this to 2,000 shares, results in the $20,000 gain.

Creating an Investment Policy

Fixed Income

As an integral component of all portfolios, fixed income investments serve a number of purposes. First and foremost, bonds generally provide the bulk of a portfolio's income. They also serve as the family's overall safety net, although bonds are not always a risk free asset class. The higher risk bonds, commonly referred to as "high yield bonds," can produce an attractive total return over the long term if they are effectively managed. Our discussion of fixed income strategies is divided into four segments. In order, we will cover the basic features of fixed income instruments followed by a review of the various sectors of the market. We will then look at some of the issues involved in managing fixed income portfolios and conclude the discussion with a review of bond swaps.

Features of Fixed Income Instruments

To provide a background for discussing some of the more specific management strategies, it is first important to cover some of the basic features inherent in most fixed income instruments.

1. **Par Value-** This is the face or principal value of the bond. It is the value that other features key off of. The amount you receive at maturity is the par value.
2. **Market Value-** Because of changes in interest rates, bonds prices will fluctuate as we will see later. When bonds are priced below their par value, they are said to be trading at a discount. Conversely, when they sell above their par value, they are trading at a premium.
3. **Coupon Rate-** This represents the interest rate that the issuer pays on the bonds. The percentage rate is applied to the bond's par value. Some bonds pay no interest and are issued at a discount. These are called zero-coupon

bonds. Still, other bonds will not pay a fixed coupon rate and instead, will pay a variable rate that changes over time to reflect current interest rates.

4. **Current Yield**- This is simply the annual income divided by the current price of the bond. As interest rates rise, the bond price will fall so that the current yield reflects present market conditions.
5. **Yield to Maturity**- As bonds will trade at premiums or discounts, the coupon rate or current yield will not give you the complete yield picture. Impacting the true yield of a bond is not just the coupon payments, but also the current bond price and its maturity date. The yield to maturity is therefore a closer approximation of the bond's yield. It is defined as the interest rate that equates the present value of the interest payments and principal repayment to the bond's current price. This rate can therefore be considered as the average rate of return an investor will earn on a bond that is purchased now and held until maturity. With a financial calculator, you can easily determine the yield to maturity given the other parameters. Consider the following functional equation:

$$\text{Price} = \text{Coupon} \times \text{Annuity factor (ytm, \# of payments)} + \text{Par value} \times \text{PV factor (ytm, \# of payments)}$$

Let's look at a live example to better illustrate the calculation:

Price = $1,157.75
Coupon = 6% or 3% semi-annually, equating to $30 semi-annually
Maturity = 10 years or 20 payments

We therefore solve for the yield to maturity. Using a financial calculator, this comes out to 4.06%.

6. **Yield to Call-** Issuers sometimes have the right to retire part or all of a bond issue prior to maturity. In that case, you would calculate the yield to call date as opposed to the yield to maturity.

7. **Weighted Average Maturity-** As the name implies, this calculation is derived by multiplying the maturity of each bond by its relative weighting in the overall portfolio. This measure will have an impact on the price change of a bond given a stated change in the interest rate levels.

8. **Duration-** This concept, originally developed by Frederick Macaulay, is a more refined measure of the sensitivity of a bond to changes in its yield to maturity. To conceptually compute duration, you start out with each interest and principal payment and time weight each cash flow. The weights are therefore the present values of each cash flow as a percentage of the present value of all cash flows. Accordingly, the weighting is proportional to the value of each payment to the total number of payments that will be generated by the bond. Duration has a few important properties in relation to other bond features. First, it is always going to be less than the maturity of the bond since you are giving weights to the coupon payments. Second, the larger the coupon, the shorter the duration, since the coupon payments will have an overall greater weighting in the total cash flow picture. Third, with a zero coupon bond, the duration matches the term to maturity since you have no coupon payments.

9. **Convexity-** As a strict definition, convexity is a measurement of the rate of change of duration as yields change. The best way to visualize this concept is to first

look at the price/yield relationship as depicted on exhibit 5-P. The relationship between a bond's price and yield is not a linear one. Instead, it is a curved or convex relationship. The curvature of the line is therefore called its convexity. You can measure the convexity of the bond at a given yield by the slope of its tangent line. What does all of this mean? It first means that price changes for a change in yield are not always symmetrical. A given increase in yield will not cause the same price movement as would a decrease. For example, with convexity, when yields decline, the rate at which the bond price increases will accelerate as the slope of the tangent line steepens. At the same time, when yields increase, the rate at which the bond price decreases becomes slower as noted by the flattening of the tangent line. Another observation is that you would prefer bonds with higher convexity. If you have two bonds with the same duration but one has greater convexity, you want the one with the greater convexity since it is likely to show better performance in both rising and falling interest rate markets. In rising interest rate environments, its price will fall at a slower rate, while in falling rate environments, its price will tend to rise at a faster rate. See exhibit 5-Q as a graphic example. In this case, bond B has greater convexity. Its slope is steeper as you move toward lower yields and flattens out a little more as you progress toward higher rates.

Convexity is related to a bond and its portfolio's coupon, maturity and yield. As to coupon, there is an inverse relationship since the lower the coupon, the higher the convexity. Lower coupons mean that less of a bond's total return will come from the income side.

Accordingly, for a given level of interest rate change, a bond with a lower coupon will experience a greater price change than would one with a higher coupon. As to maturity, there is a direct relationship, since longer maturities are, by nature, more volatile than shorter ones. As to yield, there is an inverse relationship. Exhibit 5-P shows that the price yield curve is steeper at lower yields than at higher ones.

EXHIBIT 5-P

CONVEXITY

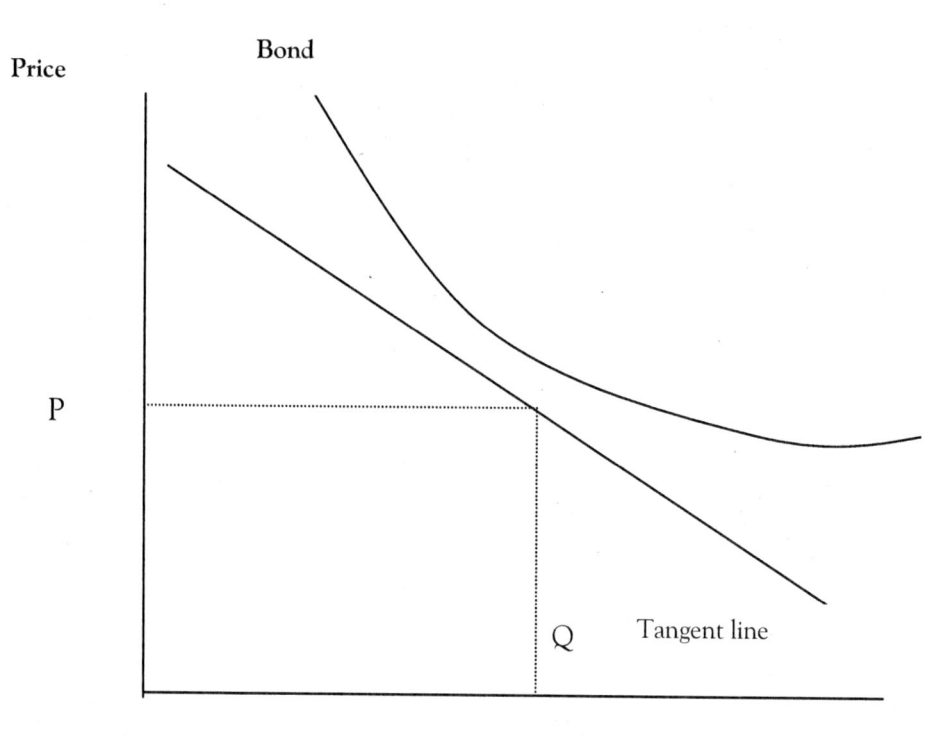

EXHIBIT 5-Q

COMPARATIVE CONVEXITIES

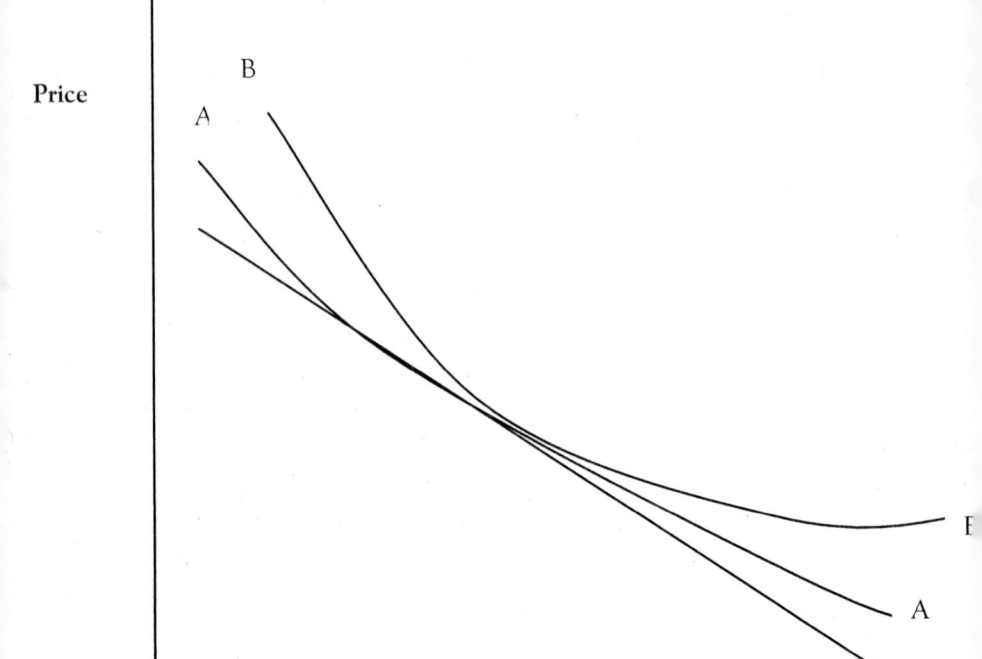

Price

B

A

B

A

Tangent line

Yield

Sectors of the Fixed Income Markets

The fixed income market offers investors a wide range of alternatives. Deciding which sectors to emphasize has a significant bearing on your portfolio's performance at any given time. In the next section, we will cover the portfolio management aspects of sector strategy, but first, we will briefly discuss what these sectors are.

- At the top of the food chain are **U.S. Treasury** securities. Without a question, the U.S. treasury is the single largest issuer of debt in the world. The Treasury issues several types of debt, each backed by the full faith and credit of the U. S. Government. At the short end, the Government regularly issues Treasury Bills with maturities less than one year. It then issues longer-term securities in two segments. First, there are Treasury Notes, which have maturities less than ten years. Then, the Treasury issues bonds, which range in maturities from ten to thirty years. There are also some specialized securities issued by the Treasury. To give investors some protection against inflation, the Treasury began to issue *Treasury Inflation Protected Securities (TIPS)* in 1997. As to mechanics, the principal value is adjusted every six months to properly reflect the inflation rate since origination. The inflation rate is the consumer price index. Then, the original coupon rate is applied to the revised principal value to arrive at an updated yield. Another specialized security are *Treasury STRIPS*. These are effectively equivalent to zero-coupon bonds. As the name implies, the Treasury Bond is stripped into its coupon interest and principal components. Investors are then given an interest in each coupon payment as well as the final principal payment. If there is a disadvantage to these securities, it is the same as for other zero-coupon bonds, in that you pay income tax on the accrued income each year.

- **Agencies** of the federal government also issue securities. These agencies can be classified into two categories. One category is those federally related institutions, which are essentially arms of the federal government. Examples include the Tennessee Valley Authority, The Export-Import Bank, the General Services Administration, the Government National Mortgage Association and the Small Business Administration, to name a few. The vast majority of these institutions are backed by the full faith and credit of the Treasury. The other category of agencies is called government sponsored enterprises. These agencies do not carry the full faith and credit of the U.S. Treasury, so there is some perceived credit risk. However, they generally carry the strong moral backing of the Government, meaning that it is unlikely that Congress will let them fail. There are five major government sponsored enterprises today. Here is a brief description of the purpose of each:

    1. **Federal Farm Credit Bank System**- Its purpose is to provide adequate credit facilities to the agricultural sector of the economy. They raise funds in both the short-term money markets as well as in the medium and long-term bond markets.
    2. **Federal Home Loan Bank System**- The system consists of 12 district banks and their individual member banks. The purpose of the system is to provide credit for the savings bank and savings & loan industries, which, in turn, insure that adequate credit facilities are in place for the housing sector of the economy. Debt obligations issued by the Federal Home Loan Banks are joint and several obligations of the 12 district banks. They will also issue debt in both the short-term as well as bond markets.

3. **Federal National Mortgage Association-** Fannie Mae was established by the Federal Government in 1938 in order to expand the pool of mortgage money, primarily for low, moderate and middle income families. They would purchase Federal Housing Administration insured mortgages, thereby continuing to provide additional liquidity to the mortgage markets. In 1968, Fannie Mae became a private company and its stock trades on the New York Stock Exchange. While it receives no federal backing, it still comes under the watchful eye of Congress. They will issue short-term discount notes as well as longer term debentures.
4. **Federal Home Loan Mortgage Corporation-** Established in 1970, Freddie Mac also provides liquidity for the mortgage markets. It does so by purchasing single family and multi-family mortgages from the originating financial institutions. It then finances these purchases by securitizing the mortgages and selling participation units in the secondary markets. It also issues straight debt instruments. Like Fannie Mae, Freddie Mac is a private company but one that comes under the watchful eye of Congress.
5. **Student Loan Marketing Association-** Sallie Mae exists to provide liquidity for private lenders who participate in various government-guaranteed student loan programs. They can fund their loan purchases through offering investors participation in loan pools. They also issue straight debt obligations.

- It is also worth a moment to briefly discuss the **mortgage-backed** securities market. Some of these structures can be quite complex, so we will only cover this topic in a general sense. The market originated as federal agencies, such as Fannie Mae and Ginnie

Mae, issued securities backed by the mortgage loans that they purchased. There are some important features of mortgage-backed securities that are different from other investments. First, each payment includes a portion for interest and principal amortization. However, there could also be additional payments in the form of a mortgage prepayment. Prepayments can be significant during periods of falling interest rates as consumers refinance their mortgages or purchase new homes. The level of prepayment will affect the overall rate of return investors can earn on these securities. The impact of prepayments will depend upon the structure of the securities as there are several variations. We will discuss the two major ones:

1. **Pass-Throughs**- Issued by GNMA, FNMA and FHLMC, these securities provide its holders with an interest in a pool of mortgages. As GNMA is an agency of the Government and its mortgages are government insured, its debt is essentially guaranteed by the U.S. Treasury. The other two agencies are private and their mortgage pools consist of conventional mortgages. However, the mortgages must conform to certain standards. The nature of the pass-through security is that all payments flow directly to each bondholder and each holder assumes the same prepayment risk.

2. **Collateralized Mortgage Obligations**- Securities have been created where investors are not necessarily subject to the same principal pay-down and prepayment risk. Under the CMO structure, there are *tranches* (perhaps three or four) and each may have a different principal pay-down schedule. For example, when each payment is received, interest is paid first and then all of the principal payments are applied to the first tranche until it is completely retired. Then, all future principal payments

are applied to the next tranche. This enables the issuer to offer bonds of varying maturities.

- **Corporate** bonds also offer investors a range of alternatives. We will look at the characteristics of this market from a couple of vantage points:

    1. **Issuer Type-** There are five primary types of corporate issuers or sectors including utilities, transportations, industrials, financials and Yankees (international entities that issue dollar bonds in the U.S.).
    2. **Collateral-** Corporate bonds can be issued with or backed by certain collateral. Mortgage bonds would be backed by properties with first and second liens on those properties. Collateral Trust bonds are backed by securities, which are held by a trustee. Equipment Trust Certificates are issued by railroads, airlines and trucking companies and their debt is collateralized by the rolling stock. A more recent and rapidly expanding debt instrument is asset-backed securities. Here the issuers securitize certain assets such as credit card receivables or automobile loans.
    3. **Maturities-** Corporations borrow in three different maturity ranges. First, they are active borrowers in the short-term money markets. They predominately do this through bank credit as well as commercial paper. Commercial paper is issued at maturities of 270 days or less. Corporations are also active participants in the long-term bond markets and generally issue unsecured, subordinated debt. The rate at which they borrow is dictated by their credit rating. They can enhance the rating on their bonds by securing a letter of credit from a bank and then it becomes a letter of credit-backed bond.

Beginning in the 1970's, corporations have steadily moved toward an alternative to commercial paper or long-term bonds. This alternative is medium-term notes, which have some unique characteristics. They offer the investor a range of maturities. Generally, investors can select among these range maturities: 9 to 12 months, 12 to 18 months, 18 months to 2 years, and continuously up to 30 years. By definition, medium-term notes are non-callable, unsecured, senior debt securities with fixed or variable rates and investment grade credit ratings. They are registered with the Securities and Exchange Commission under rule 415. This registration is termed a shelf registration, giving the borrower the ability to issue the bonds on a continuous basis with a high degree of flexibility. For example, the rate could be tied to certain derivative pricing. However, there is an important distinction in terms of how these bonds are marketed or distributed. Unlike long-term debt where the underwriter purchases the bonds and then sells to the public, thereby guaranteeing distribution, medium-term notes are distributed on a "best efforts basis."

4. **Conversion-** We covered convertible securities earlier, so we will just comment here on the advantages and disadvantages to the issuer and investor when raising funds through convertible bonds or preferred stock. For the corporation, convertible bonds will generally carry a lower interest rate than straight debt because of the conversion feature. Also, the corporation may be able to ultimately sell new equity capital at a better price than under a direct equity offering. Generally, when a company issues new equity, it may experience a decline in earning per share if the funds are not converted to earnings immediately. For example, it may take time for

a new facility to be built and to generate incremental earnings. The convertible gives the firm time to deploy the new money before it ultimately sees its bondholders convert to equity. Convertibles do have some disadvantages for the company. First, if the stock were to rise immediately, it would have been better off to wait and issue new stock at the later time. On the other hand, if the stock drops, the investors will not convert, so there is unlikely to be additional equity capital in the firm. For the investor, there are also advantages with convertibles. While waiting for the opportunity to convert, the investor enjoys a yield that is likely to be higher than the dividend on the stock. The investor also has the benefit of owning a senior debt security. As the stock rises, the investor participates as the value of the bond will rise proportionately. On the other hand, should the stock price fall, the bond would only decline to its inherent value as a straight bond. For the investor, there are also disadvantages in that he/she will be receiving a lower interest rate than what could be earned on a straight bond. This is only a factor if the stock price languishes and the bond is not exercised. Also corporations have the right to call some bonds or force conversion.

5. **High Yield-** Although they have experienced a checkered history, high yield bonds are becoming an important asset class for wealthy investors. Generally speaking, high yield bonds are corporate bonds that have a credit rating below BBB. Accordingly, they are considered to be speculative-grade securities. Some have also referred to these securities as junk bonds. Bonds are classified as part of the high yield market for a number of reasons. Certainly, the company could be experiencing problems and its debt becomes classified as below

investment grade. However, there are firms that may not necessarily be in deep financial trouble but because of their size or structure can only borrow in the financial markets at higher yields. One example is small firms who do not have substantial financial resources to receive an investment grade rating by the national rating agencies such as Standard & Poors or Moodys. Another could be large as well as small firms who are issuing debt in conjunction with a leveraged buy-out. In terms of risk, high yield bonds as an overall asset class are more risky than investment grade bonds but less risky than equities. Some investors believe it is more correlated to the equity markets than the bond market. Generally, high yield bonds offer attractive relative spreads to other bond classes during the trough of an economic recession.

- **International Bonds** have historically been part of institutional portfolios but have not enjoyed widespread appeal among individual investors. Nevertheless, they can provide additional diversification to large portfolios. One classifies international bonds into three categories.

    1. **Foreign Bonds-** These bonds are issued in a particular country by an issuer whose headquarters is in another country. An example would be foreign companies who issue dollar denominated bonds in the United States. These securities are called "Yankee Bonds." Similarly, when U.S. firms issue bonds in England, they are called "Bulldog Bonds."
    2. **Eurobonds-** These securities have the unique feature in that they are issued outside the jurisdiction of any single country. They are also traded predominately in the over-

the-counter-markets although some are registered on a national exchange so that certain institutional investors can buy them. Generally, they will be registered on the Luxembourg, London or Zurich exchanges. The bonds will be classified based on the currency in which they are dominated. Eurobonds offer investors a range of alternative features including zero-coupon issues, deferred coupon issues, dual currency bonds, convertibles, bonds with warrants and floating rate notes.

3. **Global Bonds**- These bonds are issued and traded in both the U.S. and Eurobond markets. They are generally very large issues.

Investors and analysts also distinguish international bonds between sovereign and private debt. Generally, one characterizes sovereign debt as being more secure since you have the backing of a foreign government.

- Last, but by no means least, we will discuss the **municipal** bond market. By far, this is the most popular fixed income market among wealthy investors. Municipal bonds have a number of important features and we will consider some of the more important ones below:

    1. From a credit perspective, there are two distinct types of bonds. **General obligation bonds** are issued by states and municipalities and are backed by the taxing powers of those entities. **Revenue bonds** are issued to support specific projects such as hospitals, bridges, highways, toll roads, sewage plants and stadiums. The revenues from these projects support the debt service on the bonds.

2. Municipal bonds are given a quality rating by one or several of the national rating agencies. This rating can be enhanced through the purchase of insurance to guarantee the payment of interest and principal. There are several municipal bond insurance firms with the more well known being the Municipal Bond Investors Assurance (MBIA), American Municipal Bond Assurance Corporation (AMBAC), and Financial Guaranty Insurance Company (FGIC).
3. Sometimes an issuing authority may decide to pre-refund an outstanding bond issue. It accomplishes this by collateralizing the outstanding issue with U.S. Government obligations. This portfolio of government securities is placed in trust and invested so that the cash flows from the portfolio match the obligations on the original issue. Once this process takes place, the original bonds become classified as pre-refunded bonds and essentially carry the credit rating of the U.S. Government.
4. Municipalities also issue money market securities to assist it in managing short-term cash flows. It will issue tax anticipation notes and revenue anticipation notes to bridge its treasury in anticipation of tax collections. Bond anticipation notes will be issued in anticipation of the sale of long-term bonds. They will also issue variable rate demand obligations, auction-rate preferred notes and commercial paper.

Factors in Managing Fixed Income Portfolios

Managing large fixed income portfolios can be a rather complex task as there are several economic and market forces that can significantly impact its performance over time. Before looking at some of these factors, you need to determine whether you want to have a passively or actively managed portfolio. By passive management, we commonly refer to two alternatives. One is to ladder the portfolio over a number of designated years. For example, you may instruct your manager to evenly ladder the maturities between one and ten years. You generally buy and hold the bonds until maturity. Another passive option is to index the portfolio. You can do this by replicating an industry benchmark or by purchasing exchange-traded-funds. On the other hand, should you choose to actively manage your portfolio, your manager will structure a strategy around interest rates, sector spreads, maturities and quality spreads. We will now discuss some of the aspects of active bond management.

Managing Interest Rate Changes

Without question, the dominant factor influencing bond portfolio performance is how you manage around interest rates. Managing around interest rates is not just calling their direction up or down. It involves understanding the impact on the portfolio of a movement in rates as well as how the shape of the yield curve may change. We will consider each aspect in turn.

First, it is imperative for you to clearly understand the impact of an interest rate change on the price of a particular bond and then the portfolio as a whole. Professional bond managers term this as "rate shock." An example may best illustrate this concept. Consider the case of a single bond that you purchased below par value at a price of 95 ($950 per $1,000 bond). Your investment advisor has a bond valuation model that estimates the price change in the bond for given levels of interest rate changes at a specific yield level. As an example, let's say that interest rates increase by 50 basis points, and that the valuation model provides the following bond prices based on a present yield level of 6.5 percent:

- With a 50 basis point rise in rates, the bond price will fall to 92.5 ($925 per $1,000 bond).

- With a 50 basis point fall in rates, the bond price will increase to 98.5 ($985 per $1,000 bond).

You will then want to translate this to an estimated price change per 100 basis point change in yield. This gives you the "rate shock" effect. As you see, the price change may not necessarily be symmetrical so this is just an estimate. The following formula can be applied:

$$\frac{\text{Price if yields decline} - \text{Price if yields increase}}{2 \times (\text{purchase price}) \times (\text{yield change in decimal points})}$$

Appling this formula to our example, we get:

$$\frac{98.5 - 92.5}{2 \times (95) \times (.0050)} = 6.31$$

This means that should rates change by 100 basis points from current interest rate levels, this bond is likely to experience a change in value or price by 6.31 percent. You can extrapolate this exercise to encompass the entire portfolio. Professional bond managers will likely have the software to communicate this type of impact to you.

Another facet of interest rate management is to deal with changes in the actual shape of the interest rate yield curve. When rates change, they may not change in a uniform manner throughout the maturity spectrum of the market. Again, an example will best illustrate this. Exhibit 5-R shows the three most common yield curves. The upward sloping curve is the most normal in that investors receive increasing yields as maturities are extended. This type of curve generally exists during periods of low inflation and slow to modest economic activity. It is also prevalent during recessions as the Federal Reserve tries to lower short-term rates so as to encourage borrowing and investment. The flat curve generally exists during periods of strong business activity but where inflation is not a concern; were inflation a concern, longer-term rates would climb. The inverted curve usually exists during periods of brisk economic activity and where the Federal Reserve is concerned about inflation and rising prices. It will therefore tighten monetary policy to the point of raising short rates above longer rates so as to slow down borrowing and consumption.

EXHIBIT 5–R

YIELD CURVE

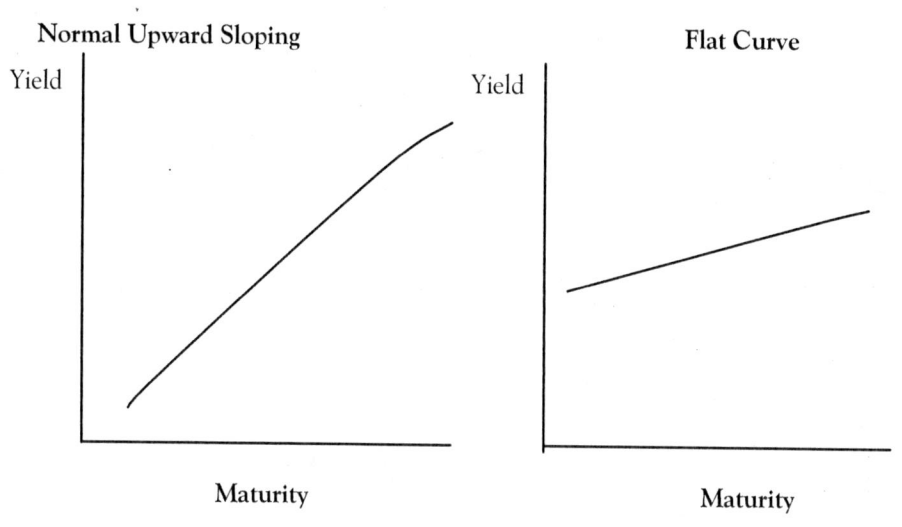

Normal Upward Sloping

Yield / Maturity

Flat Curve

Yield / Maturity

Inverted Curve

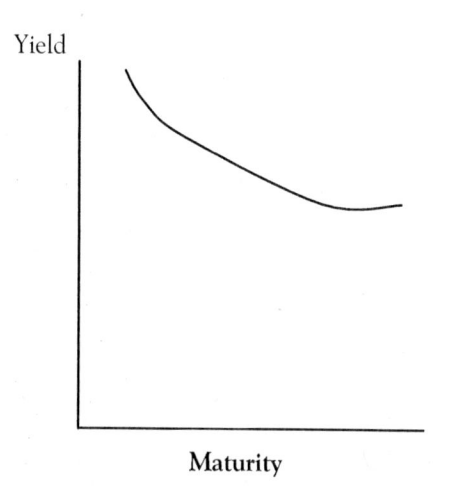

Yield / Maturity

Accordingly, as an investor, you need to be concerned about where interest rates are and where they are likely to go. At the same time, should interest rates change from their current state, they could change in a number of directions. Consider the examples in exhibit 5-S.

- The yield curve could undergo a complete *parallel* shift where rates increase along the entire curve in somewhat of a parallel fashion. This is a likely scenario when the economy is significantly expanding and the Fed is tightening.
- The curve could also *flatten*. This scenario may occur when economic activity is picking up after a recession but inflation is very much in check. The Fed is just reacting to strong economic numbers but the labor markets are not tight.
- In some circumstances, the curve will steepen. It could steepen in a way where short rates drop while long rates actually increase. The long-term bond market reflects inflationary expectations as well as supply and demand for funds. Accordingly, if investors believe that the money supply is growing too fast and that low short rates will bring about higher inflation, they may react by selling long-term bonds, thus pushing their rates up.

Managing Maturities

In line with managing interest rate changes, investors will sometimes decide ahead of time to select a specific maturity structure as opposed to having their bond investments subject to changes all along the yield curve. Investment managers generally offer short-term and intermediate term portfolio management in addition to fully discretionary management. Alternatively, investors may give their bond managers complete discretion but within a stated maturity range. For example, they may not wish to own bonds with maturities greater than 10 or 15 years.

Creating an Investment Policy

This way, they can contain some of the interest rate risk should rates climb significantly.

EXHIBIT 5-S

YIELD CURVE SHIFTS

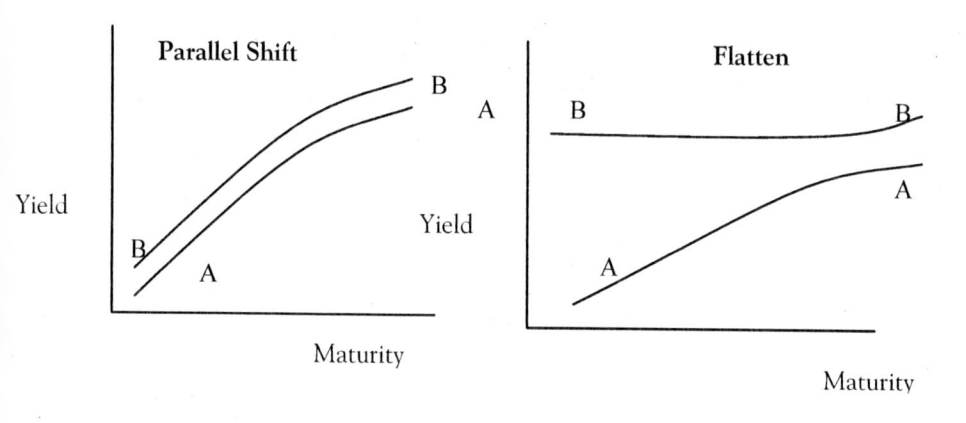

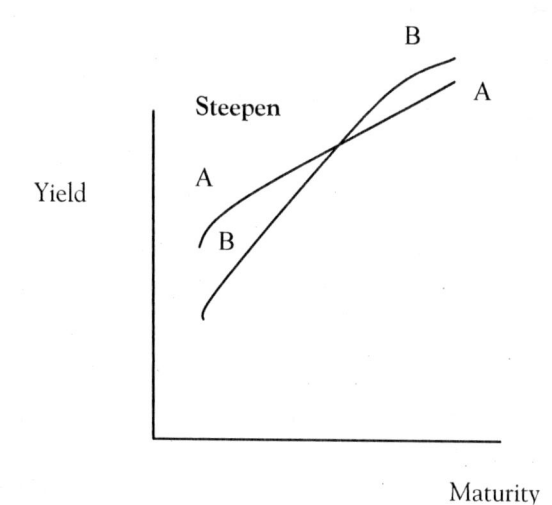

Managing Sector Spreads

While interest rates may be the key factor impacting fixed income returns, managing around sector relationships can also impact your potential return. There are several sector relationships within the bond market and we will look at a few:

- *Treasury/Municipals-* While municipal bonds are the most popular among taxable investors, they may not always be the optimal investment. You need to compare the tax-equivalent yield on municipals to comparable taxable securities. The basic formula for doing so is as follows:

$$\frac{\text{Tax-free yield}}{1 - (\text{marginal tax bracket})}$$

Applying this to numbers, assume the tax-free yield is 4 percent and your marginal tax bracket is 40 percent. The formula would work out as follows:

$$\frac{4}{1 - 0.40} = 6.67\%$$

Therefore, if Treasuries yielded more than 6.67 percent for a comparable maturity, you would be better off buying the Treasury and paying taxes.

Going back to the yield spread relationships, Municipal yields have historically fluctuated in a range against Treasuries. For example, let's say that Municipal yields have averaged 82 percent of Treasuries over time. They may have also traded in a range of 70 percent to 95 percent in the past. If today, they are trading at 91 percent of Treasuries, you would

Creating an Investment Policy

conclude that Municipals represent a good value. In the future, it is likely that the spreads may return to a more normal level either by Municipal yields falling or Treasury yields rising at a faster rate. Professional bond managers constantly look at these spreads and invest based on whether they believe the spreads will return to their historical levels. Managers could also bet that spreads may move in a certain direction. For example, if spreads are in a normal range today but there are credit problems looming in the Municipal markets or a significant supply of new issues will hit the market shortly, mangers may believe that Municipal spreads verses Treasuries will widen so they may prefer to invest new monies in Treasuries and switch back at a later date if and when the spreads widen.

- **Treasuries/Corporates-** Another common spread relationship is between Corporates and Treasuries. During strong economic times, these spreads will tighten. However, during recessions, the spreads will widen.
- **Quality-** There are also spreads between bonds of different quality. The major rating agencies, particularly Standard & Poors, Moody's and Fitch, rate bond issues according to a methodical scale. A table illustrating those scales is shown in exhibit 5-T. Generally, investment grade bonds include the first four levels down to BBB. The next two levels, down to B are considered to be speculative but at the top end of the high yield market. The C level bonds are the lower level of the high yield market, while level D is pretty much in default. Yield spread relationships exist within the Corporate as well as Municipal sectors. For investors, the common spreads are between AAA and A and between investment grade and high yield bonds.
- **Maturities-** Spread relationships also exist between maturity sectors of the market. These relationships are consistent with some of the yield spread analysis we discussed earlier.

Investors will sometimes take advantage of maturity spreads that deviate significantly from their normal patterns.

- **General Obligation/Revenue-** Within the municipal market, historical spreads developed between GO and Revenue bonds and investors will sometimes respond to differences in these relationships, expecting that they will return to the norm.
- **Mortgage Backed/Corporate/Government-** At different stages of the economic cycle, the yield spreads between mortgage-backed securities and corporates and governments will vary. When they deviate from historical norms, investment managers will adjust their portfolios accordingly.
- **Coupon-** Finally, spread relationships exist between bonds of varying coupon levels.

EXHIBIT 5–T

BOND RATINGS

	Moody's	S & P
INVESTMENT GRADE		
Prime	Aaa	AAA
High Grade	Aa1	AA+
	Aa2	AA
	Aa3	AA-
Upper-Medium Grade	A1	A+
	A2	A
	A3	A-
Lower – Medium Grade	Baa1	BBB+
	Baa2	BBB
	Baa3	BBB-
LOW GRADE SPECULATIVE		
	Ba1	BB+
	Ba2	BB
	Ba3	BB-

HIGHLY SPECULATIVE	B1	B
	B2	B
	B3	B
SUBSTANTIAL RISK		
Substantial Risk	Caa	CCC
Very Speculative	Ca	CC
Extremely Speculative	C	C
Default	-------	D

Source: *Fixed Income Analysis*, Frank J. Fabozzi

Identifying Bond Swap Opportunities

Earlier, we discussed the two major bond management approaches–passive verses active management. With active management, investment managers look at bonds much as equity managers view stocks–they are bought and sold. Selling a bond before maturity is the essence of active management. Under what circumstances does it pay to sell a bond before it matures and swap into another bond? We will consider those cases below:

- **Interest Rate Anticipation**- Perhaps the riskiest of the bond swap strategies, interest rate anticipation requires a forecast of future interest rates and the development of a strategy to position the portfolio to take advantage of that rate change. This strategy would result in changing the duration of the portfolio and by doing so you could significantly alter its risk level. For example, if you have a short-term portfolio and you expect rates to fall, an interest rate anticipation strategy will encourage you to lengthen the duration of the portfolio. If you calculate incorrectly and rates actually rise, your portfolio will be subjected to a greater erosion in value than if you left it alone.
- **Yield Spread**- As discussed above, there are a variety of yield-spread relationships in the bond market. When investors believe one of these spread relationships will change in the future, he/she

will sell the overvalued one and buy the undervalued one. For example, if the yield differential between AAA and A 10-year municipals is only 25 basis points and the normal spread is more like 65 basis points, you may think of selling the A and swapping into the AAA. Conversely, if the spreads were to widen well beyond the 65 basis points, you would do the opposite and sell the AAA and buy the A, so long as you believe the spreads will move back in the direction anticipated.

- **Pure Yield Pickup-** This swap involves the sale of one bond and the purchase of another with similar maturity and quality profiles. The objective is to pick up a higher realized yield over the remaining maturity. In many situations, you will be selling a lower coupon bond to purchase a higher coupon bond. You may take a loss on the bond sold so the yield differential plus any difference in final maturity value will have to offset that loss. Also, if you purchase a higher coupon bond and rates subsequently fall, you could be subject to a call by the issuer. On the other hand, there are distinct advantages to this swap. You are gaining an increased yield without making an interest rate call or increasing the duration risk of the portfolio. You are also not making any sector bets.

- **Substitution-** Because the pricing mechanisms of the bond market are not as efficient as the stock market, there are sometimes opportunities to take advantage of substitution swaps. Here you may find a bond in the marketplace that is nearly identical to one you have in your portfolio but it is selling at a lower price and therefore offering a slightly higher yield. These situations may sometimes develop during periods of new bond issuance, especially if there is a heavy supply of new bonds hitting the market.

- **Tax-** Becoming increasingly popular is the tax-loss swap. When you sell a stock, you cannot repurchase that same stock for 31 days or you will lose any tax loss benefit under the "wash sale rules." With bonds, you also cannot repurchase the same bond, but you can fit suitable substitutes. Accordingly, investors have been more willing nowadays to offset gains elsewhere in their portfolios with bond losses during periods of rising rates.

Futures and Options

As with equities, investors can employ derivative securities to manage the risk in their bond portfolios. We will not go into great length on the mechanics of these transactions but will share some broad features. First, investors can engage in buying or selling interest rate or bond futures. At inception, you do not have to put up the entire amount of the contract; instead, you only need the initial margin. When purchasing or selling a futures contract, you benefit or lose based on its price change over the life of the contract. Selling futures against a bond portfolio can be an effective hedge in certain market conditions. A second strategy is to buy or sell options on futures contracts. Like equity options, the buyer of a call or put option can only lose the premium and is not subject to the same change in value as under a direct futures contract. The writer or seller of options can lose a greater amount of money and must maintain a margin account to protect their position. Investors would buy a put option on a futures contract as a hedge against rising rates, particularly if they have a long duration or high average maturity portfolio. On the other hand, investors would buy a call on a futures contract if they believe rates will fall and they may not wish to extend the duration or maturity of their portfolio. They will profit if rates fall.

Hedge Funds

In 1949, a gentleman by the name of Alfred Winslow Jones created an investment fund whereby he combined the purchase of stocks with short selling and leverage. His success depended on the ability to select long equity investments that appreciated as well as short investments that fell. Consequently, his performance was not always predicated on the direction of the market. He would also magnify his positions through borrowings. Additionally, he charged his investors a performance-based fee. Thus we witnessed the birth of the hedge fund. Hedge funds grew slowly until the early 1960's when we experienced the first real hedge fund boom. However, the hedge fund market cooled off in the early 1970's as the financial markets struggled. They returned in the late 1980's and early 1990's, experiencing a nice rise through the mid-90's.

Then, in 1998, we suffered the first real crisis in hedge funds when a very large and prominent one, Long Term Capital Management, collapsed and was liquidated by its creditors (leading Wall Street banks and brokerage houses) after prodding by the Federal Reserve Bank. The catalyst for its demise was the Russian default and currency devaluation, prompting investors to jump to quality. This put enormous pressure on Long Term Capital's trading positions and high leverage position. Nevertheless, the hedge fund industry recovered and entered its greatest boom period as the equity markets began their journey through a bitter bear market. Hedge funds, on the whole, gave investor's portfolios a great cushion during the difficult bear market. Universities, foundations and wealthy individuals alike began to enthusiastically embrace hedge fund investing. They have emerged as a major force in the investment industry and may have changed the landscape forever.

Strictly speaking, a hedge fund is a pooled investment vehicle generally organized as a private partnership. They frequently have offshore status and some are organized as commodity pools. They are usually unregistered and charge performance fees in addition to a normal management fee. We compare hedge funds to traditional investment vehicles (e.g., mutual funds and separate accounts) in exhibit 5-U.

Creating an Investment Policy

We may take a moment to discuss the regulatory issues surrounding hedge fund participants. Because hedge funds are exempt from securities registration, they are limited in their ability to market their product to the public. Here are some of the general limitations:

EXHIBIT 5-U

COMPARATIVE STRUCTURES

FEATURE	MUTUAL FUNDS	SEPARATE PORTFOLIOS	HEDGE FUNDS
Legal Structure	• Registered funds under Investment Company Act of 1940	• Separate accounts	• Mostly unregistered, funds, organized as partnerships
Performance objectives	• Market benchmark driven	• Market benchmark and peer groups	• Absolute return measures
Primary sources of return	• Market and some manager skill	• Market and manager skill	• Manager skill
Correlation with general markets	• Very high	• High	• Low
Firm size	• Very large	• All sizes	• Mostly small
Liquidity	• Very high	• High (2-3 days to settle sales)	• Limitations — requires notice
Permitted investments	• By prospectus, limited to traditional investments.	• Generally traditional asset classes	• Diverse range
Fees	• Management and operating expenses	• Asset-based	• Asset based and performance incentive
Clients	• Universal	• Generally in the $1 million range and above	• Restricted to accredited and qualified investors

Business model	• Manager/firm are agents	• Agency	• Manager and client are partners; managers co-invest, sometimes significantly
Tax efficiency	• Distribute capital gains annually, most are not highly efficient	• Based on turnover. • Many are efficient as gains/losses more easily offset	• Inefficient due to trading and short-term gains. • Most income taxed at highest rates

- Hedge funds are limited to 100 accredited investors per the Investment Company Act of 1940. An accredited investor is someone who has a net worth of $1,000,000 or passes an income test. The test is for the individual to have income in excess of $200,000 in each of the prior two years, or joint spouse income of $300,000, and with a reasonable expectation that the income level will be maintained.
- Hedge funds can generally have an unlimited number of "qualified investors." These investors have at least $5,000,000 in investment assets. If the investor is an entity or institution, it must have investment assets of $25,000,000.

Benefits of Hedge Fund Investing

Before looking at specific hedge fund strategies, we should first understand the benefits investors seek when allocating assets to hedge funds. Here are some of them:

- Hedge funds have demonstrated a low correlation to the U.S. stock market.

- Individual hedge funds themselves are not highly correlated to each other.
- There is the real potential for higher risk-adjusted returns.
- Better protection in falling markets
- Access to some of the best talent in the investment industry as many of the top talent leave large firms to set up independent hedge fund firms.

Hedge Fund Strategies

To guide us in the process of looking at hedge fund strategies, consider the stages delineated in exhibit 5-V. We will look at some of these processes in this chapter and will cover the remaining ones in chapter 6.

Establishing Objectives

There are different ways to categorize hedge fund strategies. We will begin the process of categorizing them by breaking out some macro objectives.

Market Neutral/Directional

Here you are segmenting your objectives between holding virtually no net exposure to the direction of the markets versus taking a directional bet. In other words, your objective may be to reduce market risk significantly. Market neutral strategies are designed to do just that and generally involve arbitrage-related strategies.

EXHIBIT 5–V

HEDGE FUND MANAGEMENT PROCESS

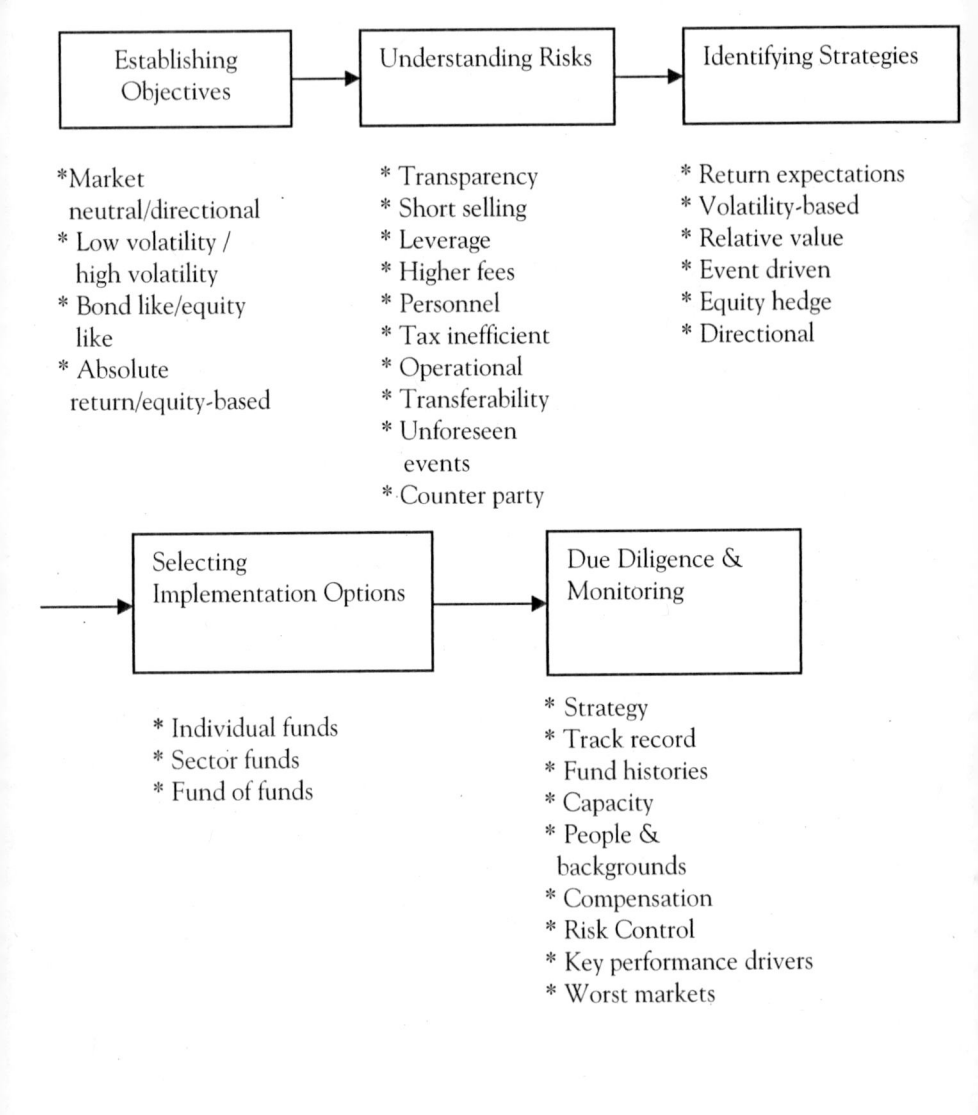

Establishing Objectives → Understanding Risks → Identifying Strategies

Establishing Objectives
- Market neutral/directional
- Low volatility / high volatility
- Bond like/equity like
- Absolute return/equity-based

Understanding Risks
- Transparency
- Short selling
- Leverage
- Higher fees
- Personnel
- Tax inefficient
- Operational
- Transferability
- Unforeseen events
- Counter party

Identifying Strategies
- Return expectations
- Volatility-based
- Relative value
- Event driven
- Equity hedge
- Directional

→ Selecting Implementation Options → Due Diligence & Monitoring

Selecting Implementation Options
- Individual funds
- Sector funds
- Fund of funds

Due Diligence & Monitoring
- Strategy
- Track record
- Fund histories
- Capacity
- People & backgrounds
- Compensation
- Risk Control
- Key performance drivers
- Worst markets

Creating an Investment Policy

Low Volatility /High Volatility

The idea here is pursue an objective of low portfolio volatility versus high volatility, or vice versa. Low volatility strategies are frequently arbitrage, market neutral and event driven, while higher volatility strategies are frequently long-short equity, sector, macro and managed futures.

Bond-Like/Equity-Like

Some investors will look to hedge funds to act as a quasi-substitute for bonds. Accordingly, they will select a portfolio of funds with an expected return between bonds and equities (or at a premium above bonds) but with a standard deviation or risk that is similar to bonds. Accordingly, they are looking for better-than-bond results with bond-like volatility. Alternatively, some investors will select a portfolio of funds that are expected to show returns that approximate the equity market returns but with a standard deviation the falls somewhere between bonds and equities. In other words, the objective is equity-like results with less-than-equity risk.

Absolute Return/Equity-Based

Some investors will pursue hedge fund investing because they are in need of absolute as opposed to market-related returns. Foundations will frequently be in this camp but many individuals find this approach attractive as well. Absolute return funds will have low volatility. On the other hand, some investors are willing to assume the risks inherent in some directional hedge fund investing and are looking at this asset class to produce equity returns, even greater than the general equity market.

Understanding Risks

Hedge funds carry many of the same market and security-specific risks as do traditional asset classes; however, they also have some unique ones of their own. Here are some of the more important risks inherent in hedge fund investing:

Transparency

In a broad sense, transparency means the ability to look inside a fund and see what the manager is investing in. To a professional advisor who may be managing a fund of funds hedge fund, transparency is the ability to receive daily positions. On the other hand, to an individual investor, transparency is the ability to gain answers on such macro issues as the amount of leverage employed, derivatives employed and short sales. These are the major risk elements. When investing in mutual funds or separate portfolios, investors have full transparency.

Hedge fund managers have resisted full transparency for a couple of reasons. First, they believe their competitive advantage lies in the marketplace not knowing what positions they are taking. Some competitors may try to duplicate it but others may even try to bet against it and potentially disrupt their strategy. Second, hedge fund professionals believe the average investor is not skilled enough in the various strategies and tactics to fully understand all of the information that would be disseminated. Third, the very best hedge fund managers will not need to fully disclose positions until regulators force them to do so. Therefore, if you insist that your hedge fund manager disclose all positions, you may eliminate some good investment opportunities.

While there may be some arguments in favor of less transparency, there are also some good reasons for it, especially for managers of fund of funds. Consider the following:

- Transparency would allow investors to spot changes in style and major bets taken.
- Leverage is more likely to be contained as the manager knows that this would be detected quickly.
- Investors can see the fees taken.
- Transparency may also enable investors to detect fraud; as a result, it could discourage fraud as managers know it might be detected more quickly.

Short Selling

As we discussed above, short selling carries a high degree of risk, which is why you must maintain a margin account in order to engage in that activity. Hedge fund managers who maintain significant short positions can face unlimited losses should the markets move against them and their short sale selections are wrong. When their long positions do not work out, the most that they can lose is the position itself. With short sales they can lose much more and they would have to pledge other assets to stay within margin requirements. Therefore, understanding the degree to which a hedge fund can engage in short selling is quite important.

Liquidity

Hedge funds generally do not allow investors to liquidate their investments on demand. Instead, investors usually have to provide redemption notice that could range from 30 to 90 days. Alternatively, some hedge funds only allow redemptions on certain dates, like quarterly or semi-annually. Other funds may also have a lock-up period where you cannot liquidate your holdings for an initial period of time, like up to one year.

Higher Fees

Hedge funds charge an ongoing management fee as traditional money managers do. These fees average between 1.0 and 2.0 percent per annum. They also charge a performance fee, which usually ranges from 10 to 20 percent of the performance above a hurdle rate. A typical hurdle rate is 5-6 percent. This means that no performance fees are earned until the fund itself earns 6 percent or whatever the hurdle rate is.

Personnel

Hedge fund firms are generally very small and depend on the skill of a few key individuals. Needless to say, one needs to always know what is happening with those key people.

Tax Inefficient

Investors consider hedge funds to be relatively inefficient from a tax standpoint. This is because of their active trading and the resulting short-term gains and losses. Here are some relevant issues related to taxes and hedge funds:

- Any dividends or interest are taxed at ordinary income tax rates.
- Dividends on short positions are netted against dividends on your long positions.
- Margin interest is deducted from overall income.
- Interest on short sale proceeds is part of overall income.
- Since hedge funds are limited partnerships, they are considered "pass-through" entities for tax purposes. This means that you pay taxes on income and net gains whether or not they are distributed.

- Many hedge funds, like other limited partnerships, may provide some temporary tax relief to current holders. This occurs as a result of investors leaving the fund. When investors redeem their positions, the hedge fund may allocate a disproportionate amount of the realized gains to them, since they will be hit with gains anyway since they are selling their positions. The remaining investors will then receive a disproportionate share of the unrealized gains, so they can escape or defer current taxation.

Operational

It is important for hedge funds to have proper operational systems to handle trading and accounting. Some may be under-investing in this area and that can pose significant risks for investors.

Transferability

Most hedge funds are not transferable. To transfer ownership, you must obtain permission from the manager as new investors must qualify.

Unforeseen Events

One lesson from the investment markets is that events do not always play out as expected. During rapid changes in such economic factors as interest rates, inflation or currencies, some hedge funds could experience significant and unforeseen volatility, based on how they are positioned.

Counter-Party

A hedge fund can experience losses should a trading partner not be able to meet its obligations under a derivative transaction. It is therefore important that the fund have internal limits on transaction exposure to other firms.

Identifying Strategies

We are now set to discuss specific hedge fund investment strategies. When deciding which strategies to employ, you will again categorize the different strategies in some organized format. There is not necessarily one and only one way to categorize the strategies. We will offer three different ways to categorize hedge funds and then go into an explanation of some specific strategies.

Return Characteristic

Absolute Return Strategies

- Convertible arbitrage
- Convertible debenture arbitrage-Regulation D
- Fixed income arbitrage
- Distressed securities
- Futures arbitrage
- Merger risk arbitrage
- Statistical arbitrage
- Equity market neutral
- Special situations
- Some fund of funds

Directional Strategies

- Global macro
- Commodities trading account
- Managed futures
- Market timing
- Emerging markets
- Short selling
- Long/short equity

Strategies based on return characteristics will respond to market conditions. For example, absolute return strategies will show performance based on the movement of interest rates. As rates decline, performance will be strong. However, when rates increase rapidly, performance could be weak, but may still outperform some long bond strategies. Directional strategies will be tied to the general direction of the equity markets even though they may not be strongly correlated to the markets. Short selling, of course, will counter the markets.

Volatility Characteristic

Another way to categorize hedge funds is in accordance with its volatility or risk. We can segment the universe into low, medium and high volatility.

Low Volatility Strategies

- Convertible arbitrage
- Fixed income arbitrage
- Merger risk arbitrage
- Statistical arbitrage
- Equity market neutral

Medium Volatility Strategies

- Futures arbitrage
- Distressed securities
- Capital structure arbitrage
- Convertible debenture arbitrage-Regulation D
- Special situations
- Some fund of funds

High Volatility Strategies

- Global macro
- Managed futures
- Emerging markets
- Market timing
- Short selling
- Long/short equity

Market Characteristic

The more general way to categorize hedge funds is by the general market and we again recategorize the above strategies. We will use this method as we define some of the specific strategies.

Relative Value Strategies

Convertible Arbitrage- This strategy takes advantage of an apparent mispricing between a convertible bond and its underlying stock. The strategy usually involves purchasing the bond and selling short the underlying stock. Profits are realized as the pricing disparities correct and the positions are sold. We can show an example to illustrate the dynamics of this transaction. Assume the following structure:

- Bond par value=$1,000
- Bond interest rate=4%
- Conversion ratio=50 (conversion price of $20)

Assume the bond and stock price increases 15 percent over a one-year period. Your annual return would then be as follows:

- Capital gain on convertible bond is 15% or $150.00.
- Short sale loss on 50 shares is $75.00.

- Bond interest of $50.00
- Short sale interest of $10.00
- Fees to lender of stock of $2.00
- Net return of $133.00
- Annualized rate of return of 13.3%

Managers will frequently employ leverage to magnify the returns.

Convertible Debenture Arbitrage-Regulation D- This strategy is similar to convertible arbitrage except that it involves privately structured investments for small capitalization companies. The structures are unregistered convertible securities and are directly negotiated with the company. They can carry either a fixed or a floating exercise price. The floating exercise price can insulate the investor from a decline in the stock price. Once the securities are sold, the company will file with the Securities and Exchange Commission to register the common shares. Afterwards, the investor can sell the shares and potentially realize a profit spread between the market price and the effective discounted price of the stock he/she converted into. An example may better illustrate this situation. Assume that a convertible security is issued with these features:

- The share price at issuance is $25.00
- The conversion ratio is therefore 40 shares per bond.
- The floating discount is 15% at time of conversion.

If the share price should drop to $20 at the time of conversion, you would be able to convert your $1,000 equivalent bond into 58.82 shares based on the floating discount of 15 percent from the current stock price. The formula is to divide $1,000 by the discounted share price. This is certainly more attractive than the fixed 40 shares or so at the original issue date. However, it is likely the original conversion ratio would be at some fixed discount from the current price as well. The floating discount is still more protective.

Fixed Income Arbitrage- This strategy involves transactions that seek to profit from the relative mispricing of highly related securities. For example, the manager would purchase one security such as a Treasury Bill and sell short a Eurodollar, trying to take advantage of any spread imbalance. Other types of arbitrage could involve trading between newly issued Treasury Bonds and those issued in the recent past. This is called "on-the-run" versus "off-the-run" Treasury arbitrage. Another transaction could be yield curve arbitrage where you would buy the five-year Treasury and sell short the four- and six-year maturities. Again, managers would likely deploy leverage with this strategy.

Statistical Arbitrage- Certain securities may show strong historical correlations with each other. Also, certain indexes will demonstrate a consistency with its underlying securities. At times, these historical relationships will deviate and there are short-term arbitrage opportunities. Traders will buy the undervalued security and sell short the overvalued one, expecting that the relationship will revert back to its mean.

Equity Market Neutral- These managers seek to take advantage of pricing inefficiencies in the market without taking a position on the direction of the market itself. They must skillfully match long and short stock positions of underpriced and overpriced companies. Statistically, they attempt to achieve near-zero market exposure. They will define net exposure in a number of ways including portfolio beta, market capitalization, manager style (e.g., value, growth), country, currency or industry.

Event Driven Strategies

Merger Risk Arbitrage- This strategy involves securities that are part of a merger. Typically, you purchase the shares of the company being acquired and sell short the shares of the purchaser. Generally, the share

Creating an Investment Policy

price of the company being acquired does not reach its announced offering price, as there is always some residual risk the deal may not close. Of course, your risk is that the deal in fact does not close and the prices of the respective stocks reverse.

Distressed Securities- This is essentially a strategy where hedge fund managers are looking to pick up investments at what they believe to be great bargains. They seek out companies that are experiencing some financial distress such as bankruptcy, liquidity problems, excess debt, regulatory difficulties or operational failings. The hedge fund manager may believe that the marketplace has overreacted and the current value of the company's securities represents good value. The manager usually purchases debt or equity in these companies. They also may take an active role in directing the future course of the company such as encouraging a merger, filing for bankruptcy or spinning off divisions. Generally, these portfolios consist of long only holdings.

Capital Structure Arbitrage- As a form of distressed securities investing, a hedge fund manager may be long and short different securities of the same issuer. For example, you would buy the debt and sell short the equity if you believe the debt will be paid off at a higher percentage than its current value, and believe the stock price may fall further. You could also arbitrage within classes of equity or debt.

Special Situations- This strategy takes advantage of capital restructurings as well as other corporate reorganizations. The manager bets that the outcome of the corporate event will be better than the market believes it will, based on the current stock price.

Equity Hedge Strategies

Long/Short Equity- This is probably the largest of the hedge fund strategies in terms of dollars committed. The strategy essentially involves selling short those stocks that the manager believes are overvalued and buying those stocks that the manager believes are undervalued. The manager will also employ options and futures to partially hedge positions. Additionally, the manager will not necessarily be market neutral as he/she will usually make a directional bet on the markets or sectors of the market. This strategy can be attractive in that the manager can play both sides of the market. You can invest on the belief that a stock will go down just as you can invest on the belief that it will go up. These strategies sometimes emphasize a particular sector of the market such as technology or Far East equities, etc.

Long Biased- These strategies are where the managers are net long all or most of the time. Their fortunes are therefore based on the market going up.

Short Biased- Conversely, these managers are net short and their fortunes are based on the market going down.

Futures Arbitrage- This strategy entails investors providing liquidity for commercial hedgers in the futures market. For example, if farmers want to lock in the price of soybean or oil producers want to lock in the high price of oil, they will sell futures on their respective commodity. Investors will take the opposite position. Generally, investors will diversify their risk by taking many different positions in the futures markets.

Directional Strategies

Global Macro- This is the broadest of all strategies whereby managers will employ long and short positions in a range of securities, futures, currencies, commodities or derivatives. The approach is top down and is based on a fundamental analysis of general macroeconomic variables including forecasted trends in interest rates, commodity prices and foreign exchange rates. Managers will frequently use leverage.

Creating an Investment Policy

Managed Futures- This strategy encompasses trading in financial, commodity and currency futures. The strategies are usually executed by Commodity Trading Advisors, who are regulated by the Commodity Futures Trading Commission.

Emerging Markets- This strategy involves taking positions in bond and equity securities of companies in emerging markets.

Market Timing- As the name implies, this strategy entails aggressively moving between cash and equities as well as between sectors of the market. The idea is to accurately time major movements in the financial markets.

Short Selling- Short selling, as we covered earlier, involves making bets on price declines in individual stocks or on the market as a whole through selling short various futures indices.

Fees, Expenses and Conditions

The terms and conditions of investing in hedge funds are also much different than investing in the traditional asset classes. Here are the general terms you may find when investing in a hedge fund:

Management Fee- This fee is similar to the standard investment advisory fee you will pay to an investment manager. For hedge funds, it generally ranges from 1.0 to 1.5 percent. The fee usually decreases with higher amounts invested.

Incentive Fee- Unlike traditional asset classes, hedge funds almost always feature an incentive fee based on performance. This fee generally ranges from 10 to 20 percent of profits. Sometimes, however, there is a "hurdle" rate that the manager must first achieve before receiving any incentive compensation. This hurdle is usually between 5 to 8 percent. Additionally, some hedge fund managers will deduct the management fee before calculating the incentive fee.

Purchase and Redemption- Hedge funds do not trade like stocks, bonds and mutual funds. Most hedge funds allow monthly purchases and some may even have lock-up periods whereby investors must keep their money with the fund for a period of time before they can cash out. With most funds, this lock-up period begins with the first dollar invested. Redemptions are typically quarterly and many funds also require advance notice for withdrawals. This advance notice can range from 60 to 90 days or even more.

Minimums- Nearly all funds will have minimum subscription amounts as well as minimum amounts on additional investments. Fund of funds almost always have much lower minimums than do successful individual hedge funds.

Investor Qualifications- As mentioned earlier, hedge funds have requirements as to the minimum net worth and income levels of its investors. These requirements are mandated by regulation.

Real Estate

Despite being the world's oldest investment asset class, real estate remains its most inefficient from a market standpoint. No two pieces of property are really identical. Real estate is driven by location and the improvements one makes to the property. Its price can also be influenced by the homes and businesses around it, the level of interest rates, the local economy and governmental policies including zoning and land use policies. Real estate is also a relatively illiquid investment. Finally, unlike nearly any other investment, real estate entails annual costs from the day

Creating an Investment Policy

you buy it until the day you sell it. These costs include taxes, insurance, legal, maintenance, capital improvements and brokerage. Nevertheless, real estate investing has generally provided individuals and families with handsome returns over the decades. Moreover, it has enabled some investors to reap great fortunes. Some investors engage in real estate as a full-time business and therefore have a highly concentrated percentage of their wealth in this asset class. Others will invest in real estate as just one asset class in a highly diversified portfolio. For these investors, real estate offers the following portfolio benefits:

- As a general investment, real estate has a low correlation to stocks and bonds.
- Even though values can fluctuate, real estate does not have the short-term volatility that equities display.
- In addition to capital appreciation, real estate offers a meaningful and somewhat stable income flow.
- If you invest in REITs, you can participate in real estate and enjoy ready liquidity as these instruments trade like stocks.
- Real estate is generally considered to be a good inflation hedge.

There are various strategies for investing in real estate and we will consider a few of these below:

Land- By far the riskiest way to invest is to purchase raw land. You must be able to tolerate a long lead time to realize the potential of your investment. Moreover, you will have annual cash outflows for taxes, insurance and security without receiving any cash inflow. If you borrow to finance the purchase, you may not be able to deduct the interest since the deduction could be limited to the net investment income on the property. Finally, you cannot depreciate land.

Core Properties- This strategy involves investing in leased properties with a stable income flow. Usually, these properties are large-scale residential buildings, as well as office buildings in large metropolitan centers. They may also include highly stable shopping malls with strong anchor tenants. If you access this strategy through real estate partnerships, the entity will likely employ low debt since cash flow is the key objective. You would expect only modest appreciation since the value would be driven largely through capitalized income and income would be favored over appreciation.

Value-Added Properties- This investment strategy involves buying properties at below market prices with the objective of investing additional monies to improve and reposition the properties. Leverage is frequently employed and the turnaround plan will usually take about three to five years. The investment objective favors capital appreciation over income. The typical property could be suburban office buildings, residential buildings and somewhat higher-end retail space.

Opportunistic Properties- This is the higher risk strategy where investors purchase properties with uncertain cash flow and prospects. They will require considerable investment to improve, reposition and then re-lease. Frequently, these investments include retail shopping areas and ultimate profitability may also depend on the development of adjacent properties.

REITs- While real estate investments have performed well throughout the years, they are not the most liquid as it generally takes some time to convert the assets into cash. However, there is a way for investors to participate in the real estate market and, at the same time, be able to liquidate their investments much as they would a stock or bond. This is through a real estate investment trust, commonly referred to as REITs. These entities are very much like public companies as they are structured as C-corporations with a board of directors. REITs are in the business of owning and managing real estate properties including commercial office buildings, shopping centers, warehouses, hotels, health care facilities and residential properties. They serve as pass-through entities as they distribute most of their income to shareholders.

To qualify as a REIT, a company must comply with a series of Internal Revenue Service tax code regulations. Here are some of those provisions:

1. It must be established as a taxable entity such as a corporation or business trust.
2. A proper governance structure needs to exist. This can be in the form of a board of directors or trustees.
3. The entity must pay out to its shareholders at least 90 percent of its taxable income.
4. There are also some shareholder restrictions. It must have a minimum of 100 shareholders and no more than 50 percent of its shares can be held by five or fewer individuals during the second half of each year.
5. As expected, a REIT is also subject to certain investment restrictions. First, it must invest at least 75 percent of its assets in real estate. Second, at least 75 percent of its gross income must come from rents or mortgage interest on real property. Third, it can invest no more than 20 percent of its assets in stocks of taxable REIT subsidiaries.
6. REIT shares must be fully transferable.

Not all REITS are alike. There are several types or REITs, including the following:

- *Equity REITs* acquire properties and then manage them as part of a permanent portfolio. They are essentially an operating company.

- *Mortgage REITs* provide credit to real estate operators. Many will also employ interest rate hedging techniques to manage their interest rate risk.
- *Hybrid REITs*, as the name implies, are entities that have both equity investments as well as mortgages in its portfolio.
- *Private REITs* also exist in the marketplace. These entities do not trade on an exchange as do general REITs. They frequently represent venture capital like deals, where the investors hope to eventually launch an IPO if the REIT is successful.

The structure of REITs is also interesting. There are three ways a REIT may be structured:

1. You can have a *traditional* REIT where the entity directly owns the assets.
2. Another form is an entity called an UPREIT. These are formed when the partners of an external partnership join with a REIT to form a new partnership, which is formally termed an Operating Partnership. The partners from the external partnership contribute their properties to the new Operating Partnership while the REIT contributes cash. Generally, the REIT is the general partner and has the majority ownership position. When the external partners contribute their properties, they do so on a tax-deferred basis. After a period of time, which is usually one year, the operating Partnership owners can convert their units or shares into regular REIT shares, which are then very liquid. They can then sell these units over a period of time, thus deferring the tax liability.
3. There is also a structure called a DOWNREIT, which has some of the features of an UPREIT, but this entity can also own properties outright in addition to those in the Operating Partnership.

It is also important to understand how REIT income is taxed. Here are some guidelines:

- Since REITs distribute most of their income to shareholders, they do not pay tax on those distributions at the corporate level. Accordingly, the shareholder will be taxed at ordinary income tax rates, currently subject to a maximum federal level of 35 percent.
- Capital gains distributions from REITs are subject to the 15 percent rate.
- Where the REIT distributes income from a taxable subsidiary and already paid a corporate tax, the shareholder will be subject to only the 15 percent rate.
- Should the REIT distribute funds where it already paid tax at the corporate level and is distributing retained earnings, receiving shareholders are subject to only the 15 percent rate.

In the next chapter, we will discuss how to select and evaluate REITs, but now we will just summarize some of the benefits of including them in your portfolio:

- Overall, they provide high stable dividends with the potential for moderate capital appreciation.
- They provide good diversification to the traditional asset classes as well as to other alternative investments such as hedge funds.
- Unlike direct real estate investments, they provide immediate liquidity as their shares are traded on major stock exchanges.
- Oversight is generally good. There is a board of directors and the REITs must disclose financial reports to the Securities and Exchange Commission.
- The REITs are professionally managed.

1031 Tax-Deferred Exchanges- Before leaving the topic of real estate, we should discuss the strategy of engaging in a 1031 exchange transaction. Assume you are ready to sell an investment property or one that is used in your trade or business. You are also willing to take the proceeds and purchase another similar type of property. Can you accomplish this with minimal tax consequences? The answer is yes. Under section 1031 of the Internal Revenue Code, an investor can sell a property and reinvest the proceeds into a like-kind property and defer the capital gain tax. As one might expect, there are a series of rules that you must follow for the exchange to work. Here are some of the critical ones:

1. The cash proceeds from the property sold must be reinvested into the replacement property. If you take out any cash at inception, you will be taxed. On the other hand, you can later refinance the new property and take cash out at that time. Many investors actually use the 1031 exchange as a way to buy larger properties, either at inception or after refinancing.
2. The value of the replacement property must be at least equal to the original property.
3. The exchange must be with like-kind properties. This means properties of a similar nature. For example, you can exchange a retail shopping center for a hotel but could not exchange a shopping center for an airplane.
4. There are time limits for completing the exchange. Two dates are important. First, you have 45 days from the sale of the original property to identify replacement properties. The sale must then take place within 180 days from the transfer of the original property.
5. There are rules for identifying replacement properties. You can select among three options when identifying a replacement property. The first is the "3-Property Rule." This specifies that you can identify three possible replacement properties. A second alternative is the "200% Rule," where you can select any number

of potential replacements so long as their aggregate market value does not exceed 200 percent of the value of the relinquished property. The third option is the "95% Exemption," where you can identify any number of replacement properties without regard to value, so long as the properties you acquire are at least 95 percent of the fair market value of those properties identified.
6. The actual transaction must be conducted through a Qualified Intermediary and no funds can pass through your hands or the hands of your agent. Otherwise, you could lose the deferred tax benefit.

Finally, it is important to note that you cannot exchange a property directly for shares of a REIT and defer taxation. However, as discussed above, you can contribute properties into an Operating Partnership where you become partners with a REIT. After a period of time, you can receive units of the REIT and then sell them as you wish. You will defer payment of taxes until you actually sell the REIT shares. This is the concept of the UPREIT that we covered above. This has been a popular way for large-scale real estate investors to sell their properties.

Private Equity

Nowhere is the risk/return trade-off more intense than with private equity investments. Successful investing in this space requires considerable skill and patience. As an asset class, private equity is very long term and highly illiquid. Each stage of the process can take considerable time to complete, whether it is the initial investment selection period, the holding period or the exit phase. As an example, a typical venture capital fund cycle could take up to a dozen years. During the first three to four years, the venture capital fund will be seeking investments and deploying the capital. Generally, capital is called by the fund as needed. The middle phase involves additional financing from banks and other investors as the companies are now producing products and are hopefully becoming profitable. This phase could take another three to five years. The final phase is the exit phase, where you hope that your companies are successful enough to do an IPO or a recapitalization, engage in a strategic merger or be acquired.

When crafting a private equity strategy, there are several points to keep in mind, including the following:

Investment Time Horizon- Timing is critical when investing in this space. Timing, however, is on two levels. First, timing involves when you commit to investing in this asset class. Investing at the end of a hot cycle can and has put investors in a vice that will take years to work out of. On the other hand, investing at the beginning of a cycle is difficult as you remember the prior market collapse and there are not always a lot of new deals around. Timing is also important within a private equity fund. Some private equity offerings involve fund of funds where the manager will buy into funds with different vintage years. This type of diversification enables investors to own underlying investments in companies that are at various stages in their development. Consequently, you will have a portfolio of varying investment time horizons which may be beneficial in managing the risk inherent in these investments.

Buyouts- This strategy involves seeking company buy-out opportunities or facilitating various forms of buyouts. Some of the common buyouts include a leveraged buyout, where the buyers take over a company with the financing coming from a third party like a bank or private equity firm. Another form is the management buy-in, where an external group takes over a company, largely with its own funding. Still another form is the management buy-out, where current management buys the company. It can do this with a combination of its own money as well as investments from private equity firms or other financing sources.

Venture Capital- A strategy for investing in venture capital is predicated on selecting the stages where you wish to participate. Alternatively, you could invest generally in this space without being specific as to a stage. The principal stages of venture capital investing are:

- *Seed Stage-*This is the very earliest stage of investing where many companies still do not have any clear revenues. The entrepreneur is still likely to be setting up the company.
- *Early Stage-*The company has begun to produce revenues but has not yet produced any profit.
- *Late Stage-*By this stage, the company is profitable and is seeking more traditional credit financing to expand its operations or acquire other companies. It now needs financial engineering skills as opposed to the creative conceptual skills that it needed earlier. These financial engineering skills will then be used to craft the appropriate exit strategies.

Special Situations- Some private equity investors prefer a strategy that emphasizes highly specific situations. Some of these more specific strategies include mezzanine financing, distressed debt and private real estate. Mezzanine financing falls between equity and debt on the risk spectrum of a deal. A typical transaction would involve a loan to the company with the receipt of some form of equity such as warrants, stock or convertible securities. In this case, the investor must be assured of cash flow and not just future appreciation.

Secondary Market- Historically, private equity posed one risk or drawback that kept many investors away. This is the lack of liquidity and the long exit cycle, particularly during tough economic times. However, during recent years, we have witnessed the emergence of a true secondary market for private equity. There have been a number of factors contributing to the emergence of secondary market transactions:

- During the past slowdown, venture capital and buyout funds significantly slowed down their distributions.
- Investors were unable or unwilling to meet capital calls.
- Some institutions exceeded their allocation targets to alternative investments or just wanted to more efficiently manage those allocations.
- Institutional private equity fund sponsors merged and wanted to reposition their portfolio of investments.

While a secondary market certainly helps investors who want to sell, it can also help buyers in some ways. In particular, some fund advisors are now establishing fund of funds with private equity funds of different vintage years. This offers potential investors much greater transparency as they can see what they are actually buying into. It also offers investors the ability to have investments at various stages of their life cycle.

The trick, of course, is to realize a good value for your investment if you are the seller. Conversely, if you are the buyer, you are looking for a great discount. As a result, secondary market advisory firms exist to structure these types of transactions.

Capital Calls- Private equity is characterized by its capital calls. When investing in this asset class, you rarely have your entire commitment invested at any point in time. For example, the manager will draw down capital as needed. When a private equity fund is established, the manager does not necessarily have all of the investments identified. It is therefore common for the fund manager to call 15 to 20 percent of the commitment at inception and another 20 to 25 percent annually until all of the capital is deployed. At the same time, it is likely that the manager will begin to distribute capital back to the investors in the fourth or fifth year after inception. The distributions occur after individual companies engage in their exit strategies, such as an IPO or merger.

Terms and Conditions- These investments generally have the following characteristics:

- **Management Fee-** There is an annual management fee, usually in the range of 1 percent. This fee may be reduced for larger commitments and may be reduced overall as the funds age.
- **Placement Fee-** Some funds will have a placement fee on the original commitment. This fee compensates the manager for the expenses associated with organizing the fund and searching for the investments. Again, this fee can vary, based on the level of commitment, and usually starts out around 1 percent. In some cases, the fee may even be eliminated for large commitments.
- **Minimum Investment-** Most funds have minimum commitment levels. These can vary greatly depending on who the manager is. The most successful managers usually have very high minimums. Fund of funds generally permit lower minimums and provide investors with access to funds that would require much higher minimums.
- **Term-** The hallmark of private equity investing is its long commitment period. Investors must be prepared to stay with their investment from seven to twelve years, again keeping in mind that you do not have your entire commitment outstanding at any one time.
- **Carried Interest-** Another distinctive feature of private equity is its profit or incentive structure. It is common for the general partner or manager to get something like 10 to 20 percent of the profits of a fund with the limited partners getting the remaining 80 to 90 percent. However, it is also very common for this profit incentive to be withheld until the investors get some multiple of their capital returned. This multiple could be something like 1.25 to 1.5 times their capital contributions.

Natural Resources

Investors today are beginning to distinguish between "real assets" and traditional financial assets. We covered real estate earlier. We will take a moment now to discuss the reason, along with some strategies, for investing in natural resources.

Perhaps no investment is a better inflation hedge than some of our natural resources. Included in the category of resource investments are:

- Energy including oil and natural gas
- Industrial metals such as copper and steel
- Precious metals such as gold and silver
- Agricultural commodities such as cattle, corn and soybeans
- Timber

Resources also offer investors an asset class with low correlation to traditional stocks and bonds. There are a couple of ways to play the resource investment field and we will cover each briefly:

1. You can just buy stocks in companies that largely represent a resource play. This includes steel, aluminum, copper and energy companies.
2. You can purchase commodities or invest with a Commodity Trading Advisor. We covered this in the section on hedge funds.
3. You can purchase interests in private energy partnerships.
4. You could purchase timber investments.

Timber has become a popular investment among wealthy families, so we will spend a moment to discuss some of its features and benefits:

1. **Diversification**- Timber displays a low correlation to stocks and bonds so it represents an effective diversification play. It has also been used as a balance against a large concentrated equity position in portfolios.

2. **Capital Preservation**- While timber may not return spectacular results, it is nevertheless known for its capital preservation. To better explain this feature, consider the various sources of return on timberland:

    - First, as you might expect, the value of the land can appreciate.
    - Timber, as a product or commodity, can appreciate. However, it is highly cyclical and somewhat dependent on the housing and construction markets.
    - Timber has a very unique characteristic, which is biological growth. Timber actually becomes more valuable as trees get larger. For example, smaller trees produce pulpwood, which is employed in paper production. Intermediate trees, which create chip-n-saw products, produce some lumber. Larger trees produce saw-timber, which is commonly known as lumber/plywood. This is the most expensive lumber.
    - This implies that timberland owners can postpone harvests during soft demand periods and actually realize increasing investment value while they are waiting.

3. **Tax Efficiency**- Timber investments are fairly tax-efficient. They offer investors depletion deductions, where they can recover capital costs against harvested timber. Timber also supports leverage, so interest deductions are available as well. When timber is harvested and sold, the profits are treated as capital gains.

4. **Time Horizon-** One drawback of timber is that it is a long-term investment with limited liquidity.
5. **Management Costs-** Timber is not an inexpensive investment to acquire and maintain. You generally pay some acquisition cost, ongoing management fees and sales commissions when you harvest and sell the products. These structures vary, however. We will discuss some of the alternative structures in the next chapter.
6. **Other Business Uses-** Timberland is also unique in that its owners can use it for business and even personal uses. You could charge fees for hunting, fishing and camping. You could also build a cabin and live there as a second home.

In the next chapter, we will discuss ways to access timber investments.

Structured Products

How would you like an investment that cannot lose money? Many investors, even very wealthy ones, have a low threshold for loss of principal, even though they may frequently forgive investment managers for under-performing their benchmark. As a result, financial institutions have engineered products that can provide its clients with exposure to certain investment strategies while preserving their initial capital. Others may provide a high degree of protection, although it may not be guaranteed. We will comment on two of these products: 1) principal protected notes and; 2) collateralized debt obligations.

1. **Principal Protected Notes-** These products have two essential features. First, there is a guaranteed return of principal at the maturity of the note. This is achieved by securing part of the investment with high-quality notes such as zero coupon instruments and depositing/pledging them with a commercial

bank that could provide the guarantee. Second, there is the investment of the remaining capital into financial strategies to achieve equity-like returns. The strategies will vary depending on the objective of each note. For example, some notes will provide protection of principal plus a percentage of the S&P 500 index returns over a specified time period. Others could be pegged to returns on international markets or commodities. It is important to mention that the returns are almost always some percentage of an index and not its entire return. You should also note that these investments are locked up for the maturity of the notes, which could range from three to seven years. Investors will sometimes employ these instruments as hedge fund surrogates.

2. **Collateralized Debt Obligations-** Likewise, these instruments can sometimes serve as fixed income surrogates. A CDO is an investment structure specifically established to raise capital for investing in pools of asset backed securities, generally commercial loans or investment grade and high yield debt. Profits are created through managing the funding gap. As an example, consider a sample structure.

- A CDO is established with several classes of investors, each considered to be part of a specific tranche. We illustrate this in exhibit 5-W.
- Those who purchase the subordinated notes have the greatest risk but also are in position to earn the highest return. They would realize profits from the funding gap as well as returns on investments from the capital raised in this tranche.
- Also, as the structure implies, the CDO will pay different returns on each tranche. It is therefore important for the manager to invest in a way to maximize the overall net interest spread.

- The priority on cash flows is also important to understand. Typically, here is how it would work. The manager takes its management fee, as well as other high level administrative expenses, first. Then he/she distributes interest income to each investor class in order of rank and preference. Then, the manager gets any incentive fees and the subordinated investors receive their residual interest payment. Also, each CDO is likely to have a reinvestment period in which maturing assets can be reinvested. After this reinvestment period, maturing assets must be used to retire investor capital. As with the priority of interest payments, retirement of capital takes place in the same order of priority, with the higher tranches being redeemed first.

EXHIBIT 5-W

SAMPLE CDO STRUCTURE

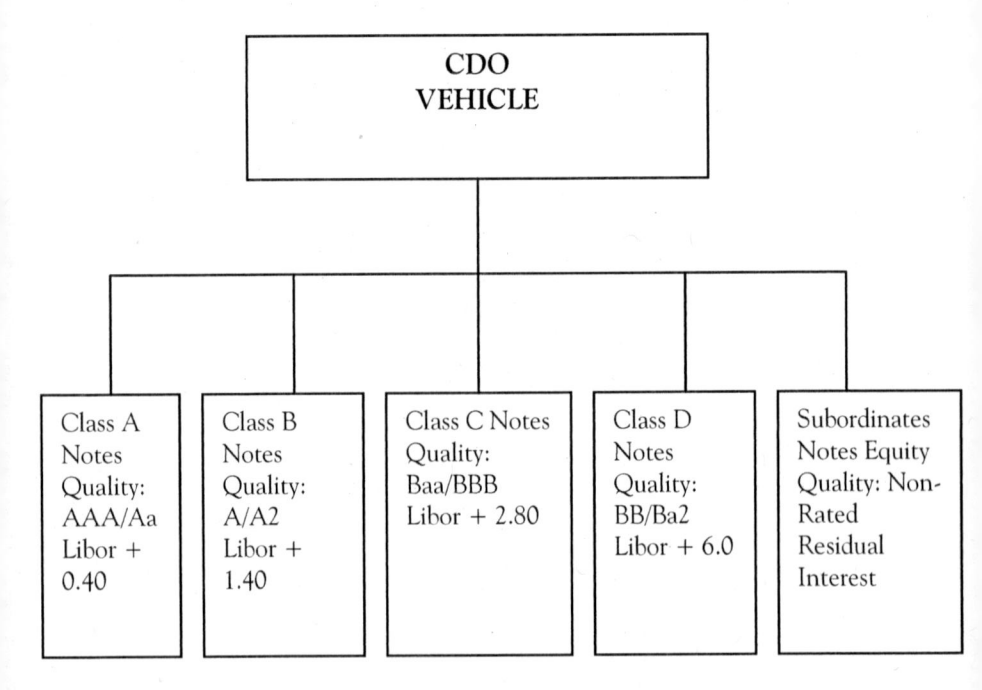

```
                    ┌──────────────┐
                    │     CDO      │
                    │   VEHICLE    │
                    └──────┬───────┘
     ┌────────┬────────┬───┴────┬────────┬────────┐
```

| Class A Notes Quality: AAA/Aa Libor + 0.40 | Class B Notes Quality: A/A2 Libor + 1.40 | Class C Notes Quality: Baa/BBB Libor + 2.80 | Class D Notes Quality: BB/Ba2 Libor + 6.0 | Subordinates Notes Equity Quality: Non-Rated Residual Interest |

Creating an Investment Policy

Both the principal protected note and the CDO offer investors strategies that may neatly fit within their portfolio risk and return profile. Keep in mind, however, that these are relatively illiquid instruments.

We have now completed our tour of equity class strategies. However, before leaving this topic, we will conclude with a few brief comments on tax efficiency.

Tax Efficiency Strategies

We will be covering a range of tax planning issues in subsequent chapters, but here we will comment on a specific technique to manage an overall investment portfolio in a more tax efficient manner. However, first, we should summarize some traditional measures to achieve greater overall tax efficiency when managing investments:

- When purchasing mutual funds, examine their portfolio turnover and after-tax returns. Many mutual funds are not tax efficient, but some are.
- All things being equal, investors have favored portfolios of individual securities so they are able to control the timing of capital gains. If they have a professional manager handling the portfolio, they can have their managers harvest losses at year-end, to offset a net gain position.
- To the extent possible, try to hold investments longer term so as to realize a long-term gain when you sell it.
- Carefully review equity investments to see which ones will qualify for the 15 percent dividend tax rate as opposed to the ordinary tax rates.

Second, there is a strategy that wealthy individuals can employ to deal with significant tax issues. As background, there are two asset categories that present tax issues for their holders. One is hedge funds, which predominately produce short-term capital gains, and the other is a concentrated stock position, which produces long-term capital gains when sold. One way to manage around these tax issues is to establish a large cap S&P-like portfolio as part of your core equity approach. With a portfolio of many companies across all of the economic sectors, you will always have winners and losers in a given year. Accordingly, you could harvest short-term losses to offset some of your hedge fund income and sell positions with long-term losses to offset any sales of concentrated holdings. Some investors may not have the asset base to have a manger create a customized index portfolio. In this situation, you could achieve a similar result by creating an index-like portfolio that has 80 to 100 names spread across the economic sectors of the market. The key is to always be broadly diversified so that you achieve two important results. First, you want a portfolio that will perform much in line with the benchmark index you are trying to replicate. Second, you want to create opportunities to offset hedge fund and concentrated stock gains so as to enhance your overall after-tax return. Perhaps a final comment on tax strategies is also in order. As you consider various techniques and tactics, keep in mind that the investment objectives must always supersede any tax objectives. The "tax tail cannot wag the investment dog."

No discussion of taxes would be complete without at least mentioning the Alternative Minimum Tax. By no means will we cover this topic in complete detail as it is one of the most complex aspects of the tax code, and you should consult you tax advisor for assistance in fully understanding it as well as in designing strategies to deal with it. When Congress established the AMT, its intent was to prevent high-income taxpayers from using deductions, tax credits and exclusions to pay very little tax. However, in practice, the AMT has reached far into the tax rolls and impacts way more people than originally intended.

The tax itself is an additional tax above what one would pay using the traditional tax tables. Stated simply, you calculate your tax liability in two ways. First, you do it the regular way and arrive at a tax. Then, you calculate your tax using a different methodology to arrive at what is called the alternative minimum tax. Whichever is higher, you pay. When comparing the two methods, the difference is that you have to add back certain deductions and exemptions when calculating the AMT. Here are some of the common ones:

- Personal exemptions
- Standard deduction
- State and local income taxes
- Interest on home equity loans where proceeds are not used to buy, build or improve you residence.
- Certain medical expenses
- Certain itemized deductions such as tax preparation fees, unreimbursed business expenses and investment related expenses.
- The spread realized when exercising incentive stock options
- Long-term capital gains in years of large gains.
- Non-AMT municipal bonds
- Some tax shelters

Once calculated, the AMT rate is 28 percent. We should also mention that there is the possibility of some good news in that you can use the AMT payment as a credit to offset tax liabilities in future years. However, it will be dependent on what caused your AMT liability in the first place and whether your future income situation is conducive to employing it. The key concept here is one of timing. For example, if you exercise an incentive stock option, you create an AMT liability in the year you exercise it. However, when you actually sell the stock in a later year, it would be subject to regular income tax. Since this type of transaction qualifies for a credit, you can use the AMT credit at any time in the future. On the other hand, a large capital gain incurred in a given year or certain large deductions may not qualify for carry-forward credit. Also, you cannot use the credit in a year when you have actual AMT liability. Nevertheless, you should consult your tax advisor for further explanations of this complex issue.

From an investment perspective, your advisors may be able to suggest certain portfolio realignments to create additional taxable income in years when you expect significant AMT liabilities.

6

Implementing Your Investment Strategy

Even though historical studies point to asset allocation as the key to performance, a good plan that is poorly executed will not give you the results you are seeking. Accordingly, we will now devote significant space to discuss implementing the investment program. We will cover this topic in two segments. First, we will cover the process for selecting investment vehicles and managers. Then, we will speak about ways to monitor your portfolios and rebalance them when it is appropriate to do so.

Should You First Hire an Investment Consultant?

Investors have multiple options when implementing their investment plan. At the outset however, the investor faces a critical decision on investment governance. This entails whether he/she should engage an investment consultant to advise on the actual selection and continuous evaluation of investment vehicles and managers. As background, you have three ways to put together a portfolio. First, you can do it yourself whereby you buy and sell specific securities, hedge funds and real estate. You essentially do your own research or rely on limited advice from brokers. Second, you can hire professional investment managers or select individual mutual funds per asset class. These managers, in turn, buy and sell the actual securities. Third, you can hire a consultant to select the managers.

What services do consultants provide? Essentially, they will provide investors with asset allocation advice, suggest asset class strategies, recommend specific investment managers and continually monitor the performance of each manager, suggesting terminating some when appropriate. Investors have embraced investment consultants for a couple of reasons:

- They have the resources and have developed processes to properly evaluate investment managers.
- Many have the technology to effectively monitor the performance of the managers.
- Some family members may have the responsibility to oversee the investments for the entire family group. Hiring an external consultant is sometimes a good way to shift some of the fiduciary responsibility or to just gain assistance in discharging these duties.

Investors generally have two considerations when deciding whether to use an overall consultant. The first issue is that you need to be prepared to pay the consultant a fee for his or her services. This additional fee can range from 20 to 50 basis points, depending on asset size. A second issue is that you are subject to the range of managers that the consultant follows and has relationships with. Should you want a provider with access to a wide range of investment managers, you may need to stick with the larger institutions that are able to establish relationships with more firms, particularly the more difficult firms to access.

Investors also have a choice in the type of investment consultant to engage. Some consulting firms are independent and only engage in providing investment consulting services. They sell no products, nor do they manage any money directly. Some investors like this business model because they view this type of advisor as being totally neutral. Another model is the comprehensive manager of managers platform that large banking and brokerage organizations offer. These platforms offer clients a full package consisting of asset allocation, manager search and evaluation, performance monitoring, custody, reporting and trading. They usually offer these services at one comprehensive price. Hence, they are sometimes referred to as "wrap accounts."

Let's say you decide to employ an investment consultant. How should you go about evaluating alternative providers? Here are some things to look for:

- Determine the range of asset classes the consultant covers and make sure they have strong expertise in those classes that are important to you.
- Assess the consultant's capacity to advise on alternative investments such as hedge funds, private equity and real estate if those classes are important to you.
- Ask about the number of individual managers the consultant follows. As a follow through question, ask about their research capabilities in terms of the number of analysts that cover that group of investment managers. Do the ratios make sense in terms of managers covered per analyst? If the ratio is too high, you may question how effectively the firm really covers each manager.

- Assess the experience of each of the principals and key personnel. Also, understand how the people are paid and whether there is any form of incentive compensation based on client results.
- Carefully evaluate the process each provider uses to select and evaluate managers. Equally important, you should understand how they continually monitor the managers and under what circumstances the firm will fire a manager. Ask each consultant how many managers they have fired over the past three years and what the underlying circumstances were for those actions.
- Ask how many clients the firm has and make sure you are comfortable with the ratio of clients per account officer.
- In this day and age, you do need to ask about potential conflicts of interest. You can attempt to assess this in a couple of ways. You could ask the firm whether any of its recommended investment managers refer clients to them. If, for example, some of the managers refer clients to the consultant, the consultant could possibly be hesitant to ever fire those managers. You could also ask whether there is any revenue sharing between the consultant and their investment managers.
- Finally, you will certainly ask about fees. Make sure you ask for total disclosure of all forms of compensation. For example, some firms may operate fund of funds hedge funds. For this service, they may get part of the management and incentive fees.

Evaluating the Different Investment Vehicles

Whether you elect to manage your portfolios yourself, select individual investment managers or engage the services of a consultant, the actual process for selecting investment vehicles and individual managers is essentially the same. To implement the investment program covering the traditional asset classes, you will first want to decide which vehicles are appropriate for each asset class, realizing that for each asset class, you may arrive at a different answer. You will want to evaluate the following three alternative investment vehicles:

- Mutual funds
- Exchange traded funds
- Separate accounts

Mutual Funds

For good reason, mutual funds are perhaps the most widely held investment vehicle. Individuals hold them in their retirement funds as well as in their personal portfolios. Mutual funds have provided investors with many benefits, including the following:

- They fall under the regulation of the Investment Company Act of 1940. As such, each mutual fund must issue a prospectus describing the objectives, management and operations of the fund. The Securities and Exchange Commission reviews these prospectuses; however, they do not issue any endorsement as a result of their review. Their role is to insure that mutual fund companies follow all of the rules of disclosure.
- They offer investors a high degree of diversification. By law, mutual funds must follow certain rules of diversification in order to be considered as a diversified management company under the Investment Company Act of 1940. For example, at least 75 percent of its assets must be invested so that no more than 5 percent are invested in any one issuer. Also, they may not own more that 10 percent of any company. The other 25 percent of the fund's assets does not have to follow these restrictions. As a result, through mutual funds, investors are able to diversify to a

- much greater extent than they can through investing on their own, particularly for smaller portfolios.
- They provide investors with professional management as they have the ability to hire top talent in the industry.
- Mutual funds offer certain operational benefits. One such benefit is the dividend reinvestment plan whereby you can automatically reinvest dividends into new fund units. Another one is the ability to transfer investments to other funds in the family without incurring load charges where they exist.

Mutual funds take on one of two major forms. First, there are closed end funds, which trade on a stock exchange just like stocks. The funds may trade at, below or above the net asset value on its underlying investments. If the fund is in high demand, it could likely trade at a premium to net asset value, while it is likely to trade at a discount when it is in low demand. Specific country funds usually trade as closed end funds. The second form is open end funds. These funds are issued directly from the fund company or its distributor and are issued at net asset value. The funds are open for purchase and redemption until 4:00 pm on each trading day. After the close of trading, the funds are valued and all inflow and outflows are transacted at that price. Open-end funds are offered with a load or sales charge, or they are sold on a no-load basis.

Mutual funds cover nearly all traditional asset classes and management styles as there are probably as many mutual funds as there are stocks. Services exist that evaluate mutual funds, with the best known ones being Morningstar and Lipper. Some of the common issues to consider when evaluating mutual funds are:

- Risk-adjusted performance
- After-tax performance
- Turnover and tax efficiency

- Expense ratio, which includes management, custodial, accounting and marketing fees
- Personnel stability
- Size

Investors today can purchase mutual funds directly from the fund family, from a brokerage firm, through banks or from large financial service firms that act as "supermarkets." These firms offer its clients the ability to purchase mutual funds from a large variety of fund families. They offer clients not only access to the funds but also consolidated custody and reporting on those assets.

Exchange Traded Funds

While this investment vehicle has been around in some form since the late 1970's and really came into its own with the introduction of the Standard and Poor's Depository Receipt (commonly referred to as Spiders) in 1993, it is only recently that ETFs have become one of the fastest growing investment vehicles. In many respects, exchange traded funds are a combination between closed end and open end mutual funds. Like an open end mutual fund, ETFs can be issued with virtually no limit and represent ownership in an underlying portfolio of securities. In this case, the securities replicate a specified index. Also, like closed end funds, ETFs are traded on a securities exchange and could trade at a premium or discount to the net asset value of its underlying securities. There are a number of important features and benefits to these popular, fast-growing investment structures and we will consider some of these below:

Mechanics of Creating and Redeeming Shares

Exhibit 6-A illustrates the process for creating ETF units. There are a couple of key steps in this process:

- We first need to identify the key players. The "Authorized Participants" are responsible for the creation and redemption of ETF units on behalf on their customers. These players are large financial institutions with sophisticated investment capabilities.

EXHIBIT 6–A

EXCHANGE TRADED FUND STRUCTURE

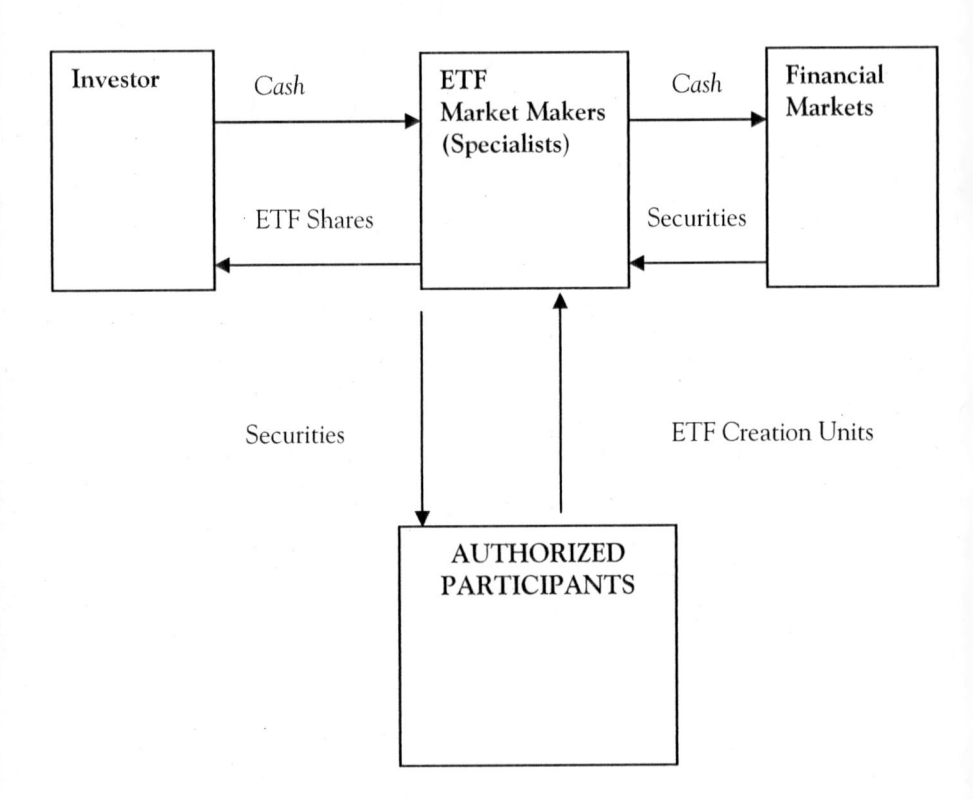

```
┌──────────┐   Cash    ┌─────────────┐   Cash    ┌──────────┐
│ Investor │ ────────► │     ETF     │ ────────► │Financial │
│          │           │Market Makers│           │ Markets  │
│          │           │(Specialists)│           │          │
│          │ ◄──────── │             │ ◄──────── │          │
└──────────┘ETF Shares └─────────────┘Securities └──────────┘
                         ▲         ▲
                         │         │
                  Securities    ETF Creation Units
                         │         │
                      ┌──────────────┐
                      │  AUTHORIZED  │
                      │ PARTICIPANTS │
                      └──────────────┘
```

- The other key player is the exchange specialist or market maker, who is responsible for maintaining an orderly market price.
- ETF units are issued in share amounts of 50,000. Each 50,000 block is called a creation unit.

- When purchasing an ETF, an investor places an order much like he or she would do when buying a stock. The order is directed through an authorized participant to the exchange where the market makers exchange cash for ETF units, if available. If there is not a supply/demand balance, the market maker will take the cash and purchase securities to represent the underlying index of the ETF. The ETF fund advisor then issues a new unit. Alternatively, orders can be placed through the AMEX–Automated Routing Order System for *i* Shares.

A key feature of ETFs is that redemptions can take place with the in-kind transfer of the underlying securities. Accordingly, you will not realize a capital gain when you sell your units. However, you may realize some capital gains while holding the ETF as the underlying index is rebalanced.

Price Maintenance

An important aspect of ETFs is the stability of its price versus the net asset value of its underlying securities. A drawback of some closed end mutual funds is that their market prices can and frequently do trade at discounts to their net asset value. The easy ability for ETF market participants to arbitrage any difference of this nature has provided for a very orderly market for these securities. Consider how the arbitrage process would work:

- Assume the S&P 500 *i*Share sells for $50, which means that a new creation unit would have a market value of $50 times 50,000 or $2,500,000.
- Also, assume that the market value of the underlying basket of securities would cost $2,435,000. This leaves an arbitrage gap of $65,000.

- The Authorized Participant could establish a new creation unit by selling the *i*Share to a buyer in the market and using the $2,500,000 proceeds to buy the underlying market basket for $2.435,000. This leaves a profit of $65,000. Technically the Authorized Participant or its institutional clients would continue this process until the price differential narrows.

On the other hand, should the *i*Share be selling below its net asset value, the following set of transactions could take place until the price narrows.

- The Authorized Participant would buy the *i*Shares in the market and then sell short the basket of stocks underlying the index.
- At the same time, the Authorized Participant would redeem the *i*Shares for the actual basket of stocks and use those stocks to close out the short position.

Portfolio Efficiencies

ETFs can provide a portfolio with a range of efficiencies. Here are some of the more important ones:

- Today, one can access multiple sectors and indexes of the marketplace. These indexes cover: large, mid and small capitalization equities; growth, value and core styles; global and international sectors; fixed income and industry sectors.
- The expense ratios on ETFs are generally lower than their mutual fund counterparts as they do not have the same custodial and recordkeeping requirements.
- Tax efficiency is high. Capital gains occur when the funds are rebalanced to reflect changes in the makeup of the index itself. Unlike mutual funds, ETFs do not need to worry about raising

cash to meet redemptions and thus create more capital gains in the process.
- Pricing is continuous throughout the day compared to mutual funds where the pricing is done only after the end of the trading day at 4 pm.
- You can short-sell ETFs, and can even do so on down-ticks. Generally, when you engage in short selling, you can only do so on an up-tick, where the sale must be at a price higher than its previous price.

Strategies

ETFs lend themselves to supporting a number of portfolio strategies. Here are a couple to consider:

- ETFs can assist investors in tax loss selling and in particular, to mitigate the impact of the Wash Sale Rules. Under these rules, an investor cannot purchase a security that is substantially identical to one that it has sold within 30 days prior to or after the sale. If you do, you will not be able to realize any tax loss on the sale. Accordingly, one of the risks in tax loss selling is that you are out of the stock for 30 days and possibly out of the market as well. To maintain at least the market exposure, you can purchase an ETF that closely resembles the stock or its sector after you sell a stock for a tax loss. After the 30-day period, you could always buy the stock back and sell the ETF. Therefore, you remain invested in the market for this 30-day period via the ETF.
- ETFs are good vehicles to use when conducting tactical asset allocation. For example, should you wish to add emerging market exposure to your portfolio but do not want to hire an individual manager and cannot decide upon a mutual fund, buying the ETF

is very efficient as you can sell it rather easily when you wish to reduce your exposure later. Another example is when you may want to temporarily have more exposure to healthcare, for example. You could buy the iShares Global Healthcare Sector Index Fund.
- You could also employ ETFs in hedging an overweighted exposure to a segment of the market. For example, if you had too much allocated to small cap equities, you may short the relevant small cap ETF and therefore not have to sell out a specific manager or mutual fund. However, I should advise you to always engage competent financial advice before engaging in any short selling transactions as they are inherently risky in and of themselves even when used to hedge a portfolio.

Separate Accounts

Investors with over $1 million have tended to gravitate toward separate account management. This industry has expanded considerably over the past decade. As mentioned earlier, you can access separate accounts in at least one of three ways. First, you could hire individual investment managers. Second, you could hire an investment consultant to select and monitor managers. Third, you can engage a full-service banking and brokerage firm that would provide a platform combining manager search and evaluation, custody, trading and reporting.

Separate account management has gained popularity versus the other investment vehicles for a number of reasons including:

1. Separate accounts give you the ability to selectively manage tax loss selling. It is easy to sell individual stocks in specific portfolios to offset gains elsewhere.
2. Like its mutual fund and ETF counterparts, separate account management is now available across multiple asset classes and management styles.

3. With separate account management, you can generally negotiate fees for larger dollars invested.
4. Certain high performing boutique managers may not be available in mutual fund form.
5. Separate accounts provide direct transparency to the individual securities. With mutual funds, you generally receive periodic reporting.

While separate accounts have great appeal, there are some issues investors should be aware of. For portfolios under $5 million, their costs may be higher than comparable mutual funds. Also, managers will have minimum investment levels. However, you can circumvent this to some extent when you utilize a brokerage/banking platform.

Selecting Traditional Equity Managers

There are more mutual funds than listed companies and there are probably over 20,000 independent investment managers. As a result, it can be a formidable task to select the ten or so managers to handle your single portfolio. How does one get there? Whether you hire an investment consultant or do the selecting yourself, there are certain fundamental steps one could follow. Exhibit 6-B offers a template for organizing your approach to selecting equity managers and we will refer to this as we discuss the process. As the exhibit indicates, you should approach the selection process from the standpoint of evaluating performance, process and people.

EXHIBIT 6-B
DECISION PROCESS
INVESTMENT MANAGER SELECTION
MANAGER ATTRIBUTES

PERFORMANCE	PROCESS	FIRM
• 1,3,5 and 10 year numbers	• Investment philosophy	• Size
• Annual performance	• Research methodology; how securities are selected	• Assets under management
• Rolling period analysis		• Growth over time
• Up/down market capture ratios		• Business model
	• People involved in the process	• Key personnel
• Tracking error to benchmark		• Succession of key personnel + Turnover history
• Batting average (short term consistency)	• Sell disciplines	
	• Diversification policies	• Ownership structure
• Peer group rankings	• Tax efficiency	• Compensation structure
• Risk adjusted returns		• Administration & operations capacity
• Attribution analysis		
• Backtesting and blend analysis		• Pricing of services

Investment Performance

There is a common saying in the industry that when selecting investment managers, you must not get swayed into "chasing the hot dot." This means that you should not put together a lineup of managers who have been the hottest performers over the recent past. Studies have shown that of those managers who have performed in the top quartile over a given five-year period, only about a quarter of those remained in the top quartile over the next five-year period and only about half even remained above the median. Also, when looking at performance, there are several layers of analysis and we will consider a few at this time:

- As a starting point, you will naturally look at the annualized one, three, five and ten year numbers if available. To support this, you should also look at calendar year numbers over ten years to see if any one or two years stand out in either a positive or negative way. For example, if a manager has good numbers over five or ten years, but largely achieved them with one or two good years, you need to be cautious. One of the drawbacks of just looking at performance in this way is that the evaluation points in time are

static. It largely depends on the beginning and end points in time.
- One way to better evaluate the consistency of performance is to look at what is called rolling period analysis. Here you maintain the long-term time period of, let's say ten years, but evaluate three-year performances at many different intervals over that period. This way, you vary the beginning and ending dates. You would compare the performances against established benchmarks to determine the manager's consistency against it.
- In addition to evaluating managers against relevant index benchmarks, it is instructive to compare them against peer groups of like style managers.
- Evaluating returns is only part of the process. How a manager achieves returns is also important. In particular, you will want to assess the risk a manager takes to achieve his/her results and to determine whether that level of risk is acceptable to you. There are a few ways to evaluate risk. A standard yet simple way is to measure the return over the manager's standard deviation of returns. A further extrapolation is the sharpe ratio, which is the return minus the risk-free return (e.g. treasury bills) divided by the standard deviation. Performance consistency is also a measure of risk and there are two common measures. One is the batting average, which defines how consistently a manager beats the benchmark. As an example, here you could measure, over a ten-year period, the number of quarters a manager beats the benchmark against the total number of quarters in the period. Another measure of consistency is the information ratio, which measures the manager's annual excess return versus benchmark against the manager's standard deviation over the evaluated time period, say ten years.
- As you put together a portfolio, you might be interested in how various managers perform in both up and down markets. If you

are conservative, for instance, you will lean toward a collection of managers that beat their benchmarks in down markets and be willing to give up something in the up markets. More aggressive investors may not be as concerned about down market performance so long as overall long-term performance is superior. Accordingly, there are two performance indicators to help you assess managers in this way. First, there is the upside market capture ratio, which measures a manager's performance relative to the market benchmark during up market periods. Specifically, you calculate this ratio by dividing the performance of a manager during up market periods by the return of the market benchmark during those periods. The period is usually calendar quarters. Conversely, the downside capture ratio is calculated by dividing the performance of the manager during down periods by the market benchmark during those same periods. For example, a manager with an upside/downside capture ratio of 92/68 means that it captures only 92 percent of market returns during up markets but captures only 68 percent of the market returns during down markets.

- For those who want to more intensively evaluate the sources of a manager's return, you could review its attribution analysis, which segments a manager's return among the impact of asset class, manager style, economic sector and security selection. For international managers, you will, of course, want to also look at country allocation impact.
- Concluding the review of performance, you need to perhaps consider the most important part of the manager construction process. This involves how you blend the managers into an overall portfolio. Do you want all of your managers to perform in the same direction or do you want diversification in the individual results so as to have a smoother performance cycle? If you have an investment consultant, he or she should be able to

run a composite blend of selected managers to back-test risk/return results. The trick is to have a stable of managers so that the majority, even if it is a slight majority, will outperform benchmarks in any measurement period. Exhibits 6-C and 6-D at the end of this chapter, offer templates for displaying investment performance.

Investment Process

Great performance is nice, but can a manager sustain it? How do you evaluate this capability? One way is to carefully understand the investment process employed by the firm. Here are some of the process features to look at:

- What is the manager's investment philosophy? Do they follow certain themes or do they believe in rigid quantitative analysis?
- How do they actually get stocks into their portfolios? You will want to understand the role of quantitative screening, fundamental security analysis and market technical analysis.
- Who are the people involved in the process? You will need to determine if one person drives the process or if there is a collaborative effort. Examine whether there are checks and balances in the system.
- Does the manager have some form of sell discipline and do you get the impression that he/she follows it?
- What is the manager's policy regarding diversification, including sector and industry limits, cash levels and size of individual positions?
- How tax efficient is the manager?
- Finally, is the entire process easy to understand? If not, you should be suspicious.

The Firm

In the long run, an investment manager will not sustain its performance if the business model of its firm is flawed. Therefore, when evaluating an independent investment manager, you should also evaluate the firm itself. Here are some of the things to look for:

- Check out the size if the firm and ask how the assets under management have grown over the past five years. Determine the ultimate capacity of the firm to grow and still service its clients effectively.
- Ask about the ownership structure of the firm and inquire about the ages of the key principals. Determine whether you feel the firm is being positioned to sell.
- Definitely ask how people are paid and what their incentive compensation is based on.
- Check the staff turnover in recent years.
- Figure out whether the firm has a well running back office.
- Are its fees reasonable?

Selecting Fixed Income Managers

When deciding how to implement your fixed income program, you first need to answer the key question raised in the prior chapter. That question is whether you wish to follow a passive or active approach to bond management. If you elect to adopt a passive approach, you essentially have two implementation options:

1. You could utilize a brokerage account and have your account representative buy and hold bonds until maturity. A common approach is to ladder the portfolio between maturity ranges. For

Implementing Your Investment Strategy

this service, you pay the broker's spread on the bonds when you buy them.
2. You also have the alternative of hiring an investment manager to manage the portfolio in a passive manner. Generally, the fees would be lower than for active management.

On the other hand, should you adopt an active approach as outlined in the prior chapter, your options increase.

1. Again, you can hire an investment manager to actively manage the portfolio based on parameters you may set and agree upon.
2. You can purchase a fixed income mutual fund. With mutual funds, you acquire the advantages of diversification, professional management and access to supply. However, there are also some disadvantages with mutual funds. As with equity funds, they can be tax inefficient if they trade actively and create significant capital gains. You are also not guaranteed a return of principal as bonds are marked-to-market daily. This is unlike a portfolio of individual bonds where you can always hold the bonds to maturity should interest rates rise.
3. As with equities, you also have the ability to access ETFs.

When finally deciding on an approach and a manager, here are some additional thoughts:

1. Decide whether you believe active management is worth the extra management fee, keeping in mind that you are likely buying and selling the bonds absent the broker markup.
2. Check into how the manager and especially the broker will conduct due diligence on the bonds. Buying and holding bonds without reviewing them periodically can be dangerous as bonds are frequently downgraded.
3. For active managers, review performance versus benchmarks.

4. Check into the provider's ability to gain access to supply of bonds, which is not always easy to do.

Implementing a Hedge Fund Strategy

Determining your hedge fund strategy in the first place is difficult enough. Having to design an implementation plan can be just as tricky. There are at least five ways one can invest in hedge funds:

1. Directly investing in single hedge funds.
2. Engaging a professional investment advisor to construct a customized portfolio of hedge funds.
3. Selecting a specific sector or sectors and selecting funds that fit within those sectors.
4. Investing in index hedge funds.
5. Investing in fund of funds.

We will consider each of these in turn:

Direct Investing

This approach involves buying individual hedge funds that you either heard about or that your advisors are recommending. Some investors will buy one or a few funds and do so because of the funds' performance and reputation. The strategies may or may not fit together as you are buying the managers and not necessarily have any particular strategy. Drawbacks of this strategy are that individual funds may have high minimums and you could end up with high concentration in either a single manager or strategy or both.

Customized Portfolio

Here you engage a manager to construct a portfolio much as you would for stocks and bonds. The portfolio could contain ten to thirty-five individual hedge funds and you would, in essence, have your own fund of funds. To accomplish this, you will need to commit significant dollars, generally around $10 to $25 million.

Sector Strategy

You may wish to establish a hedge fund approach where you only have exposure to certain segments of the market. Some financial providers, such as the large bank/brokerage platforms, may give you such access. Here you would specify a sector, such as market neutral, event driven or long/short directional. The provider will then manage a portfolio of funds around that sector. The provider will generally have full discretion within that portfolio.

Index Funds

As with other asset classes, hedge fund investing also features index style portfolios. This is attractive to investors who just wish to have exposure to the general market. There is a range of indexes with the Hedge Fund Research, Inc. being the prominent gatherer of this information. They have thirteen major index groupings, including the following:

- HFRI Convertible Arbitrage Index
- HFRI Distressed Securities Index
- HFRI Equity Hedge Index
- HFRI Event Driven Index
- HFRI Fixed Income Index
- HFRI Fixed Income Arbitrage Index

- HFRI Macro Index
- HFRI Emerging Markets Index
- HFRI Market Timing Index
- HFRI Merger Arbitrage Index
- HFRI Relative Value Arbitrage Index
- HFRI Short Selling Index
- HFRI Fund of Funds Index

Fund of Funds

For investors who cannot or will not commit substantial monies to hedge funds, there is a good alternative—the hedge fund of funds. As the name implies, this is a fund that consists of investments in a variety of selected hedge funds. Each fund of funds will follow a specific approach but all are generally well diversified. Sometimes there will be distinctions between low volatility, market neutral funds and higher volatility, directional fund of funds. As with any investment vehicle, there are advantages and disadvantages and fund of funds are no different. Here is an evaluation of the advantages:

- They give you access to individual funds where you may not reach the minimums required for single investments. Also, fund of funds generally have lower minimums to get into them in the first place.
- There is the information advantage with these investments. As we mentioned earlier, transparency is a risk inherent with hedge fund investing, but professional fund of fund managers will get better access to information than most private investors.
- It goes without saying that you achieve greater diversification.
- You gain the due diligence resources of a professional manager and his/her firm.
- You have the benefit of consolidated reporting.

Implementing Your Investment Strategy

There are also a couple of drawbacks that we should mention:

- As with mutual funds, you have to deal with cash flows into and out of the fund; therefore, you are subject to other investors' cash flow patterns.
- You do pay another layer of fees, which generally average 1 percent annually with a 10 percent incentive.
- Customization is difficult.
- Performance is usually around the average, but many good funds will give you a relatively steady absolute return.

The next step in this process is to determine the important factors in selecting specific hedge fund products. We will look first at how you might evaluate individual managers if you are going that route. Next, we will look at how to select a fund of funds advisor.

Individual Manager Selection

Performance

Naturally, you want to look at performance. With hedge funds, however, there are different levels and factors to consider.

- How has the fund performed against its most relevant index?
- How consistent have those returns been? You could look at the standard deviation.
- Another important feature is what we call the maximum drawdown. This is the largest decrease experienced from a high water mark. For example, you would look at various high points in performance and then examine the largest drop from those points. This can give you some feel for how much risk you may be

taking on if you are jumping in at a high point in the fund's history.

Investment Approach

To the best you can, you will want to understand the manager's approach to investing, looking at some of these factors:

- What factors drive returns? How much is top down investing versus transaction execution?
- What range of strategies are employed/
- In what market conditions will the fund manager perform best? Alternatively, which market conditions pose the greatest risk?
- Does the manager use various quantitative models? Have they been very reliable and predictive?

Risk Control

Everyone is certainly interested in risk measures when it comes to this type of investing and here are some features to look for:

- Determine the level of diversification among strategies. Are there limits for specific types of transactions?
- What is the use of derivatives and short selling. Are there limits on short selling?
- What is the overall liquidity of the fund?
- Find out what happened in the fund's worst drawdown period. Did they make any adjustments to their strategy as a result?
- Does the manager do any stress testing as to what might happen in a severe stock market drop?

Firm Characteristics

- Are the results audited?
- What is the fund's maximum capacity and how far are we from that point?
- Do the firm's principals invest in the fund alongside clients?
- Has the manager closed down any funds in the past and what were the reasons for it? What was the fund's performance prior to closing down?
- Does the firm have an offsite disaster recovery plan?
- Are you comfortable with the firm's operational reputation?

People

- Who are the principal owners of the firm and what are their professional backgrounds?
- If you are not familiar with their prior firms, will they provide references?
- Can you get client references?
- Check the ADVs that are on file with the SEC.

Fund of Funds Selection

When evaluating fund of funds, there are some characteristics that are similar to evaluating individual hedge funds, but there are also some very unique features to examine. We will consider each.

Performance

You may wish to look at performance from this perspective:

- Annual returns since inception.

- Monthly returns over the past three years. This will give you an indication of the style employed and the level of volatility.
- Annual standard deviation.
- Largest drawdown period loss.
- Performance relative to comparable fund of funds.
- Correlation to various equity capitalization and manager styles in your portfolio.

Portfolio Construction

How the manager constructs a fund of funds is also of great interest. Here are some things you should look for:

- The specific strategies employed by the fund of funds manager.
- The total number of funds usually present in the fund.
- The average allocation per fund manager and the maximum that would be placed with any single hedge fund.
- Maximum leverage that the fund can undertake.
- Liquidity for fund investors
- Whether the fund is constructed to be defensive, aggressive or moderate compared to the general hedge fund market.

Due Diligence Process

Key to evaluating a fund of funds is to understand the way the manager conducts due diligence of the underlying hedge funds. Some of the questions you could ask are as follows:

- How many people are allocated to the process?
- What is the annual turnover of managers? Why are managers fired?

- Do you visit managers at their offices and how often do you do that?
- How much capacity do your managers generally have? Is this a factor in adding new hedge fund managers to your platform?
- How many managers have closed down or gone out of business during the time you have offered the fund?
- Do you monitor style drift?
- Describe your degree of access to top managers?

Implementing a Private Equity Program

When executing your private equity program, you have a couple of options. First, you can buy individual companies and run them. Certainly, some investors are quite capable of doing this as they may have started companies of their own and later successfully sold them. A second option is to buy into individual private equity funds. Should you have access to some of the top funds and have the minimum capital to invest, this is a viable approach. However, many investors do not have access to such funds. Once again, a third option is to invest in a fund of funds that may be offered by large banking/brokerage institutions. For many investors in private equity, the fund of funds approach again offers some distinct advantages, including some of the following:

Access

Perhaps more so than in any other asset class, the ability to gain access to product is most important in the private equity space. Many of the very best managers frequently close their doors to new investors. Moreover, when they start new funds, they generally offer slots to old investors first before going out to new clients. Additionally, many have high minimums on top of that. As a result, going with an established fund of funds player may give you access to these top managers and at minimum investment levels that you can meet.

Diversification

As you might expect, a private equity fund of funds will give you extensive diversification across the private equity field. Achieving the same level of diversification would require significant capital, which many investors would either not have or want to commit to this asset class.

Due Diligence

Once again, a key benefit of this structure is the extensive due diligence they are capable of conducting. They have experience in seeking out private investments and are knowledgeable in monitoring them.

Implementing a Real Estate Program

With real estate, you have several alternative ways to implement your investment program, including the following:

- You can certainly buy individual properties and either manage them yourself or hire someone to manage them.
- You can purchase REITs or even hire a REIT investment advisor who would manage an individual REIT portfolio.
- There are many real estate partnerships in the marketplace and you could purchase interests in them.
- Some financial advisors, such as banks and brokerage firms, will put together individual real estate funds and offer them to their clients. These funds are generally well diversified and provide for professional portfolio management.

Purchasing Timber Investments

Having gained significant popularity among wealthy investors, timber offers several different access points. Here are a few of those:

- The easiest way is to just buy pure forest product companies on the stock exchange. This requires little capital and offers high liquidity. The major disadvantage is that the investment will be somewhat correlated to the overall stock market so you lose some of the diversification appeal. Also, the underlying value of the timberland may not factor into the stock price to as great a degree as other forms of investing.
- You can also buy into timber REITs, although there is not a great supply of these. Again, on the plus side, you have high liquidity and the capital required is low.
- There are also commingled funds in the market. As you begin to venture into these investment structures, you start to realize the direct impact of the timber value as well as the land underneath it. However, the initial capital required begins to climb. Moreover, liquidity begins to tighten as the exit strategies narrow.
- Moving along the ownership curve, you can access timber investments through undivided fee ownership or tenants in common structures. These are offered via limited liability structures. The minimum investment required may be quite high, but you now are in a position to own the actual timber and your investment value will totally reflect the value of the timber which is the primary factor of your return. However, your liquidity is low and exit terms are set and relatively inflexible.
- A final ownership form is to own timber properties outright in full fee ownership, without any partners. The obvious advantages are that you are the boss and can initiate exit strategies at your

time of choosing. You can also develop alternative activities on the properties including hunting, fishing and camping. The disadvantages are, again, low liquidity and very high capital as you will have difficulties finding small timber properties to purchase.

Portfolio Rebalancing

Before leaving this chapter, we should say a word on portfolio rebalancing. The 2000-2002 bear market taught all of us a lesson on the importance of having a disciplined approach to asset allocation and adhering to that approach.

First, let's define what rebalancing is:

- Simply put, it is the periodic adjustment of the portfolio to restore your target asset allocation and manager style mix.
- Some will say that it is selling the winners and buying the losers.
- To a certain extent, it is practicing contrarian investing.
- It can also be a form of dollar cost averaging.
- It is also disciplined profit taking.

The case made for rebalancing is that it secures better results in down markets and is a good form of risk reduction. On the other hand, detractors claim that active rebalancing has opportunity costs in bull markets, high transaction cost and only very incremental returns. Having said this, rebalancing is generally most effective in these situations:

- During periods of high market volatility.
- Where there is low cross correlation among asset classes so that when you rebalance, you will be going in a different direction.

- Where the long-term performances between the asset classes is tight. This way, you can feel more assured that you will revert back to the mean when rebalancing.
- When an asset class is far from your original target.

Regardless of your position on the need for rebalancing, if you do establish a rebalancing policy, here are some of the components you may wish to consider:

- **Timing-** Generally, a rebalancing policy will call for periodic review at either monthly, quarterly or annual intervals.
- **Target Threshold-** You also need to determine how you are going to rebalance the portfolio. Where you have expressed your asset allocation in terms of specific targets, the rebalancing can be triggered when an asset class or style exceeds its target by a stated percentage. For example, you may have a policy of rebalancing when an asset class exceeds its target by 5 percentage points. At that time, you rebalance to the target allocation.
- **Range Rebalancing-** Alternatively, you may express your asset allocation in terms of a range where you not only have a target, but may have minimum and maximum parameters. You would then rebalance when the outer bounds of the range are pierced.
- **Volatility Based Rebalancing-** Some investors do not like to operate under rigid numerical structures and want flexibility based on the types of asset classed in their portfolio. As such, you can base your rebalancing trigger points on the volatility and even liquidity of each asset class. For instance, you may allow greater ranges for equities than fixed income and will allow for wider bands for hedge funds and private equity since you cannot govern your exit strategy in each case.
- **Partial Rebalancing-** Some investors will not want to be confined to always move back to their target, so they will build in the flexibility to partially rebalance. For example, when an asset class exceeds its maximum range, you may adopt a policy with

your investment advisor to rebalance halfway to the target if you still believe the prospects for the asset class are strong. This way, you add an element of tactical asset allocation, which is not a bad practice.

Regardless of your approach, the important thing is to have a rebalancing program that you and your investment advisor are committed to follow. Otherwise, you are open to riding the market rollercoaster.

While portfolio rebalancing is an essential risk control method, it may not work effectively if you do not occasionally revisit and reconfirm your strategic asset allocation. Markets, as we know, do not stand still and one must stay current with the times. Therefore, you should revisit and change your overall asset allocation targets and ranges under some of these circumstances:

- Your investment objectives change.
- Your risk tolerance changes in either direction.
- Your time horizon changes where, for instance, you no longer need to have as much invested short term and can tolerate more volatility in short-term performance.
- New products are introduced and you believe they have a place in your portfolio. This will necessitate changes in the allocations to other classes.
- Over time, there are changes in the expected return, standard deviation or correlation of asset classes. In other words, the assumptions that you employed to build your original asset allocation have changed significantly to warrant adjustments.

Performance Monitoring

Exhibits 6-C and 6-D provide illustrations for monitoring the performance of your individual investment managers. Exhibit 6-C shows an appropriate benchmark for each asset and style category, while exhibit

6-D applies it to each manager. There are also some statistical measures that capture the level of risk and sources of return. We offer some definitions to some of the terms:

Return/Risk

This shows the return adjusted for each unit of risk. The formula is the return divided by the portfolio's standard deviation.

Up and Down Market Capture Ratios

These measures show how a manager performed in up and down markets relative to the market benchmark itself. A down market is characterized by quarterly returns that are negative, while an up market is any positive return. To further illustrate, the down market capture ratio is calculated by dividing the return for the respective manager during down market quarters by the performance of the market benchmark during those same quarters. Conversely, the up market capture ratio is calculated by dividing the performance of the manager in up market periods by the performance of the market benchmark during those same periods. You will want to have a down market capture ratio of less than 100% as it would indicate that the manager captures less of the downside. Alternatively, you like to have an up market capture ratio that exceeds 100% as it would indicate that your manager is capturing more of the market gains during positive markets. While it is difficult to " have your cake and eat it too", most people would be willing to give up some of the upside so as to not under-perform during the down markets.

Batting Average

This is a measure of a manager's ability to consistently beat the market benchmark. You simply calculate it by dividing the number of quarters that a manager beats or matches the market benchmark by the number of quarters in the measurement period. For example, a manager who hits or beats the benchmark half the time would have a batting average of 50.

Alpha

This statistic represents the manager's return that is not dependent upon the market itself. In other words, it is the return attributed to the skill of the manager. A positive alpha means that the manager has added value over the movement of the market. Conversely, a negative alpha means that the manager has detracted from the performance of the market.

Information Ratio

The information ratio then translates alpha into a measurement against a unit of risk. Simply stated, the information ratio is alpha divided by the standard deviation during the measurement period. An information ratio of 0.50 is considered to be good, a ratio of 0.75 is considered to be very good, while a ratio of 1.00 is outstanding.

EXHIBIT 6–C

SETTING PERFORMANCE BENCHMARKS – EQUITIES

	Value	Core	Growth
Large Cap	S & P 500 Barra Value	S & P 500	S & P 500 Barra Growth
Mid Cap	Russell Midcap Value	Russell 1000	Russell Midcap Growth
Small Cap	Russell 2000 Value	Russell 2000	Russell 2000 Growth

EXHIBIT 6–D

PERFORMANCE REVIEW

JOHNSON FAMILY
FOURTH QUARTER, 2003
EQUITY MANAGERS

Equity Manger Performance
December 31, 2033

Manager	Return/Risk 1 Year	Return/Risk 3 Year	Return/Risk 5 Year	Standard Deviation 5 Year	UP MKT Capture Rate 5 Year	Down MKT Capture Rate 5 Year
Large Cap Core						
Manager A	1.08	(0.60)	0.13	18.6	81.67	75.00
S & P 500	1.54	(0.46)	0.05	21.3	100.0	100.00
Large Cap Growth						
Manager B	1.32	(0.46)	0.27	26.1	91.82	58.33
Russell 1000 Growth	2.01	(0.67)	(0.09)	28.7	100.00	100.00
Mid Cap Value						
Manager C	1.08	0.51	0.61	21.2	107.7	79.42
Manager D	1.26	0.99	0.88	14.7	81.89	39.71
Russell Mid Cap Value	1.58	0.32	0.45	18.8	100.0	100.00
Small Cap Value						
Manager E	1.74	0.30	0.75	20.6	103.0	74.29
Russell 2000 Value	1.38	0.45	0.50	21.6	100.0	100.00

Small Cap						
Growth						
Manager F	1.96	(0.22)	0.23	34.1	94.75	79.31
Russell 2000 Growth	1.81	(0.34)	0.08	35.2	100.0	100.00
International						
Manager G	1.06	(0.30)	0.20	20.5	91.76	73.66
Manager H	1.10	(0.55)	0.02	27.2	125.6	123.95
MSCI EA	1.17	(0.38)	0.04	21.5	100.0	100.00
REIT						
Manager I	2.49	1.40	1.11	12.6	104.5	77.23
S & P Reit	2.02	1.26	0.87	13.3	100.0	100.00

EQUITY MANAGER PERFORMANCE
December 31, 2003

Performance	Quar-ter	YTD	1 Year	3 Years	5 Years	10 Years
Large Cap Core						
Manager A	0.81	11.31	16.66	(10.91)	2.44	10.97
S & P 500	2.65	14.72	24.40	(10.31)	1.00	10.05
Large Cap Growth						
Manager B	5.65	20.83	18.96	(9.76)	6.99	N/A
Russell 1000 Growth	3.91	17.51	25.91	(19.05)	(2.46)	8.54
Mid Cap Value						
Manager C	4.47	19.02	25.70	11.54	12.88	14.76
Manager D	5.32	16.16	22.14	15.12	12.98	N/A
Russell Mid Cap Value	5.94	19.82	28.29	6.63	8.42	11.43
Small Cap Value						
Manager E	7.19	20.37	24.45	6.64	15.44	N/A
Russell 2000 Value	7.72	25.48	31.65	11.06	10.83	11.28

Small Cap Growth

Manager F	7.90	29.65	35.20	(6.57)	7.99	12.19
Russell 2000 Growth	10.47	31.83	41.73	(12.67)	2.75	4.45

Internat'l

Manager G	4.03	12.63	22.50	(6.47)	4.05	N/A
Manager H	9.07	20.88	27.63	(13.94)	0.58	N/A
MSCI EA	8.17	18.83	26.54	(8.45)	0.88	3.24

REIT

Manager I	10.58	26.35	27.45	16.12	14.05	N/A
S & P Reit	9.46	24.67	25.42	15.68	11.62	N/A

EQUITY MANAGER PERFORMANCE
December 31, 2003

PERFORMANCE CONSISTENCY FACTORS

Manager	Information Ratio 5 years	Batting Average 3 years	Batting Average 5 years	ALPHA 5 years
Manager A	0.21	0.42	0.45	0.96
Manager B	0.80	0.75	0.70	7.90
Manager C	0.60	0.67	0.55	3.90
Manager D	0.46	0.50	0.55	3.90
Manager E	0.43	0.33	0.50	5.23
Manager F	0.38	0.58	0.60	4.84
Manager G	0.46	0.75	0.65	2.84
Manager H	(0.40)	0.33	0.40	0.23

7

Investing for Charitable Entities

Thus far, our investment focus has been on individual portfolios that are subject to income taxation. However, many individual investors also handle retirement and charitable portfolios today. Managing these portfolios requires many of the same principles of investing, but there are also some important differences. Accordingly, we will consider some of the important elements in constructing and managing charitable portfolios. We will specifically discuss investing for charitable trusts and family foundations. In a companion book, *The Philanthropic Executive*, I go into much further detail on the investment concepts and practices in managing charitable portfolios.

Charitable Trusts

As we will discuss in chapter nine, there are two general types of charitable trusts. One is the charitable remainder trust while the other is the charitable lead trust. We will consider each in turn.

Charitable Remainder Trusts

As we will discuss later, the charitable remainder trusts pays you, or a designated individual, an annual annuity or unitized payment for a number of years. At the end of the term, the remaining assets go to charity. From an investment perspective, you have two important decisions. First, what assets will you use to fund the trusts and secondly, how should you manage the portfolios. From the standpoint of funding the trusts, one of the more popular assets is low basis stock as you can defer the capital gain over several years. Also, you can use real estate but must watch out for the unrelated business income tax issues discussed below.

With charitable remainder trusts, you also need to consider two tax parameters. The first is how the annual distributions will be taxed to you. Essentially, there is a four-tier system governing the taxation of each annuity or unitrust payment. The payment is broken out into a hierarchy along these lines:

1. **Ordinary Income-** To the extent that the distribution has ordinary taxable income, these amounts are considered to be distributed first. Also, there is a carryover from prior years in that any undistributed ordinary income from last year is considered to be distributed before you distribute any of this year's income.
2. **Capital Gains-** To the extent that the CRT has short-term capital gains in the current year as well as in the prior year, these are considered to be distributed next. Then, you go through the same process for long-term gains.
3. **Tax Exempt Income-** Once you exhaust your taxable income and capital gains distributions, you then report your tax free income.
4. **Return of Capital-** The last component that is distributed is your original capital.

An example may better illustrate how this works:

- Assume your CRAT has an annual distribution of $120,000.
- The CRAT earns $20,000 in ordinary income this year along with $40,000 of tax free income. It also sold some low basis stock this year and incurred a long-term capital gain of $30,000. This is on top of a similar long-term carryover gain from last year of $24,000.
- As a result, the current year's distribution is taxed as follows:

    Taxable income.................$20,000
    Long-term capital gains.........54,000
    Tax free income..................40,000
    Return of capital...................6,000

    Total distribution..............120,000

These tax regulations have a bearing on how you may want to position your portfolio. For example, you will likely include municipal bonds in the asset mix and will also want to time the sale of any low basis stock so long as it is prudent to do so from a valuation standpoint.

Another important tax regulation surrounds the unrelated business tax. Simply stated, unrelated business income is any income earned from a trade or business that is not substantially related to the mission or purpose of the charitable entity. This definition also extends to debt-financed income from such activities as real estate, margined securities and certain hedge funds. Should you violate this restriction in a charitable remainder trust, not only will the trust be taxed on the unrelated business income earned that year, but the entire income earned by the trust that year will be taxed. In other words, the trust itself would lose its tax exemption and the income effectively double taxed.

We might say a word about the charitable remainder unitrust investment strategy. As the CRAT pays a constant annuity each year, the CRUT, on the other hand, pays an adjusted amount each year based on revaluing the principal. Accordingly, you may wish to adopt a higher growth strategy so as to have a higher corpus from which to calculate your annual unitized payment. This will generally call for allocating a higher percentage to equities. Additionally, you may want to fund these trusts with closely held stock if you expect to sell the company in the near future. Real estate is also an alternative.

Charitable Lead Trusts

A mirror image of the charitable remainder trust, the charitable lead trust is structured so that an annual annuity or unitrust payment goes to a charity, while the remainder interest goes to an individual family member. As a result, we need to modify the investment strategies. We first need to realize that there are two types of charitable lead trusts. One is a grantor lead trust, where the grantor gets an up-front charitable deduction based on the present value of the annuity payments. However, the grantor is then taxed on the annual income of the trust, whether it is distributed to charity or not. This implies that the trustee should invest the fixed income portion of the assets in municipal bonds. The second type of charitable lead trust is the non-grantor trust where the grantor receives no up-front income tax deduction but also has no ongoing tax liability. However, the trust itself could be subject to tax liability to the extent that it does not distribute earned income. Consequently, when you establish this trust, you should specify in the document that distributions should occur from income in the following order:

1. Ordinary income
2. Short-term capital gains
3. Unrelated business income

4. Tax-exempt income
5. Return of capital

A key investment issue of charitable lead trusts centers around the remainder interest, which goes to an individual, most likely your children. One of the factors determining the gift tax on the remainder interest is the applicable federal rate. To the extent that the trust outperforms that rate, the differential passes to your children's estate and gift tax-free. As a result, you will want to position the portfolio for growth.

Private Family Foundations

We will now consider how foundations design, implement and monitor their investment programs. The overseers of a family foundation have a fiduciary obligation that extends beyond the family itself. Specifically, they have an obligation to the community and, in many states, are accountable to the attorney general of the state in which they reside.

Before getting into the investment process itself, we will take a look at the investment governance process. As with managing large family wealth, you will first want to determine who will decide how the assets are allocated and how the investment advisors will be selected. Here are some of the options:

- The foundation board of directors could empower the foundation president or executive director to run the investment process and report performance back to the board. This is likely to be the set-up with smaller family foundations.
- Larger foundations may actually hire a chief investment officer.
- The board may establish a formal investment committee to directly oversee the investment portfolio.

- The investment committee may then hire an investment consultant who provides asset allocation, manager search and performance monitoring services to the foundation. The consultant could be in the form of an independent firm or a bank/brokerage company that would provide a comprehensive platform that includes custody and trading.

Regardless of the governance structure, the actual investment process would likely follow the template shown in exhibit 7-A. We will use this as a guide as we discuss some of the more important aspects of foundation portfolio management.

Foundation's Risk Profile

From a global perspective, the key to understanding the true risk when formulating investment policies for a foundation is to clearly spell out the way grants are or will be administered. If the foundation generally gives single-year grants and does not tend to give all of its money to the same organizations every year, you have a low risk profile. The rationale is that you have no implied obligation to fund recipients at any stated level. On the other hand, if the foundation tends to make multi-year grants and at large dollar amount, the risk profile is much larger. Organizations will tend to depend upon your funding in order to operate This will consequently put added pressure on your investment performance. You will therefore need to structure the portfolio so that effective risk controls are in place.

Pure investment risk, however, is very similar to what is involved when managing private family assets. Some of the more important ones for a foundation are:

- Ability to absorb a loss in any given year
- Willingness to invest with contrarian managers
- Liquidity needs or preferences

EXHIBIT 7-A
FOUNDATION INVESTMENT PROCESS

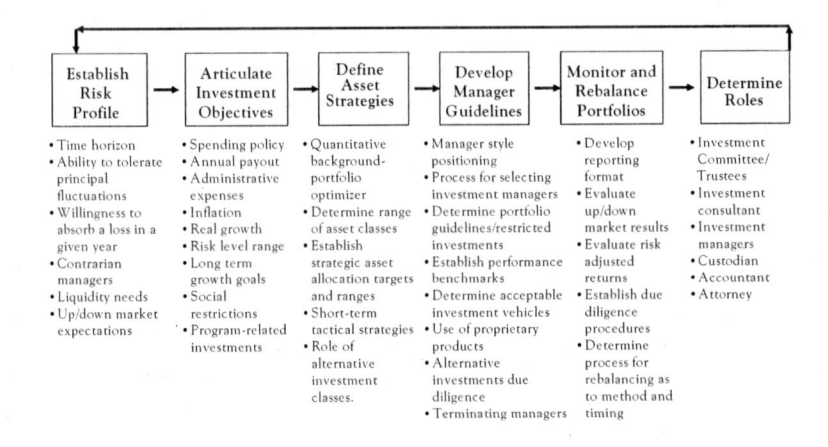

Establish Risk Profile	Articulate Investment Objectives	Define Asset Strategies	Develop Manager Guidelines	Monitor and Rebalance Portfolios	Determine Roles
• Time horizon • Ability to tolerate principal fluctuations • Willingness to absorb a loss in a given year • Contrarian managers • Liquidity needs • Up/down market expectations	• Spending policy • Annual payout • Administrative expenses • Inflation • Real growth • Risk level range • Long term growth goals • Social restrictions • Program-related investments	• Quantitative background-portfolio optimizer • Determine range of asset classes • Establish strategic asset allocation targets and ranges • Short-term tactical strategies • Role of alternative investment classes.	• Manager style positioning • Process for selecting investment managers • Determine portfolio guidelines/restricted investments • Establish performance benchmarks • Determine acceptable investment vehicles • Use of proprietary products • Alternative investments due diligence • Terminating managers	• Develop reporting format • Evaluate up/down market results • Evaluate risk adjusted returns • Establish due diligence procedures • Determine process for rebalancing as to method and timing	• Investment Committee/Trustees • Investment consultant • Investment managers • Custodian • Accountant • Attorney

Establishing Investment Objectives

Portfolio objectives are set at a couple of levels. The top level objective is the foundation's spending policy. This represents the long-term rate of return that the foundation would like to exceed so as to perpetuate the growth of its asset base. Falling short of matching the spending policy will prevent the foundation from doing greater things unless you contribute additional funds. The spending policy is comprised of these components:

- **Annual Payout**- This is the 5 percent statutory payout ratio. As this must always be distributed, it becomes the baseline performance bogey regardless of what happens in the financial markets.
- **Administrative Expenses**- A foundation will have a variety of expenses including the president's and staff's salaries, rent, utilities, travel and equipment.

- **Inflation-** Most foundations expect their portfolios to achieve an excess return above inflation.
- **Real Growth-** To be in a position to achieve greater distributions in the future, you are not just satisfied to meet costs and inflation. You will want some real growth.

To illustrate a typical spending policy, consider the following:

- Annual payout.................................... 5%
- Administrative expenses...........................1%
- Inflation... 2%
- Real growth....................................... 1%
- Total expected return........................... 9%

The next level objective is to set performance benchmarks per asset class and investment manager. Generally, you will have a market index benchmark as well as a peer group benchmark for each investment manager.

Define Asset Class Strategies

The exercise is very similar for managing foundations as it is for handling family wealth. With foundations, these are some of the more critical issues:

- You will need to determine the global allocation between real or hard assets and financial assets. Real assets such as real estate, timber and natural resources will offer the portfolio considerable diversification to the domestic stock market. Moreover, the asset valuations of real estate and timber tend to move slowly so you will not be subject to volatile asset value changes year over year.

- Foundations have embraced the concept of hedge funds and the role they can play in providing portfolio stability. You will have to determine the overall allocation to hedge funds and then determine how you want to segment your allocation between lower volatility and higher volatility funds, much as we discussed in the previous chapters.
- To what degree are you willing to invest in illiquid asset classes such as private equity?

Implementing the Investment Program

The implementation process is again very similar to the process for implementing strategies for individual family portfolios. Foundations offer a couple of additional factors:

1. Many foundations have social investment restrictions. For example, you may not want your investment managers to invest in companies that manufacture tobacco, alcohol or firearms. These are common restrictions.
2. Some foundations have restrictions on the investment instruments that its traditional managers may employ. Examples include the use of derivatives such as uncovered call options, short selling or commodities.
3. Some may also prohibit managers from using certain proprietary products without the approval of the foundation's investment committee.

A foundation's investment program is best illustrated through its formal investment policy statement. In appendix V, we include a sample statement for a private foundation.

8

Wealth Transfer Techniques

Certainly the core activity in managing family wealth is investing the assets. On the other hand, it is almost equally important sometimes how you title your assets and efficiently transfer them to the next generation or even to charity. Much is written on the tax code and the estate and tax planning techniques necessary to deal with it. The purpose of this book is not to go into a comprehensive analysis of all of these techniques as others are far more qualified to do so. Moreover, this is a very technical field and investors should hire and consult with competent legal and tax advisors where their estates are large and/or complex. Instead, I want to just show how it fits within the context of managing one's wealth. We will provide you with a framework for organizing your wealth transfer process and briefly describe some of the important strategies for efficiently transferring wealth to your heirs.

We organize the discussion around three ways to transfer family wealth. First, the most common way has been to do it at death through the terms of your will. This has not always been the most efficient way, although it does give you the most control of your assets for the longest period of time. A second way is to transfer assets during your lifetime and there are several ways to do this. Still a third way is to establish certain estate freeze structures that will not only affect the transfer efficiently, but may position the assets for further after-tax growth. Before going into these three methods, we offer some background information on the transfer tax system.

It is first important to understand the way individuals are taxed when they transfer assets to family members and others. To that end, the transfer tax system includes four separate but somewhat interrelated taxes.

1. The **federal estate tax** is assessed at death and covers those assets transferred in an unprotective manner. The tax rates have been graduated and essentially top off at around 50 percent. However, the 2001 Tax Act phases out the estate tax by 2009, but the law then sunsets in 2010 unless Congress enacts further tax legislation at that time or before. The process for determining your estate tax involves consideration of a number of deductions and exemptions, with the most important one being the personal exemption equivalent. Exhibit 8-A shows how the exemption equivalent increases over this time period.

EXHIBIT 8–A

Estate and Gift Tax Changes: 2003 through 2011

Year	Exemption	Rate
2003	$1 Million	49%
2004	$1.5 Million	48%
2005	$1.5 Million	47%
2006	$2 Million	46%
2007	$2 Million	45%
2008	$2 Million	45%
2009	$3.5 Million	45%
2010	Tax repealed	Top individual income tax rate-gift tax only
2011	$1 Million	55%

* Note that the gift tax exemption remains at $1 million from years 2003

2. Transfers made during lifetime are subject to **gift tax.** This tax has historically been integrated with the estate tax so that a uniform system existed. However, under the 2001 Tax act, the gift tax will remain in force even if the estate tax is repealed. The gift tax exemption is pegged at $1 million.

3. Individuals who receive an inheritance are subject to **state inheritance tax.** Prior to the 2001 Tax Act, states shared in the estate tax paid to the federal government. Should the federal estate tax be phased out, the states will need to find other ways to make up the lost revenues, including a separately levied estate tax that is paid directly to them.

4. At first glance, you might think one could reduce future estate taxes by transferring assets to grandchildren and even great-

grandchildren so that successive generations are not subject to the estate tax system.
5. You are not so lucky, as the tax drafters deal with this and it is called the **generation skipping transfer tax.** Simply, this is a tax that is assessed on transfers during your lifetime or at death to individuals that are two or more generations below yours, such as grandchildren or trusts for their benefit. We will cover this subject in further detail below.

We will now cover the three ways to transfer assets.

Transfers at Death

Transfers taking place at death or testamentary transfers, as they are commonly referred to, are governed by a number of legal documents and preexisting legal structures including, but not limited to, some of the following:

- Last will and testament
- Terms of an existing living trust
- Retirement plans
- Life insurance policy or trust
- Partnership agreements
- The state, through its intestate laws governing transfers where the descendent had no will or estate plan.

To look at the various ways an estate plan unfolds, refer to exhibit 8-B and 8-C. We will use these as guides in describing the general setup of an estate. Let's first take exhibit 8-B where GST tax planning is not a factor. When planning for transfers at death, two important features of the tax code take effect. First, there is an unlimited marital deduction on transfers between spouses, so you can leave your entire estate to your

Wealth Transfer Techniques

spouse without paying any estate tax. The second feature is that you have an individual exemption equivalent that enables you to give assets to anyone else up to a certain limit. As of this writing, the exemption equivalent is $1,500,000. This effectively means that a husband and wife can pass $3,000,000 to their children tax free.

EXHIBIT 8–B

TESTAMENTARY ESTATE PLAN –LIMITED GST

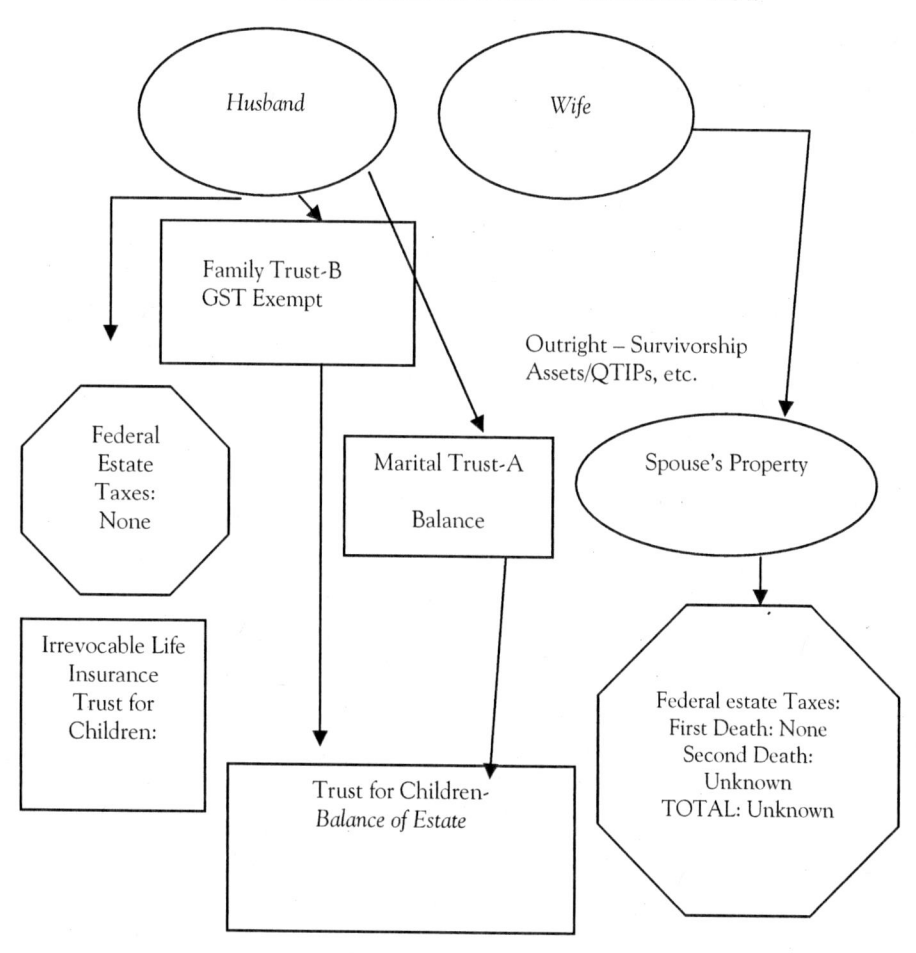

```
         ┌─────────┐              ┌─────────┐
         │ Husband │              │  Wife   │
         └────┬────┘              └────┬────┘
              │                        │
              ▼                        │
     ┌──────────────────┐              │
     │  Family Trust-B  │              │
     │   GST Exempt     │              │
     └──────────────────┘              │
                                       │
              Outright – Survivorship  │
              Assets/QTIPs, etc.       │
                                       ▼
  ┌─────────┐   ┌──────────────┐   ┌──────────────┐
  │ Federal │   │Marital Trust-A│  │Spouse's      │
  │ Estate  │   │              │  │Property      │
  │ Taxes:  │   │   Balance    │   └──────┬───────┘
  │  None   │   └──────────────┘          │
  └─────────┘                             ▼
                                  ┌────────────────┐
  ┌─────────────┐                 │Federal estate  │
  │Irrevocable  │                 │Taxes:          │
  │Life         │                 │First Death:None│
  │Insurance    │                 │Second Death:   │
  │Trust for    │                 │Unknown         │
  │Children:    │                 │TOTAL: Unknown  │
  └─────────────┘                 └────────────────┘
              │
              ▼
     ┌──────────────────┐
     │Trust for Children-│
     │ Balance of Estate │
     └──────────────────┘
```

As a result of the exemption equivalent and the unlimited marital deduction, individuals have approached their estates by setting up two trusts, called A and B trusts, in an effort to take maximum advantage of the tax code. The first step is to establish a bypass or exemption equivalent trust (B) that would be funded with the amount of the exemption. In today's terms, that would be a trust of $1,500,000 upon the death of the first spouse. This trust generally has some of these features:

- It can provide income for the surviving spouse. This could be all of the income, a specified amount or left to the discretion of a trustee.
- The trust may also give the surviving spouse a non-cumulative right of withdrawal. This withdrawal right is 5 percent of the principal or $5,000, whichever is greater. Generally, this right is given once the marital trust is depleted. This does not impact the survivor's estate as the trust will not be taxed at his or her death.
- The grantor may allow his/her surviving spouse a limited power of appointment to direct the corpus to a class of beneficiaries, most likely their children. This also will not affect the taxability of the trust upon the death of the survivor.
- At the death of the survivor, the trust usually distributes to the surviving children or into a trust for the children for a period of years.

The next phase of distribution is to the marital trust, usually referred to as the A trust. This trust holds the residual estate in excess of the exemption equivalent that funds the B trust. This trust holds those assets that are covered by the unlimited marital deduction, hence the term "marital trust." The terms of this trust are generally as follows:

Wealth Transfer Techniques

- The surviving spouse is entitled to all of the trust income annually.
- He/she is also entitled to invade the principal for almost any purpose.
- The survivor also has a power of appointment over the proceeds at death.
- As a result, the trust is included in the survivor's estate

Sometimes you may not want the surviving spouse to have a complete power of appointment over the trust assets. There are several valid reasons for this. First, you can protect the children in the event the spouse remarries. Second, you may wish to provide for your children from a previous marriage. As a result, you are able to actually split your marital deduction assets into two trusts. The first is the A trust we just described. The second is called a Qualified Terminable Interest Property, or what is commonly referred to as a QTIP trust. Under the terms of this trust, the grantor decides how it will be distributed upon the death of his/her surviving spouse. The other relevant terms of this trust are accordingly:

- All income must be paid to the surviving beneficiary.
- The trust cannot allow distributions for any party other than the surviving spouse.
- The trust may be written to allow the beneficiary to direct the trustee to provide more income producing assets.
- The trust assets are included in the surviving spouse's estate.

We can now turn to exhibits 8-C and 8-D to add another dimension to the estate plan. This involves generation skipping tax planning. The GST tax has always been one of the tax code's most onerous tax. The rate was historically set at a flat 55 percent and was on top of any gift or estate tax paid. However, this tax is also subject to revision by the terms of the 2001

EXHIBIT 8–C

FAMILY ESTATE PLAN WITH FULL GST

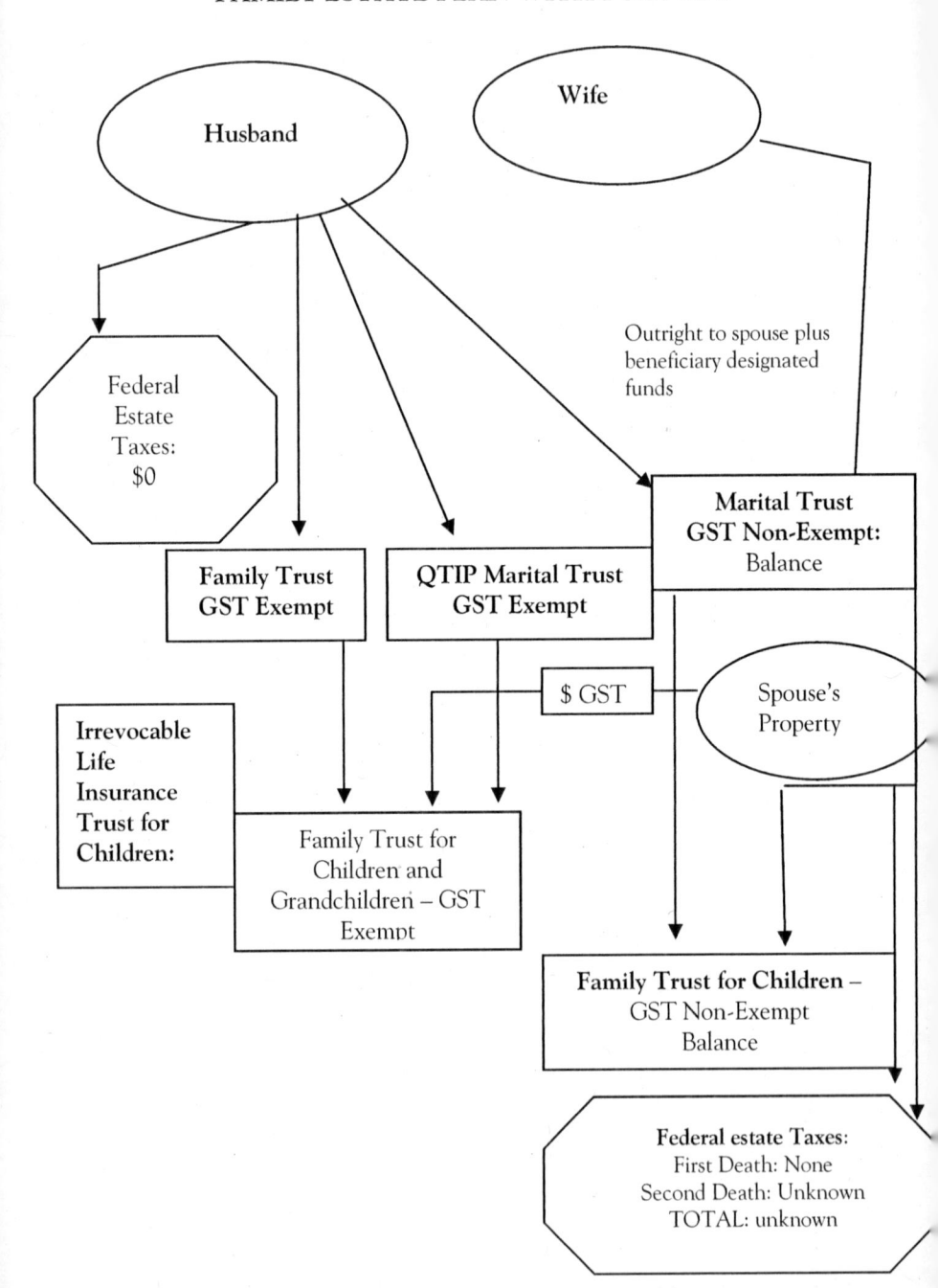

- Husband
- Wife

Outright to spouse plus beneficiary designated funds

Federal Estate Taxes: $0

Family Trust GST Exempt

QTIP Marital Trust GST Exempt

Marital Trust GST Non-Exempt: Balance

$ GST

Spouse's Property

Irrevocable Life Insurance Trust for Children:

Family Trust for Children and Grandchildren – GST Exempt

Family Trust for Children – GST Non-Exempt Balance

Federal estate Taxes:
First Death: None
Second Death: Unknown
TOTAL: unknown

Tax Act. As with the federal estate tax, the GST tax is scheduled to go away in 2010 but reemerge in 2011, unless new legislation is enacted to extend the current tax law. As with federal estate taxes, the GST tax carries an exemption. In 2001, when the current law was enacted, the exemption per individual was $1,060,000 and was expected to increase to $1,500,000 in 2004. This is the same exemption equivalent that we have for the estate tax. The amount then escalates in the same increments as the estate tax thereafter, going to $3,500,000 by 2009. Should the tax law be allowed to sunset in 2010, the exemption equivalent for the GST tax would again revert to the $1,060,000 that existed in 2001. Exhibit 8-D shows how the GST exemption will progress until 2009.

EXHIBIT 8–D

GST EXEMPTIONS

Year	GST Exemption
2004	1,500,000
2005	2,000,000
2006	2,000,000
2007	2,000,000
2008	3,500,000
2009	N/A
2010	1,120,000

Note: After 2011, in the absence of legislation, the exemption will be indexed for inflation.

There are several ways to allocate your lifetime GST exemption and the process is not always that straightforward. You can allocate the exemption at death or during your lifetime. The key issue is to make sure the allocation selected is not unused. For example, if you allocate your exemption to a trust that first goes for the enjoyment of your children, you need to feel comfortable that the children are unlikely to use all of the assets in their lifetime. Otherwise, you will have wasted your GST exemption. Another way you can lose some of your allocation is when you allocate it to a trust that loses value on a bad investment. That loss cannot be replenished. On the other hand, there are ways to leverage the GST allocation and we will consider those ways as well. We will consider lifetime transfers in the next section so here we will look at employing the GST exemption as part of your estate plan.

Exhibit C demonstrates how to incorporate GST planning into your testamentary estate structure. The first strategy that many families employ is to allocate as much of it as possible to the exemption equivalent trust since these funds will not be subject to any estate tax. When this is done, the trust then becomes classified as a GST exempt trust. Beginning in 2004, the GST and the estate tax exemption equivalents are equal so you could technically use your entire allocation on the exemption equivalent trust. However, prior to 2004, the GST exemptions were higher than the estate tax exemption, so you needed to find other places to allocate the remaining GST exemption. A common place was to split the QTIP trust into exempt and nonexempt trusts. The remaining GST allocation went to the QTIP exempt trust. This trust was commonly referred to as a "reverse QTIP," as it was treated as part of the grantor's estate for GST purposes but as part of the marital trust and subject to estate tax upon the death of the surviving spouse.

Another way to efficiently utilize GST exemptions is for spouses to establish lifetime QTIP trusts and make lifetime gifts to each that are equivalent to the GST exemption. As married couples can transfer assets to each other free of estate and gift taxes, any monies placed in these lifetime QTIP trusts will not be taxed at inception. At the death of each spouse, the assets in the QTIP trusts will be subject to estate tax to the extent the estate tax exemption has been already utilized. However, no GST tax will ever be paid on these funds and the assets will get a step up in cost basis.

Wealth Transfer Techniques

Lifetime Transfers

Many wealthy families begin the process of transferring their estate assets well before death in an effort to minimize the long-term impact of wealth transfer taxes. There are several techniques, some simple and others more complicated, that one can employ to achieve their aims:

Lifetime Gifts

Direct lifetime giving is one way to begin transferring your wealth to children and grandchildren. Perhaps the most common method is to take advantage of the $11,000 annual gift tax exclusion where each individual can give away $11,000 each year without incurring any gift tax. As a result, both spouses can give $22,000 annually to each child and grandchild. Another way to benefit children and grandchildren is to pay their educational expenses. The tax laws enable you to pay an unlimited amount of tuition bills so long as the payments go directly to the academic institutions. The same concept is true for medical payments that go directly to the health care providers.

We spoke frequently about the lifetime estate tax exemption equivalent. While this can take effect at death, one can also use it up during lifetime. Accordingly, you could gift out your exemption equivalent amount during lifetime without payment of any gift tax. You may wish to do this if you have assets that are very likely to appreciate and wish to get them in the hands of children as early as possible. At the same time, you could gift assets in excess of your lifetime exemption equivalent and elect to pay the gift tax. One advantage of paying a gift instead of an estate tax is because the gift tax is exclusive of the tax while the estate tax is inclusive. For example, when calculating the estate tax, the IRS includes the entire gifted amount. Therefore, if you transfer $1,000,000, you would pay a transfer tax on the entire amount. Let's say this is 50 percent, as an example. The recipient receives $500,000. On the other hand, if you follow the path of a gift, you pay tax only on the amount that the recipient actually receives. In this case, you would pay a gift tax of $250,000. As a result, your total outlay would be $750,000 instead of the $1,000,000. There are some other advantages and disadvantages of taxable lifetime gifts including the following:

- Advantages include the ability again to transfer property to children as early as possible if you expect the asset to highly appreciate. You also remove the gift tax paid from your estate so long as you survive three years from the date of the gift (section 2035 of the IRS Code). Also, the basis in the asset can be adjusted upward for any gift taxes paid.
- There are some disadvantages, however, in making taxable lifetime gifts. First, the recipient acquires your cost basis, even though it is adjusted for gift taxes paid. At your death, the estate gets a step up in cost basis so any assets transferred will have a cost basis at current market levels. You also lose use of the gift and the taxes paid. Finally, under the 2001 Tax Act, gift tax rates are not adjusted as favorably as estate tax rates. The gift tax exclusion is $1,000,000 and remains at that level while the estate tax exclusion climbs to $3,500,000 by 2009.

Limited Liability Companies

Borrowing from the corporate world, families have adopted some business-like structures to house their assets. One such structure is the limited liability company. Two aspects of the LLC are of keen interest to families. First, they offer limited liability for its members, as they are not financially liable for any obligations beyond their investment. Second, the structure is treated as a partnership for tax purposes. This means that there is no double taxation of income and losses can be passed through as with partnerships. LLCs operate under state laws but there is great uniformity among those laws today. One of the critical issues surrounding these structures is the rule for dissolution. Generally, the LLC will dissolve upon the death or withdrawal of any member unless there is a unanimous consent of the partners for its continuation. Also, when a member leaves the LLC, he/she is entitled to realize the net asset value of their share of the partnership's investments. This could impact the discount that partners will claim on making intra-family transfers of LLC units. We will look more closely at LLCs after we examine the family limited partnership.

Family Limited Partnerships

This structure has emerged to become a centerpiece in managing the estates for wealthy families. Exhibit 8-E-1 illustrates how FLPs are established. Here are its general features:

- Individuals, usually parents, transfer assets into a family partnership structure in a tax-free exchange.
- The parents generally retain a 1 percent general partnership interest and serve as the controlling directors of the partnership. Their remaining investment is in the form of limited partnership interests.
- The parents then begin gifting the limited partnership interest to their children. This gifting can be outright, utilizing the annual gift tax exclusion, or can be through various trust arrangements we will examine later.

EXHIBIT 8–E1

FAMILY LIMITED PARTNERSHIP

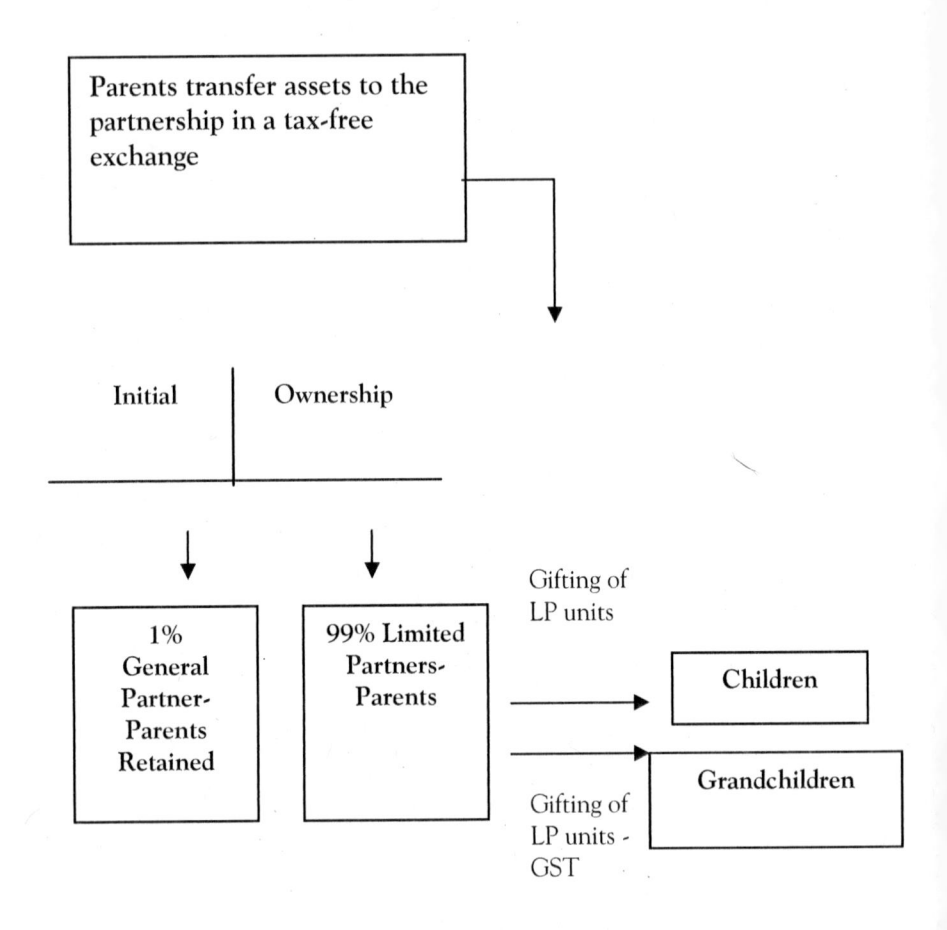

```
┌─────────────────────────────┐
│ Parents transfer assets to  │
│ the partnership in a tax-free│
│ exchange                    │
└─────────────────────────────┘
```

Initial | Ownership

```
┌──────────────┐   ┌──────────────┐    Gifting of
│     1%       │   │ 99% Limited  │    LP units         ┌──────────────┐
│   General    │   │  Partners-   │    ──────────────▶  │   Children   │
│   Partner-   │   │   Parents    │                     └──────────────┘
│   Parents    │   │              │
│   Retained   │   │              │    ──────────────▶  ┌──────────────┐
└──────────────┘   └──────────────┘    Gifting of       │ Grandchildren│
                                       LP units -       └──────────────┘
                                       GST
```

The FLP offers these advantages among others, for a family unit:

1. Limited partnership interests can be gifted at discounted values due to their limited marketability, lack of control and liquidity.

2. FLPs can be constructed to insure that partnership interest always remain in the family. This is accomplished through a right of first refusal for transfers of units. You may also limit the voting rights of an assignee partner.
3. There is also some asset protection with FLPs as creditors have difficulty gaining access to partnership interests. Also, they can be protected from divorce by further putting ownership units in trusts.
4. The FLP will not dissolve at the death of a partner. Instead, units can be transferred to heirs so long as permitted by the partnership agreement.
5. Families that own businesses and expect that they may ultimately do an IPO will find the FLP to be an attractive vehicle to contribute pre-IPO shares. The valuation will be pre-IPO and will also carry a valuation discount.

FLPs also carry some risks with the most critical one being the constant challenges posed by the Internal Revenue Service. The IRS has repeatedly attacked the discounts applied to partnership transfers and valuations at death. They have also contested the purpose of some partnerships, alleging that some have no business purpose. Two landmark cases, *Strangi* and *Kimbell*, have highlighted these challenges. In these cases, the IRS has alleged that the partnerships had no viable business purpose and their discount valuations should not stand. While the IRS won in the *Kimbell* case in lower court, it was overturned in the appeals court. There will certainly be other cases. In any event, these cases highlight the importance of structuring and then operating these partnerships in a prudent manner. Here are a couple of pointers:

- Be reasonable on the valuation discounts applied.
- Make sure there is a clear business purpose. It needs to be operated as an investment partnership and should not appear

that you just loaded all of you assets into it for the purpose of transferring them to your heirs.
- Partnership distributions should be somewhat restrictive and take place at designated times or under specified circumstances.
- Keep good records and be able to produce transaction histories.
- It does not hurt to include some illiquid assets such as real estate, private equity or even timber investments. Some legal experts believe that you can still fund FLPs with just securities but you improve your position against any challenges if the entity looks more like an operating investment business beyond managing securities.
- Hold regular partnership meetings and keep minutes.

Let's look at an example to highlight the impact of gifting discounted limited partnership interests over time.

- A family establishes a family limited partnership and funds it with stock in the family company. They transfer 250,000 shares at the current market price of $2 per share.
- The parents are the general partners and control the activities of the partnership.
- The parents then gift 240,000 shares or the equivalent of $480,000 to each of their ten children and grandchildren. These shares are gifted within limited partnership units so they are valued at a 30 percent discount. This means that the value of the gift is $336,000.
- Assume the value of the shares increases to $3.50 in three years. This increases the gift value to $840,000.
- The parents can continue to transfer units to the partnership and gift limited partnership units at discounted valuations. You can certainly see why this structure has become so popular as a means of managing and transferring wealth.

FLP or LLC?

It would be instructive to look at which format is most appropriate for your situation. While there are many similarities between the two, there are certainly some differences as well. Let's look at some of these:

- FLPs do not dissolve upon the death or withdrawal of individual members. The process for LLCs is not all that clear as some will dissolve unless the operating agreement provides otherwise.
- With an LLC, the parents do not have to be general partners with the inherent liability. Under an LLC, they can still be elected as the managing agent by the voting partners or the operating agreement could specify that they are the managing partners.
- However, parents can limit their liability as general partners in an FLP by forming an S corporation or even a separate LLC to act as the general partner.
- The IRS is more likely to challenge discounts in LLCs if the partnership will dissolve upon the withdrawal of a member. Also, it will challenge discounts if withdrawing members can realize their net asset value upon leaving. The idea of a FLP or LLC is that units are discounted for lack of control and marketability, so if a departing partner can get full value for his/her interests, the IRS will want to be treated the same. Some states are actually beginning to modify their laws to restrict the right of members who withdraw from partnerships to necessarily receive full value for their interests.

Restricted Management Accounts

A variation of the family limited partnership structure is the restricted management account. Some practitioners believe that this device can be an effective way to manage family investments and achieve wealth transfer objectives at the same time. Here are some of its features:

- You would establish an investment management account with a non-registered investment advisor, bank or trust company.
- You would sign a management agreement for a specific term, where the manager has the exclusive right to manage the portfolio with full discretion and the funds may not be withdrawn except for mutual agreement to terminate the account.
- The agreement could be extended by mutual consent.
- You could direct the manager to distribute the income to you.
- You could transfer interests in the account to your children. Because the accounts have restricted withdrawal rights and do not terminate for a period of time, you can affect the transfers at discounted values, as you would transfer limited partnership interests.
- Generally, you would restrict transfers to immediate family members, which further restricts its marketability.
- Because the investment manager does not need to worry about withdrawals and has full discretion, some believe that performance would be enhanced.

Private Annuity

Assume that you have low basis property that you would like to get out of your estate and transferred to your child. Or, consider your options if you have a significant piece of non-income producing property you would like to transfer so as to generate some income or cash flow. Do you have ways to accomplish this? Yes, as you can establish a private annuity with a family member. The transaction essentially involves transferring ownership of the property to another family member (e.g., a child) in exchange for a series of annuity payments over a period of time. If the annuity payments are based on a single individual, it is called a single payment annuity. On the other hand, if the annuity is paid over two lives (such as husband and wife), it is called a joint and last survivor annuity.

When setting up the annuity, the payments are based on the life expectancy of the annuitant and the IRS Section 7520 discount rate, which determines the growth rate of the underlying annuity assets. Present value tables are then applied to arrive at the annual annuity payments. A key aspect of the annual annuity payment is its components, which ultimately determine how you are taxed. Part of the annuity payment is return of principal, which of course is not taxed. Part of the payment could be capital gains and part is ordinary income. Another important feature of private annuities is that the property transferred is removed from the estate of the transferor since the transaction was for full and adequate consideration.

Trusts for Children

Nearly all types of trusts would ultimately benefit children and other heirs. However, there are numerous issues involved when trying to transfer wealth to children, particularly minor children. Here are some of the considerations:

- You do not usually want to give substantial assets to minors where they would have control over its use. In other words, most parents want to still control when the children can use the money and sometimes, for what purposes.
- When giving money to minors, you need to give it away so that it qualifies for the annual gift tax exclusion of $11,000. To do so, the gift must be considered a completed gift for gift tax purposes. To insure that you meet this test, the trusts must provide the children with what is called a "crummy power," which is the right

to withdraw the amount of the gift or the annual exclusion amount. This is named after a court case that sanctioned this approach.
- For children under 14 years of age, any income they earn will be taxed at the parents' marginal tax rates.

As a result, there are three types of trusts that are available to begin holding long-term assets for children. The first is called an **IRC Section 2503(b) Trust**. This trust enables you to contribute the annual $11,000 and get the gift tax exclusion. However, the child is entitled to receive all of the annual income. On the other hand, there are no mandatory principal distributions at any age, as there usually are for other trusts. The income can be placed in a Uniform Gifts to Minors Act trust until the child is of age to receive it. For gift tax purposes, only the present value of the income payments will qualify for the annual exclusion. Accordingly, you will generally invest the principal in income generating assets.

A variation of this trust is the **IRC Section 2503(c) Trust.** Like its counterpart, the 2503(c) trust will qualify for the annual exemption. Also, income can be distributed to the beneficiary or held until he/she reaches 21 years of age. At that time, all principal and accumulated income must be distributed to the beneficiary. The trust can last beyond the time the child reaches 21, but he/she has the right to demand all of the assets at any time thereafter. The trust pays income tax on income that it does not distribute. Because of the mandatory distributions at age 21, some parents do not favor this structure.

Another way to ultimately transfer assets in trust is through **life insurance trusts**, which we will cover in a later chapter.

Asset Freeze Techniques

Perhaps the most effective and tax-efficient way to transfer assets to heirs is through a range of asset freeze structures. These structures are set up in ways that enable you to fix the price of the assets transferred, even though the actual transfer may not occur for several years. Also, they frequently enable you to leverage your gift tax annual exclusion, lifetime estate tax exemption and generation skipping tax exemption. We will consider a few of these techniques, showing how they may fit into an investor's wealth management and transfer plans. When considering these techniques, it is important to hire and consult with highly competent legal and tax advisors. Each of these structures have important income, estate and gift tax opportunities as well as consequences, so it is critical that you establish them correctly and that they fit appropriately within your wealth management plans.

Installment Sales

As the name implies, you can actually sell assets among family members instead of gifting them. The installment sale may work well where you have a low basis asset and wish to monetize it without incurring an immediate capital gain on the entire asset. It may also be an effective devise when you have an asset likely to appreciate over time. By agreeing to a fair market value today, you fix the price of the sale so that any future appreciation goes to your children.

A variation of the straight installment sale is the self-canceling installment note, the SCIN. Here, the note is cancelled upon the death of the seller or at a specified date. However the date or term of the note must be less than the life expectancy of the seller. Otherwise, the SCIN will be treated as a private annuity for tax purposes. From an estate tax standpoint, the installment sale is excluded from the estate of the seller.

However, should the decedent die before all of the payments are made, there are taxable gains reported on the final income tax return. There are several other tax issues with installment sales and SCIN and you should consult your tax advisor before considering them. For example, you cannot engage in an installment sale with marketable securities and other types of assets could have restrictions. Also, the purchaser in a SCIN transaction must pay a risk premium to avoid a gift tax on the seller. The premium would be in the form of a higher than market interest rate or a higher purchase price.

Defective Trusts

An important concept in estate freeze structures is that of the defective trust. These trusts form the basis for the next several techniques that we will discuss. Essentially, a defective trust works as follows:

1. You, the grantor, would transfer property to a trust. This transfer would be irrevocable. As such, it would be considered a completed gift for gift tax purposes.
2. By doing this, you will be removing the assets from your estate.
3. However, you could remain the owner of the trust for federal income tax purposes. In other words, you would continue to be taxed on the income whether you receive it or not. By doing this alone, you are providing further gifts to your heirs.

We will now turn to the various ways to employ defective trusts.

Grantor Retained Annuity Trusts

One of the more popular techniques for transferring assets to children or to a non-spouse, is the grantor retained annuity trust, commonly referred to as a GRAT. Here is how it generally works:

1. You would transfer assets to a trust for the benefit of your children or some other designated heir.
2. The trust would have a defined term. During this term, you would receive an annual annuity payment. At the end of the term, the remaining assets will go to the designated beneficiary.
3. The transfer to the trust represents a gift of a future interest, so you would be subject to gift taxes. The gift is based on the discounted value of the remainder interest going to your heirs. Therefore, the longer the term, the lower the discounted value of the gift and accordingly, the lower the gift tax liability. Also, the higher the annuity payment to you, the lower is the future value of the gift. The factors in valuing the remainder interest are the trust term, annual annuity payment and the applicable federal rate (AFR). The federal rate is published monthly by the Internal Revenue Service. It is the rate that the IRS assumes an investment will grow over a period of time and they use it to value the annuity streams and remainder interests in trusts and annuity structures. Therefore, when you apply this rate to the principal balance, you will determine the growth of the portfolio over time. From the projected ending value, you then subtract the present value of the annuity stream to arrive at the remainder interest and this figure is used to calculate the gift tax.
4. To the extent that the trust assets outperform the applicable federal rate, that additional appreciation goes to your heirs without any further gift tax liability.
5. It is important that you outlive the GRAT term. The assets are removed from your estate so long as you do. Should you die before the term ends, the assets would be brought back into your estate.
6. As this is a defective grantor trust, you would, of course, be taxed on the income generated by the assets.
7. If the trust does not generate adequate income to make the annual annuity payment, you can transfer assets in kind.

This structure is particularly appealing in certain circumstances. First, you may wish to establish GRATs when you have assets that are likely to appreciate and therefore outperform the APR. This way, you get additional wealth to you children without paying gift taxes. It is also common to establish GRATs with family closely held business stock if you are contemplating a future sale or IPO.

There are some variations to the GRAT. For example, there are Grantor Retained Unitrusts (GRUT), where the annuity payment is reset annually and is based on the fair market value of the trust. There are also Grantor Retained Interest Trusts, which are generally deployed when transferring tangible assets like art.

EXHIBIT 8–E2

FAMILY WEALTH TRANSFERS:
Grantor Retained Annuity Trusts

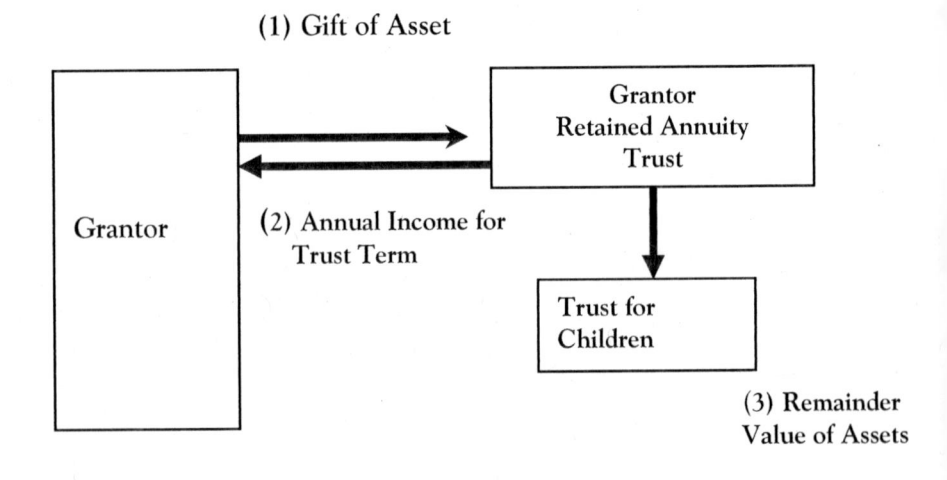

(1) Gift of Asset

Grantor	(2) Annual Income for Trust Term	Grantor Retained Annuity Trust
		↓
		Trust for Children

(3) Remainder Value of Assets

Exhibit 8-E-2 illustrates how a GRAT works. To further illustrate this technique, consider the following example:

Wealth Transfer Techniques

- Assume you establish a GRAT and transfer $2,000,000 to it.
- You want an annuity payment of 5 percent or $100,000 annually.
- The term is to be ten years.
- The applicable federal rate is 4.2 percent.
- Payments will take place annually and at the end of the year.
- The annuity factor for ten years and an AFR rate of 4.2 percent is 8.0307. This is derived from the Term Certain Factors for annuities.
- The valuation of the GRAT annuity payments is calculated by multiplying the annual annuity payment by the annuity factor. Accordingly, 8.0307 times $100,000 is $803,070.
- Then, the value of the GRAT remainder interest is $2,000,000 less the $803,070 annuity value. Therefore, the value of the remainder gift is $1,196,930. This is the value used for gift tax purposes.

As you look at the above example, consider a situation where the remainder interest is much lower. In other words, can you arrange the GRAT structure so that the remainder interest is actually zero? The answer is yes and the resulting structure is referred to as a zeroed-out GRAT. Exhibit 8-F illustrates the cash flow for a zeroed-out GRAT. Here we start with $2,000,000, an AFR of 4 percent and an annuity of 12.3 percent. Because the remainder interest is expected to be near zero, there is no effective gift tax value. However, should the trust outperform the AFR, the additional value will go to the remainder beneficiaries estate and gift tax-free. Consider the example in exhibit 8-G. Assuming the trust earns a return of 8 percent, the heirs could get $745,465 free of estate and gift tax.

EXHIBIT 8–F

Zeroed-Out GRAT

Year	Beginning Balance	Growth 4%	Annuity Payment	Ending Balance
1	$2,000,000	$80,000	$(246,600)	$1,833,400
2	1,833,400	73,336	(246,600)	1,660,136
3	1,660,136	66,405	(246,600)	1,479,941
4	1,479,941	59,198	(246,600)	1,292,539
5	1,192,539	51,701	(246,600)	1,097,640
6	1,097,640	43,906	(246,600)	896,946
7	894,946	35,798	(246,600)	684,144
8	684,144	27,366	(246,600)	464,910
9	464,910	18,596	(246,600)	236,906
10	236,906	9,476	(246,600)	(218)

EXHIBIT 8–G

GRAT @ 8% Growth

Year	Beginning Balance	Growth 8%	Annuity Payment	Ending Balance
1	$2,000,000	$160,000	$(246,600)	$1,913,400
2	1,913,400	153,072	(246,600)	1,819,872
3	1,819,872	145,590	(246,600)	1,718,862
4	1,718,862	137,509	(246,600)	1,609,771
5	1,609,771	128,782	(246,600)	1,491,953
6	1,491,953	119,356	(246,600)	1,364,709
7	1,364,709	109,177	(246,600)	1,227,286
8	1,227,286	98,183	(246,600)	1,078,869
9	1,078,869	86,310	(246,600)	918,579
10	918,579	73,486	(246,600)	745,465

Wealth Transfer Techniques

Minority Interest Grantor Retained Annuity Trusts (MIGRAT)

A powerful wealth transfer technique involves combining the family limited partnership with the grantor retained annuity trust. By doing this, you can achieve discounting at two levels. Exhibit 8-H shows how this works:

- You first establish the family limited partnership.
- Then, you transfer limited partnership interests to a GRAT, employing an appropriate discount for those interests.
- The valuation of the GRAT remainder interest is based on the discounted FLP units.
- Within the GRAT, the assets have the chance to appreciate and will go to the remainder heirs. The value of the assets transferred is essentially frozen at inception.

EXHIBIT 8–H

Minority Interest Grantor Retained Annuity Trust (MIGRAT)

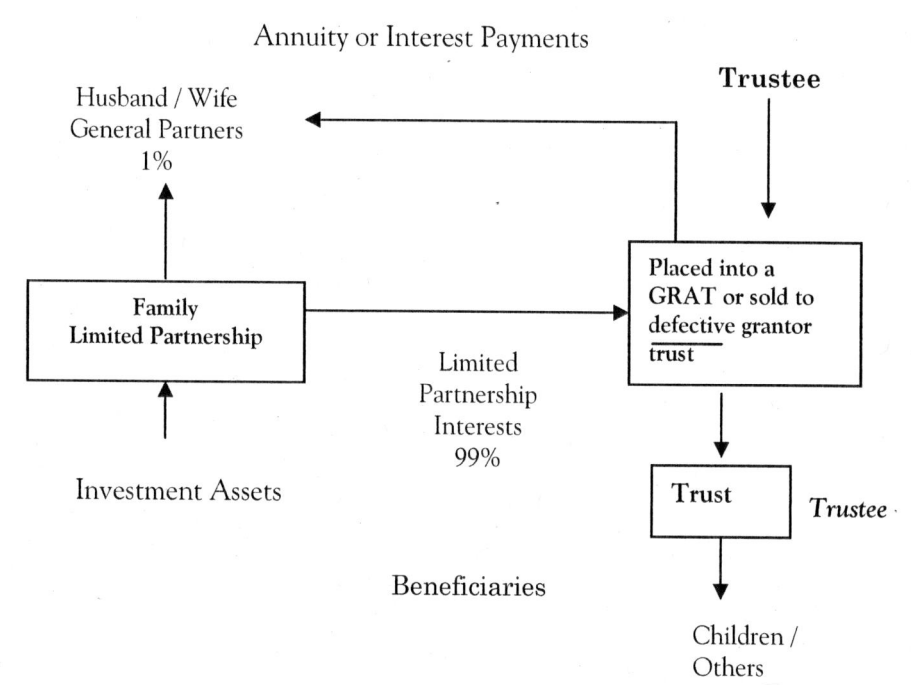

```
                    Annuity or Interest Payments
                                                        Trustee
    Husband / Wife  ◄─────────────────────────────┐       │
    General Partners                              │       │
         1%                                       │       ▼
          ▲                                    ┌──────────────────┐
          │                                    │ Placed into a    │
    ┌──────────────┐                           │ GRAT or sold to  │
    │   Family     │ ────────────────────────► │ defective grantor│
    │ Limited      │                           │ trust            │
    │ Partnership  │       Limited             └──────────────────┘
    └──────────────┘       Partnership                   │
          ▲                Interests                     ▼
          │                  99%                    ┌────────┐
    Investment Assets                               │ Trust  │  Trustee
                                                    └────────┘
                        Beneficiaries                    │
                                                         ▼
                                                    Children /
                                                    Others
```

If you were to add the FLP feature to the above example on GRATs, you could, for example, transfer $3,000,000 to an FLP and transfer it to the GRAT. You would transfer it at a 33 percent discount, so that $2,000,000 would be the actual valuation of the gift. As a result, you are able to move an additional $1,000,000 by employing an FLP in conjunction with the GRAT.

Sale to an Intentionally Defective Grantor Trust

Up to this point, we looked at gifting assets to trusts. Now let's consider selling assets to a trust instead of gifting them. Here is how it works:

- First, you would establish a defective grantor trust, where the grantor (parents) is taxed on the income but the assets are removed from the estate.
- The initial funding of the trust is subject to gift tax since you are removing the assets from your estate.
- Paying income taxes on the trust is almost like an additional gift. It currently does not incur gift taxes although the IRS sometimes tries to challenge this.
- The trust could also be established as a dynasty trust, which is intended to last in perpetuity. You could also apply your GST exemption to this trust, thereby further leveraging your GST exemption.
- You then sell an asset to this trust. The sale would be set up as an installment sale. Accordingly, there would be no capital gain for income tax purposes since you are technically selling the asset to yourself. The rationale is that the trust is considered a defective trust where you, the grantor, pay tax on the income generated.
- To further boost the leverage in this type of transaction, you could sell units of a family limited partnership at discounted values.

- The intent is to again freeze the value of the assets sold and hopefully realize capital growth in the future. This growth would accrue to your heirs in a tax-free manner.
- Upon the sale, you create a note with interest and would continue paying the note until maturity. It is possible that, at a later date, you may wish to pay off the note and even buy back some of the assets. Buying back some assets might be attractive in situations where you wish to have the appreciated assets included back in your estate and get the step up in basis. However, not everyone will want to do this.
- If the grantor dies before the note matures, only the remaining note value is in his/her estate.

The SIDGT raises several estate, gift and income tax issues as it can be a highly efficient transaction in dealing with these taxes. It is frequently compared to the GRAT, so we have prepared a summary comparison in exhibit 8-I. A key difference lies in the leveraging capacity of the SIDGT as you can significantly leverage your GST exemption, where in a GRAT, you cannot allocate the GST exemption until the GRAT terminates. On the other hand, the GRAT has enjoyed clear regulatory guidelines and the SIDGT has not and could therefore be subject to future challenges by the IRS.

EXHIBIT 8-I

Family Wealth Transfers
Comparison of GRAT and ISDGT

GRAT	ISDGT
• All future appreciation removed	• All future appreciation removed
• Permissible S shareholder	• FLP not permissible S shareholder, although trust is
• Mandatory current income stream	• Current income stream if desired
• Valuation discounts	• Valuation discounts
• Gift taxes removed	• No gift tax consequences (except for initial gift to trust)
• Payment of income taxes further reduces estate	• Payment of income taxes further reduces estate
• Interest rate is 120% of midterm AFR	• Interest rate is AFR
• Statutory "blueprint"	• No direct legal precedent
• GST exemption cannot be allocated	• GST exemption can be allocated
• Mortality risk	• No mortality risk
• Cannot prepay income interest	• Can prepay note

Sale of Remainder Interest in a GRAT (or CLAT) to a Dynasty Trust

Keep the concepts of a GRAT and a defective dynasty trust in mind. Exhibit 8-J illustrates a further advanced technique whereby you do the following:

- First, you have established a GRAT, which has an annuity stream that goes back to you and a remainder interest that ultimately goes to your heirs.
- You also established a family dynasty trust, which is essentially a defective trust that lasts in perpetuity. You would allocate at least some of your GST exemption to the trust.
- Among other things, such as purchasing FLP units as we showed above, the family dynasty trust can purchase the remainder interest from the GRAT. The price it pays can be equivalent to its present value. In some cases, this value can be quite low. This transaction can ultimately pay off nicely if the underlying assets in the GRAT appreciate significantly.

- The result is that the dynasty trust will gain from the appreciation while freezing the purchase price at today's value. The appreciation will therefore benefit future generations without subjecting the trust to further estate, gift or GST taxes.

EXHIBIT 8-J

Sale of Remainder Interest in CLAT (or GRAT) to Dynasty Trust

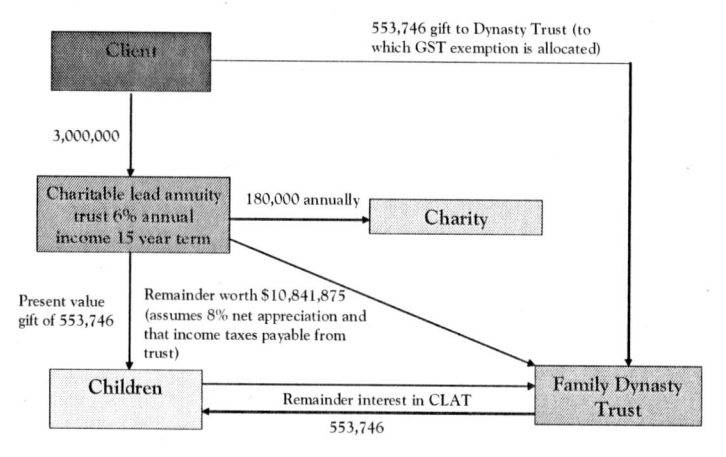

```
                          553,746 gift to Dynasty Trust (to
   ┌────────┐             which GST exemption is allocated)
   │ Client │─────────────────────────────────────────────┐
   └────────┘                                             │
        │                                                 │
        │ 3,000,000                                       │
        ▼                                                 │
   ┌──────────────────┐                                   │
   │ Charitable lead  │  180,000 annually  ┌─────────┐    │
   │ annuity trust 6% │───────────────────▶│ Charity │    │
   │ annual income    │                    └─────────┘    │
   │ 15 year term     │                                   │
   └──────────────────┘                                   │
        │         │                                       │
        │         │ Remainder worth $10,841,875           │
        │         │ (assumes 8% net appreciation and      │
Present value     │ that income taxes payable from        │
gift of 553,746   │ trust)                                │
        │         └──────────────────────────┐            │
        ▼                                    ▼            ▼
   ┌──────────┐                         ┌───────────────────┐
   │ Children │◀────────────────────────│ Family Dynasty    │
   │          │  Remainder interest in  │ Trust             │
   │          │  CLAT    553,746        │                   │
   └──────────┘                         └───────────────────┘
```

Qualified Personal Residence Trust (QPRT)

So far, we have discussed transferring or selling financial or business assets to the various trusts. One of your most valuable assets is likely to be your home. There is actually an asset freeze structure that enables you to efficiently transfer this asset to your children. With a QPRT, you can transfer your residence at a discounted value and continue to live there for a stated period of time. Here is how that works:

1. You establish a QPRT, naming your children as the beneficiaries.
2. You then transfer your home into the trust for a period of years. The value of the trust is determined by applying certain IRS interest rate factors to the current value. The remainder interest

is then the taxable gift. The formula is more favorable during higher interest rate environments because the present value of your lifetime interest will be higher.
3. Appreciation beyond the current value will accrue to your children without any further gift tax liabilities.
4. As this is again a type of defective grantor trust, all income tax benefits are recognized by the grantor. This includes deductions for property taxes and mortgage interest.
5. Also, as a grantor trust, you are able to replace the property with another one should you sell your original residence. On the other hand, if you sell your home and do not replace it in the trust, you can establish a GRAT with an annual annuity until the termination date.
6. Should you die prior to the end of the trust, the residence will revert back to your estate.
7. If you survive the trust, your children will then own the home. You can still live there, but you must then lease it from them.
8. Neither the annual gift tax exclusion nor the GST exemption apply to this structure.

As of this writing, we are at an important crossroad in the estate planning field. There is still much debate about the likelihood of a permanent repeal of the estate tax. Additionally, the IRS continues to challenge some of the more creative structures employed to transfer wealth to successive generations. The next few years will be critical as lawmakers shape the landscape for how the baby boomers may or may not inherit their family's wealth.

9

Establishing Charitable Structures

No complete wealthy family goes without creating a philanthropic plan. Most, if not nearly all successful families, are more than willing to give something back to the very communities where they made their fortunes. Fortunately, the tax code provides these individuals with an avenue of alternatives by which to provide this charitable support. These alternatives include the following:

1. Outright Gifts
2. Life Income Gifts
    - Charitable Gift Annuities
    - Deferred Gift Annuities
    - Pooled Income Funds

3. Charitable Trusts
    - Charitable Remainder Annuity Trusts
    - Charitable Remainder Unitrusts
    - Charitable Lead Annuity Trusts
    - Charitable Lead Unitrusts

4. Foundation Structures
    - Community Foundations
    - Donor-Advised Funds
    - Supporting Organizations
    - Private Foundations

We will briefly cover the highlights of each method of charitable giving. I refer you to a companion text called *The Philanthropic Executive* to get more details on each of these techniques.

Outright Gifts

By far, the least complex way to give to charity is to make an outright gift of cash, securities or other property including real estate. When doing so, you need to be aware of some of the important issues surrounding charitable gifts:

- The ability to deduct the value of the gift from your income taxes is limited to a percentage of your adjustable gross income.
- The type of charity you give to will also impact the nature of your deduction.
- Income tax deductions are also impacted by the appreciation built into each asset. With some assets, you can deduct the entire fair market value, while with other assets, you can only deduct the cost basis.
- Some deductions are also predicated on whether the recipient organization has immediate use of the money.

Exhibit 9-A summarizes the tax deductions for charitable contributions.

EXHIBIT 9–A

Charitable Tax Deductions

	Public Charities/ Community Foundations	Private Foundations
Cash	50% of adjusted gross income (AGI)	30% of AGI
Ordinary Income and Short-term Capital Gain Property	50% of AGI, valued at cost	30% of AGI, valued at cost
Long-term Capital Gain Property	30% of AGI, valued at market	20% of AGI, valued at market for marketable securities. Valued at cost for others.
Tangible Property	50% of AGI, valued at cost	30% of AGI valued at cost

Life Income Gifts

Life income gifts are split-interest gifts that provide benefits to you as well as the charity. Generally, these gifts provide an income stream for life with the remainder interest going to the specified charity that underwrote the gift. There are three common forms of life income gifts:

Charitable Gift Annuities

This is one of the more popular forms of charitable giving. Structurally, it is a contract between you and a qualified charity where you transfer cash, securities or saleable real estate in exchange for a promise to pay a lifetime annuity to you and possibly your spouse as well. The charity then gets the remaining assets upon your death. Universities, hospitals and religious organizations generally issue gift annuities. When you give funds to these organizations, they will provide you with a calculation as to the components of each annuity payment. The payments will be comprised of a return of capital, ordinary income and capital gains. Looking at an example, let's say you establish a $100,000 gift annuity with a local hospital. You are currently 65-years old and contribute a stock with a cost basis of $30,000. Also, assume that the hospital agreed to pay you an annuity of 6.8 percent and that the APR is 5 percent. Without going into all of the mathematical steps, let's assume that the charity advises you that you will receive a $6,800 annuity for life. The breakdown of the payment is $3,026 of ordinary income, $2,643 of capital gains and $1,131 as a return of capital. You will also be advised as to the tax deduction, which is based on the size and timing of your annuity payments and your age.

Deferred Gift Annuities

This is similar to the gift annuity except for the fact that the annuity payments to you do not begin until some time in the future. As a result, your income tax deduction will be greater since the charity has use of the funds until your annuity begins. Everything is factored into the equation to determine your deduction, including your age, the timing of your initial payment and the discount rate the charity can earn.

Pooled Income Funds

Where you wish to just provide a small gift to an institution, establishing a pooled income fund may be the appropriate vehicle. The operation of a pooled income fund is similar to that of a mutual fund. You contribute assets to a commingled fund and receive the earned income for life. At your death, the assets go to the sponsoring charity. The fund offers investment choices, but you must select among those choices. When you establish the gift, you will receive a current income tax deduction and the assets will be removed from your estate. Another important benefit is that when you contribute low basis stock, you will not incur a capital gain, either at inception or in the future.

Charitable Trusts

As you proceed to make larger charitable gifts, the concept of a charitable trust becomes more appealing. Charitable trusts are complex trusts, meaning that they are constructed with split interests. There is both a current income (or annuity) beneficiary as well as a remainder beneficiary. One of the beneficiaries is always a charity while the other is the grantor, a spouse or another individual. Where an individual is the current income or annuity beneficiary and the charity is the remainder beneficiary, the trust is called a charitable remainder trust. On the other hand, where the charity is the current income beneficiary and an individual is the remainder beneficiary, the trust is called a charitable lead trust. We will look at each in turn.

Charitable Remainder Trusts-CRT

These trusts can be one of two types, either a charitable remainder annuity trust or a charitable remainder unitrust. Under a **charitable remainder annuity trust** structure, the trust pays the individual a stated percentage annuity each year. The annuity is established at the inception of the trust. At termination, the assets in the trust are turned over to the charity. Here are the parameters of this trust:

1. The CRAT term can be your lifetime or for a period certain. If you elect a period certain, the maximum years are 20.
2. Your annual annuity can range from 5 to 50 percent.
3. The present value of the remainder interest going to charity must be at least 10 percent for the trust to be valid.
4. You cannot contribute any additional assets once originally funded.
5. The annuity amount is constant and cannot be changed.
6. Upon creating the trust, you get an immediate income tax deduction equal to the present value of the charitable remainder interest. The factors contributing to this value are your age, the term of the trust, the annual annuity and the applicable federal rate. Accordingly, the longer the term, the lower the charitable tax deduction. Also, the higher the annuity payment, the lower the deduction.
7. The IRS also has what is called a "5% probability test." The IRS subjects the trust to a test whereby there cannot be greater than a 5 percent actuarial probability that the trust will be exhausted before the charity gets its money. If the trust does not pass this test, you do not receive the charitable deduction.
8. If someone other than your spouse is the current income beneficiary, you may have gift and estate tax consequences.

It may help to show an illustration.

- Assume you wish to set up a CRAT with $4 million
- Your age is 57

- Annual annuity is 7 percent or $280,000, payable semi-annually
- The IRS AFR is 5 percent
- The term is for your lifetime.

Without going through all of the math, the value of the reminder interest is $419,734, which is your current income tax deduction.

Exhibit 9-B illustrates how this trust operates. While there are considerable advantages to this trust, there are also some issues you should be aware of. The trust is irrevocable and no entity outside of the trust can guarantee the payments. Also, should the lifetime annuitant die before his/her life expectancy, the charity may end up with more funds than you originally intended.

The CRAT is especially attractive for investors with appreciated securities as it is one of the strategies you can employ to diversify away from a concentrated position. Moreover, one may wish to establish a CRAT in a year when your company is sold or when you have an extraordinary gain. Also, if you are an insider or control person, you can contribute stock to a CRAT and not have a constructive and reportable sale until you actually sell the stock inside the trust. Finally, it is an effective way to support a second-marriage spouse for life and then benefit a charity.

EXHIBIT 9–B

Charitable Remainder Trusts

(1) Gift of Asset

```
┌─────────────┐       ────────────►      ┌─────────────────┐
│             │                          │                 │
│             │       ◄────────────      │   Charitable    │
│  Investor   │  (2) Charitable Deduction-│ Remainder Trust │
│             │      Income Tax Saved    │                 │
│             │                          │                 │
│             │       ◄────────────      │                 │
│             │  (3) Annual Income for Trust Term          │
└─────────────┘                          └─────────────────┘
                                                  │
                                                  │ (4) Remainder
                                                  │     Value of Assets
                                                  ▼
                                          ┌─────────────┐
                                          │   Charity   │
                                          └─────────────┘
```

Another type of charitable remainder trust is the **charitable remainder unitrust (CRUT).** This follows the same pattern as the CRAT and has many of the same features and benefits. However, there are some variations:

- While the CRAT has a constant annual annuity that is set at inception, the CRUT is a variable annuity based on a stated percentage of the fair market value of the trust, revalued annually.
- Unlike the CRAT, with the CRUT you can add assets after the trust is established. Some people like to use this trust as a place to contribute some of their retirement assets after death.

- The CRUT offers three alternative arrangements which can be very attractive to investors in certain situations. The first is the *Net Income Charitable Remainder Unitrust (NICRUT)*. Under this arrangement, the annual payment can be the lesser of the unitrust percentage or the actual net income earned during the year. The advantage is the trustee does not have to invade principal, which can be attractive if the trust is funded with low-trading volume or closely held stock. The second alternative is the *Net Income Make-Up Charitable Remainder Unitrust (NIMCRUT)*. In this situation, you also receive the lesser of the net income or the unitrust percentage. However, there is a provision that enables you to make up prior shortfalls from the stated unitrust payment. Accordingly, in later years, to the extent that the current net income exceeds the unitrust percentage, you can distribute funds to make up for prior shortfalls. This can be an attractive strategy when you initially fund the trust with low-yielding assets that are sold years later and reinvested to produce higher income. The third alternative is the *Flip Trust*. This trust is actually a combination of all of the above. It starts out as either a NICRUT or a NIMCRUT and then changes (flips) to a straight CRUT upon a triggering event specified in the trust document. This event must be something that is beyond the direct control of the donor, beneficiary or trustee. Additionally, the flip event can only occur once and is generally something like a marriage or sale of an asset such as real estate. This is attractive when you fund the trust with an asset like real estate that you may sell later on.

Charitable Lead Trusts

Charitable lead trusts are the mirror image of the charitable remainder trust. In this case, the income beneficiary or annuitant is the charity, while the remainder beneficiaries are your heirs. As a result, the remainder interest would be subject to gift tax but this presents some important planning opportunities in that you can transfer assets to your heirs tax free to the extent the portfolio inside the trust outperforms the federal AFR. Accordingly, this structure may especially be attractive during periods of low interest rates when the federal AFR is low.

The charitable lead trust has some important income tax implications as well. These implications depend upon the structure of the trust and there are two basic structures or forms. The first and more common form is the *non-grantor charitable lead trust*. With this trust, you do not get a current income tax deduction, but at the same time you are not the ongoing owner of the trust and will therefore not be subject to further income taxes. As such, the CLT is considered a complex trust and will be taxed on income not distributed to charities. You can establish this trust during your lifetime or as part of your estate plan at death. If you establish it at death, your estate gets a charitable deduction for the present value of the lead interest. The second form is the *grantor charitable lead trust*. Here you are actually considered to be the owner of the trust and will be taxed on the income earned. Accordingly, you will want to invest in tax-free bonds to the extent possible. As a result, you will get an up-front income tax deduction for the present value of the charitable lead payments. Should you die prior to the termination of the trust, your estate will have to pay a "recapture tax" that is the equivalent of the initial charitable tax deduction less the initial present value of the charitable lead interest that has been paid. Also, as with the non-grantor trust, the future remainder interest is subject to gift tax. This trust can only be established during your lifetime.

Like its CRT counterpart, the charitable lead trust can be either an annuity trust (CLAT) or a unitrust (CLUT). We will first consider some of the features of the charitable lead annuity trust.

Establishing Charitable Structures

- Unlike the CRAT, the CLAT is not limited to a specified time limit. It can last for the lifetimes of all living family members at the time it is created and could even last for a specified number of years beyond that.
- You are not restricted as to the annual annuity percentage.
- Like a CRAT, you cannot add assets once the trust is established.
- Like with the grantor retained annuity trust, you can sell the remainder interest to a family dynasty trust.

Once again, an example might better illustrate this concept. Consider these parameters:

- The term is 20 years and is a non-grantor trust
- The trust is funded with $6 million
- The annuity is 6 percent
- The present value of the annuity payments is $4,642,560 and the remainder interest is $1,357,440.
- The remainder interest is subject to gift tax.

As with the grantor retained annuity trust, you have the ability to design a CLAT where the remainder interest is close to zero. You can accomplish this by increasing the annuity payment or extending the term. Then, to the extent you can accumulate more than the original remainder interest, that differential will pass to your heirs estate and gift tax free.

Exhibit 9-C illustrates how this trust operates.

EXHIBIT 9–C

Charitable Lead Trusts

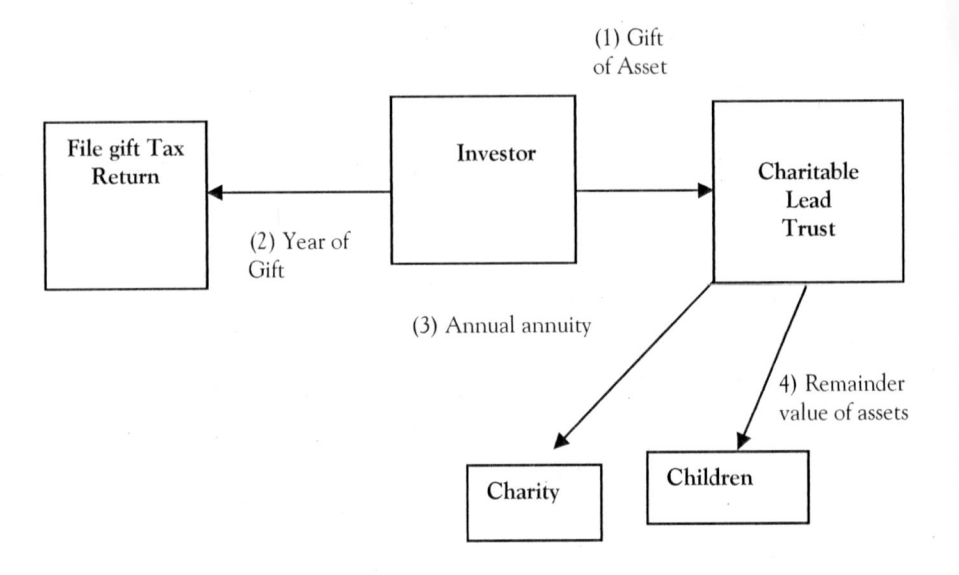

```
                        (1) Gift
                       of Asset

┌───────────┐      ┌──────────┐          ┌───────────┐
│File gift Tax│◄────│ Investor │─────────►│ Charitable│
│  Return   │      │          │          │   Lead    │
│           │  (2) Year of    │          │   Trust   │
│           │     Gift        │          │           │
└───────────┘      └──────────┘          └───────────┘
                  (3) Annual annuity        │      │
                         │                  │      │
                         ▼                  │      │ 4) Remainder
                                            │      │ value of assets
                     ┌────────┐      ┌──────────┐
                     │ Charity│      │ Children │
                     └────────┘      └──────────┘
```

We will now consider the *charitable lead unitrust*. It has many of the same features as the CLAT, but there are some differences. First, you can add assets to the trust after it is established. Also, the annuity is reset annually and is based on the revalued asset base of the trust. A key aspect of the CLUT is that the full remainder interest qualifies for the generation-skipping tax exemption. With the CLAT, only a partial interest may qualify. The CLAT is subject to a clause in Section 2642(e) of the IRS Code whereby the GST exemption is adjusted by an inclusion ratio. This fraction is derived by dividing the adjusted GST exemption by the value of the CLAT remainder at the end of the trust's term. The adjusted GST exemption is the amount of GST exemption originally allocated to the CLAT, compounded annually at the original federal AFR rate throughout the term of the trust. Accordingly, if the CLAT outperforms the AFR, you can be subject to an adjusted GST amount. The CLUT, on the other hand, is not subject to Section 2642(e) and any further adjustments. This can also be attractive if you sell the remainder interest to a family dynasty trust.

Foundation Structures

We are now ready to look at the foundation options:

Private Family Foundation

When you wish to make a substantial commitment to philanthropy, a private family foundation may be appropriate. It may also be appropriate under these circumstances:

- You want to support many different charities and may also want to change those recipients over time. The foundation gives you the structure to evaluate and process grants.
- You may want to have a forum in which your children can work together for the good of the community. It sometimes helps to build a more cohesive family unit.
- You want to leave a lasting legacy on the community.
- You want direct control over the entire process, even how the funds are invested for future growth.

A great challenge when selecting the foundation form is that you must make sure you establish sound governance. This involves selecting trustees or directors as well as officers and staff. Additionally, you will need to establish a mission and grants policy. There are also a series of tax compliance issues you must be familiar with so as to protect the tax-free status of the foundation. Here is a brief rundown of those tax compliance rules:

1. **Excise Tax on Investment Income-** This is a tax on the net investment income, which includes capital gains. However, investment related expenses can be deducted. The tax is 2 percent of income but can be reduced to 1 percent if the foundation meets certain payout requirements.
2. **Minimum Payout Ratio-** Foundations must pay out 5 percent of their asset value. The asset value is based on the monthly averages of the prior year. Failure to do so results in a penalty of 15 percent of the shortfall and the foundation has one year to make up the shortfall.
3. **Tax on Self Dealing-** This is a penalty assessed when a foundation conducts a financial transaction with certain disqualified persons. These are predominately trustees, directors, staff and their family members. The penalty for these conflict of interest transactions is 5 percent of the value of the transaction and is assessed to each individual.
4. **Tax on Excess Business Holdings-** Foundations cannot control an operating business and are therefore restricted to their percentage ownership. It is either 20 or 35 percent based on the composition of ownership by disqualified persons. The penalty is 5 percent on the investment held in excess of the applicable limit. However, the foundation has five years to divest ownership of donated shares before any tax is imposed.
5. **Unrelated Business Income Tax-** This penalty is designed to prevent foundations from earning income from a trade or business that is unrelated to its mission or purpose. Included in this definition could be certain limited partnership interests and debt-financed real estate. The penalty is that the foundation would be taxed on the earned income at corporate rates.
6. **Tax on Jeopardy Investments-** This penalty is designed to discourage foundations from making imprudent investments. The tax is 5 percent on the amount of the investment, but the tax is

imposed on the foundation executive that directed the investment.

7. **Tax on Taxable Expenditures-** To prevent grants from going to non-charitable causes, there is a penalty assessed on both the foundation and its director. The prohibited grants usually include lobbying, political contributions and grants to individuals. The tax is 10 percent on the amount involved along with a 2.5 percent tax on the foundation director.

Donor Advised Funds

A popular alternative to a full family foundation is the donor advised fund. By definition, it is a charitable fund established at a public charity. You have the ability to advise on the distributions to qualified charitable recipients. Historically, these funds were offered through local community foundations and still are. However, more recently, financial institutions with large mutual fund complexes have begun to sponsor donor advised funds. Some of the features and benefits of this structure are:

- It is less costly than a foundation and you can set it up with far less money.
- Like a foundation, you can time funding and distributions. For example, should you wish to contribute a large block of low basis stock this year and gain the tax deduction, you can do so. On the other hand, you do not have to distribute the funds until you are ready to do so at a later date.
- You can use this fund to accumulate funds over a period of years and then make a large gift to a favorite institution later on.
- Your children can become involved in the grantmaking.
- You are not subject to the 2 percent excise tax as are foundations.

You should also be aware of some of the drawbacks:

- There are additional layers of fees as you will need to compensate the sponsoring organization for its efforts.
- You are restricted to the investment options of the sponsor.
- Some charities will have rules on grant size, etc.
- Most sponsors have a stated termination date, when they would take over running the fund. Usually the funds can run a generation or two.

Supporting Organizations

Suppose you have closely held stock, restricted stock or real estate and wish to contribute some of it to charity. Also, suppose you are willing to contribute most of it to one organization, such as the local community foundation. A private foundation or a donor advised fund may not be feasible options. An attractive structure to accomplish your goal could be a supporting organization. By definition, a supporting organization is a charitable corporation or trust that is created in direct affiliation with a public charity. It enjoys many of the same tax and operating benefits of foundations. There are some added advantages as well, such as a lower payout ratio (85 percent of the earned income) and no excise tax on investment income. On the other hand, there are a range of legal requirements to set up and operate these structures, so you need to engage competent legal counsel to assist you.

10

The Role of Insurance

Insurance is a means of transferring and sharing the risk of certain life events. These life events encompass risks to your health, property, business and life. Losses in any of these areas could be catastrophic to you and your family. Insurance, in some other instances, can also serve as an effective tax efficient investment.

Much has been written on the insurance field so the purpose of this chapter is not to recreate a complete text on the subject. We leave it to the reader to consult other texts to gain a firm understanding of the topic, as insurance is a very complex field in the financial services arena. Accordingly, our intent is to show how insurance fits into the overall program of managing family wealth. To that end, we will discuss some of the new products in the market and show some of the advanced techniques of using insurance to build wealth. Additionally, we will talk about some of the service options available in the property and casualty and health care fields today.

Life Insurance

We begin with life insurance, which essentially comes in two basic forms—term or permanent. Before looking at the differences between the two, let's look at the basic features of life insurance. When comparing insurance, you generally compare each type as well as each policy alternative according to:

- Death benefit
- Cash vale build-up
- Premiums
- Investment options

With this as background, we can consider the difference between term and permanent insurance. With term insurance, you generally have lower initial premiums at younger ages, but the premiums then increase as you get older. The policies also have no cash value and terminate at a fixed date. Permanent insurance, on the other hand, may have higher initial premiums, but they stay constant and there is a cash value component, which can offset some of the premium in the future. There may also be dividends that you can use to offset premiums in later years. The cash value build-up is tax deferred and may never be taxed if the insured is not the owner of the policy. Both term and permanent insurance can be written on one or two lives. Where two lives are insured, the policies are referred to as survivorship or second-to-die insurance. There are many other investment and tax-related issues with insurance and we advise you to consult a licensed agent to determine which insurance programs and policies are appropriate for your family situation.

The Role of Insurance

At this juncture, we will examine the role life insurance can play in helping families manage and preserve their wealth. First, here are some of the common uses of life insurance:

- Support surviving dependents of young breadwinners
- Provide liquidity to pay estate taxes and settlement costs
- Shift income from one generation to another
- Support special needs of handicapped heirs
- Implement charitable plans
- Fund buy-sell agreements

Getting beyond the risk protection side of life insurance, there are some important investment elements in some insurance programs and we have summarized some of these investment-oriented programs in exhibit 10-A. We compare each program as to the basic death benefit, premium and cash value components and also look at each from the standpoint of investment control and securities ownership. Using this as background, we will devote the rest of this section to discussing some of the specialized techniques available to wealthy families. Again, you must consult your insurance agent or advisor to first get more extensive information on each technique and to then determine how appropriate any of these are for you and your family. We will look at the following programs:

- Irrevocable life insurance trust
- Private placement life insurance
- Premium financing/leveraged life insurance
- Wealth replacement trusts
- Private annuities with variable universal life insurance
- Life insurance in a dynasty trust
- Life settlements
- Policy replacements

EXHIBIT 10-A

Comparisons of Alternatives-Investment Products

Insurance Feature	Universal Life	Variable Life	Variable Universal Life
Death Benefit	Flexible, but must consider MEC rules	Guaranteed minimum, can increase with investment performance	Flexible. Also can take option of pure insurance level plus cash value
Premium	Flexibility, at option of policy owner	Fixed and level	Flexible at option of policy owner
Cash Value	Dependent upon premium, face amount and guaranteed interest rate	Based on investment performance of funds – no guarantee	Based on premium and investment performance
Investment Control	Control with insurance company- generally fixed income	Choice of fixed and equity investments. Allocation left to policy owner	Choice left to policy owner within line-up of company funds/products
Security Ownership	Assets under ownership and control of insurance company, part of company's general account	Separate accounts not part of company's general account. Death benefits in excess of cash values are backed by general account.	Same as variable life

Insurance Feature	Private placement life	Annuities
Death Benefit	Like variable universal life	Based on accumulation and payment option chosen.
Premium	Flexible, at option of policy owner	Fixed or Flexible
Cash Value	Based on investment performance	Fixed annuities have minimum guaranteed interest; variable depends upon investment performance of holder's funds
Investment Control	Control rests with policy holder; can also select specific, external investment managers	Choice of fixed verses variable. Variable includes allocation among company's investment products. The policy-holder decides upon allocation.
Security Ownership	Separate account is not part of company's general account. Death benefits supported by general account in excess of cash value coverage.	Separate account and payments in excess of separate account balances paid from firm's general accounts.

Irrevocable Life Insurance Trust

Life insurance is popular for a number of reasons and one of those is because most people believe it can pass to your heirs free of estate tax. This is true, but only if the deceased does not own the policy at death. One way to avoid this is to set up an irrevocable life insurance trust and have the trust own the policy. So long as you do not die within three years of transferring insurance to the trust, it will not be included in your estate. When establishing the trust, you need to avoid gift tax implications. Contributions to the trust can qualify for the $11,000 annual exclusion but only if the beneficiaries, presumably your children, are given the power to withdraw funds. Governing this process is a court case involving the Crummey family. The court ruled that the gifts to such a trust can qualify for the annual exclusion if the beneficiary has the right to withdraw the gift or the annual exclusion amount, whichever is smaller. Thus, these powers are referred to as "crummey powers," and life insurance trusts are frequently called crummy trusts.

Private Placement Life Insurance

This is a form of variable universal life insurance, which is essentially a program that features flexible death benefits, premiums and cash values. A further feature of variable universal life is that you can select your investments from among a group of insurance company equity and fixed income products. With private placement life insurance, you have even further flexibility in that you can select your own investment manager. Because the policies carry high minimums, usually around $1 million, they can provide this flexibility. Other aspects include somewhat lower seller's commissions as you can negotiate due to higher face values. Also, the mortality costs are generally lower than on other products.

There are certain other benefits to using this arrangement in certain situations:

1. Investors can effectively use this as a deferred tax vehicle, taking advantage of the way insurance policies can build their cash value on a tax-deferred basis.
2. While you need to be careful how you execute this, you can employ certain tax-inefficient vehicles such as hedge funds in the portfolio. Keep in mind that the IRS is carefully looking at this.
3. The death benefit is tax free to your heirs if the policy is owned in an irrevocable trust.
4. The offshore version of the policy may save on some state premium taxes.

On the other hand, there are some issues you need to consider before setting these up:

The Role of Insurance

1. The policy cannot violate the modified endowment contract rules. These rules state that the premiums paid must not be in excess of what a standard permanent policy would charge over the first seven years.
2. The IRS has rules for diversification of investments within variable life insurance policies. These rules are contained in section 817-h of the IRS code. The rules spell out how much can be invested in any single investment product.
3. While you can select your own investment manager, you have to give that manager full discretion and control over the management of the portfolio and the insurance company needs to be in control of monitoring the manager.
4. The investment manager must be managing this specific type of portfolio only for insurance programs. In other words, the investment cannot be available directly to the public except within the insurance wrapper.
5. If the policy is offshore, you need a trustee.

Premium Financing

There is always debate as to the merits of life insurance as an investment. However, one such technique where life insurance can be a wealth-building vehicle is leveraged or premium-financed insurance. With this, life insurance is purchased with credit provided by a third-party institution. This technique is generally employed by older individuals (over 60) with substantial net worth (over $20 million) and a willingness to purchase a large policy. The family typically has a business and other assets that it may not wish to liquidate. Here is how the program generally works:

- You, the grantor, establish an irrevocable life insurance trust.
- The trust applies for insurance on the life of the grantor. The policy would likely incorporate a special rider that escalates the death benefit at the same rate as the debt is growing.

- The trust enters an agreement with a lending institution to provide financing for the premium payments. In some cases, interest payments could be included, but it generally is not.
- The policy is assigned as collateral to the lending institution. It is also possible that additional collateral, in the form of investment-grade securities, would be pledged so as to better support the loan. Generally, the current loan balance would be supported by the margin on the life insurance cash value and the investment portfolio.
- The grantors would gift the value of the loan interest payments to the trust, which in turn pays the lending institution.
- At death, the insurance proceeds are paid first to the lender to retire the loan and then to the trust. Any remaining collateral is then released.

There are some advantages as well as some risks with this type of program and we will look at each:

Advantages

- You can purchase a large amount of life insurance without incurring a substantial gift tax on the premiums paid. Your gift tax exposure would pertain only to the annual interest on the loan.
- You also do not have to liquidate assets to pay premiums. Accordingly, you can maintain your current investment portfolio.
- You enjoy the same estate tax benefits associated with life insurance as the proceeds would be removed from your estate.

Risks

- The policy death benefit must grow at the same rate as the debt or you may not have the desired level of net insurance proceeds in the future.

- You could also encounter poor policy performance where the cash value does not grow as expected. You could therefore face a situation where additional premiums are required to insure that the death benefit is reached. Consequently, paying additional significant premiums may trigger gift taxes.
- You will likely have to pledge an investment portfolio as additional collateral so as to make the loan work.
- On the other hand, if you personally guarantee the loan, you could be subject to further gift tax exposure unless the trust pays you a type of surety fee.
- You, the grantor, could outlive the policy. To deal with this possibility ahead of time, you may want to fund the trust with other assets that have the possibility of appreciating. This way, you can use those assets to reduce the loan in future years.
- The insurance company could become insolvent.
- You always want to be in a positive arbitrage position where your investments are returning more than your loan interest rate.

As we have said before, we are just presenting some of the highlights of an approach. To clearly get complete details and to determine the suitability of the technique, you need to consult your insurance advisor or agent.

Wealth Replacement Trusts

Insurance can play an important role in your charitable planning. In particular, it fits neatly within a charitable remainder trust program where you are concerned with reducing the inheritance of your children. Exhibit 10-B provides an illustration on how the program works, but here is a brief summary:

EXHIBIT 10–B

WEALTH REPLACEMENT TRUSTS

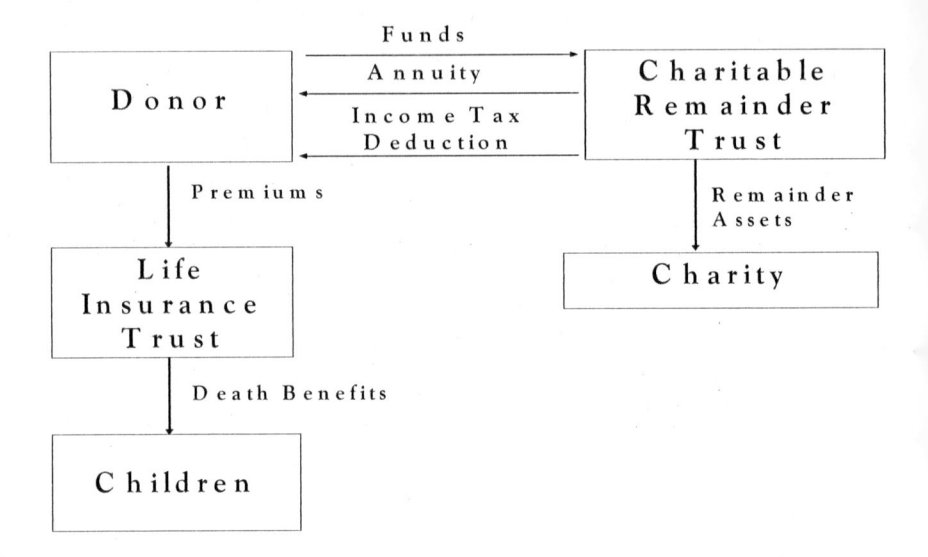

```
                    Funds
   ┌──────────┐  ─────────────→  ┌──────────────┐
   │          │      Annuity     │  Charitable  │
   │  Donor   │  ←───────────    │  Remainder   │
   │          │   Income Tax     │    Trust     │
   └──────────┘    Deduction     └──────────────┘
        │ Premiums                      │ Remainder
        ↓                               ↓ Assets
   ┌──────────┐                   ┌──────────────┐
   │   Life   │                   │   Charity    │
   │ Insurance│                   └──────────────┘
   │   Trust  │
   └──────────┘
        │ Death Benefits
        ↓
   ┌──────────┐
   │ Children │
   └──────────┘
```

- You first establish a charitable remainder trust.
- Upon doing so, you receive a current income tax deduction equal to the present value of the reminder interest going to charity.
- You would receive an annual annuity for life or a period certain. If you elect a period certain, it must be for less than 20 years.
- You also establish an irrevocable life insurance trust and purchase an insurance policy, with the tax deduction proceeds, on the life of the grantor.
- The death benefit could be established close to the expected remainder interest going to the charity.
- Your children could be the beneficiaries of the policy.
- The children therefore receive their inheritance.
- You also have the ability to invest the annual annuity and those assets will grow for the benefit of your family as well.

The Role of Insurance

Combining a Private Annuity with a Variable Universal Life Policy

Here is another advanced life insurance technique. We will discuss how it works along with the benefits and issues to consider.
First, here is how it works:

- You would establish a private annuity, either with a family member or a trust. For example, you transfer $5 million to a family member or trust in return for annual annuity payments to begin in ten years.
- The annual payments could be for life or for the period of life expectancy under the IRS tables.
- The family member would purchase a variable universal life insurance policy on his or her life. Alternatively, if the annuity is provided by a trust, the trustee would purchase life insurance on the life of a family member.
- You could purchase the policy with a single premium or in segments over a period of years to avoid being a modified endowment contract.
- When initial payments are due to begin in ten years, you can use any cash or other liquid assets to begin the annuity payments.
- When there is not adequate liquidity, you would borrow against the cash value of the policy to make the annuity payments. So long as the policy is not a modified endowment contract, the borrowing is tax free.
- Annuity payments subject the annuitant to the usual tax treatment of partial interest, partial capital gain and partial return of capital. The formula for this allocation is based on IRS tables.

The benefits of this strategy are accordingly:

- Investments in the policy grow on a tax-deferred basis during the first ten years.
- You have a good chance of having the insurance policy outperform the interest rate applied to the annuity; accordingly, your life policy will grow at a faster rate than needed to meet the annuity obligation during the grantor's life expectancy.
- The death of the insured will likely create a significant death benefit for his/her estate (or trust), which would be obligated to assume the annuity payments to the grantor.

There are also some issues you should consider:

- The value of the annuity could be included in the obligor's estate; however, the annuity obligation itself would be a deduction against the estate.
- If the annuitant dies before receiving full value for the assets transferred, the obligor will need to recognize a gain on the difference. The annuitant's estate, in turn, will exclude this difference.
- The annuitant, on his/her final income tax return, would be eligible to report a loss to the extent that he/she did not receive annuity payments equal to the cost basis in the assets transferred.
- The annuitant could outlive his/her projected life expectancy. This could be mitigated by having a specified period for payments.

Life Insurance in a Dynasty Trust

One option within a dynasty trust is to use life insurance in combination with leveraging your generation-skipping transfer tax exemption. Essentially, you would first fund the dynasty trust, allocating your GST exemption. You then purchase life insurance, particularly survivor life if both spouses are alive. You would continue to transfer funds to pay premiums, allocating additional GST exemptions. The policy proceeds will then escape estate as well as GST taxes.

Life Settlements

Recently, a market has developed for selling your life insurance to specialized life settlement firms. The sale value is somewhere between the current cash value and the death benefit. Some of the motivations for selling a policy are:

- Low performing investments on your variable life policy.
- Better opportunities to invest the funds elsewhere.
- It may be more feasible to liquidate the policy and purchase a long-term care policy.
- Your estate may now have adequate funds to cover taxes.

On the other hand, there are some considerations. First, you will have to accept a significant discount from the policy's face value. Second, you need to be 65-years old to qualify.

Replacement Policies

Sometimes, it may make sense to replace a life insurance policy. For example, new products may come to market that are superior to the policy you have. Your existing policy may not be performing well from the standpoint of cash value buildup. Should you believe that a replacement policy might make sense, you may want to follow these steps among others:

1. Look at how the current policy has performed compared to how it was supposed to perform.

2. Ask both companies to prepare "in-force illustrations," projecting future performance based on dividend rates, interest rates and investment return projections.
3. Look at the new policy to see if it has a term rider to reduce insurance costs.
4. Compare both policies at the same premium level.

Property and Liability Risk Management

Historically, property and liability insurance was a "commodity" product, influenced by aggressive pricing. Post September 11th and post Enron, it is a new ball game. Insurance rates have steadily climbed, some coverages have been eliminated or decreased and wealthy families now need as much "advice" as they do "product" from their insurance providers. The insurance industry has responded to serve the needs of its high net worth clients by establishing specialized private banking-like or family office units to handle them. These units predominately approach the high end client in the following manner:

1. They will look at the extended family and family office as one client, thereby leveraging the family for broader coverage, more flexible underwriting and better pricing.
2. They provide a comprehensive risk review on a family's real assets covering real estate, collectibles, vehicles, watercraft, planes and other valuables.
3. They will provide a comprehensive review of potential liabilities.
4. A key aspect of their analysis is to show potential gaps in coverage as well as opportunities to revise the insurance structure to achieve cost efficiencies or enhanced coverage.
5. The firms will also service the policies on an ongoing basis.

The Role of Insurance

Insurance firms in this field will operate under one of three service models. They can operate as a direct underwriter, a broker or as a consultant, where they do not get a brokerage fee for placing policies, but charge an annual fee for its services.

For high net worth clients, there is a wide range of coverage that is generally provided by the major firms. Included are some of the following:

Properties

- Homeowners residence and vacation homes
- Rental properties
- Flood and excess flood
- Farm and livestock
- International property coverage

Personal Items

- Personal property
- Fine art and antiques
- Jewelry and collectibles
- Collector vehicles

Vehicles

- Automobiles and recreational vehicles
- Yachts, houseboats and watercraft
- Aircraft

Commercial and Specialty

- Family unit health care

- Workers compensation
- Kidnap and ransom

Liability

- Underlying liability in each policy
- Excess/umbrella liability

Family Office

- Trustee and director liability
- Group health

There are at least five major players in this field and we offer their names as points of reference:

Company	Program	Delivery Model
American Int'l Group	Risk Mgt for Life	Direct underwriter
CHUBB	Masterpiece Signature Solutions/Family Office Pak	Direct underwriter
Marsh	Family Office Practice	Brokerage
PLI Brokerage	Family Office & Insurance Consultant	Brokerage
AON	Maestro	Consulting

Healthcare Insurance

Securing healthcare insurance is one of the more difficult services as most of it is underwritten in group plans or provided through the Medicare system. Therefore, if you are middle age and not working, you can have difficulties securing a cost-effective plan, even if you are in good health and wealthy. One insurance carrier, Marsh, has developed a service for its clients to make this process easier. The Marsh Health Insurance Mart brings together an array of medical insurance plans and their representative will help you sort through it to arrive at an appropriate form of coverage. They offer three basic types of coverage:

1. **Preferred Provider-** Here you have a choice from a network of providers and medical facilities.
2. **Full Indemnity-** This is the traditional program where you have freedom of choice among providers. Their array of plans offers varying sets of deductibles and out-of-pocket limits to provide lower premiums and the right fit of services.
3. **Health Savings Accounts-** Effective January 1, 2004, the IRS allows individuals to establish tax favored accounts at financial institutions for the purpose of covering specified medical expenses. These accounts, combined with high deductible health insurance, can provide individuals with the means to better manage the costs of health care. Contributions to these accounts are tax deductible and interest earned is tax-deferred. For individuals, the contribution limit is $2,600 and for families, $5,150. Some of the approved medical payments are prescription drugs, eyeglasses, dental, insurance deductibles and co-pays.

Another emerging concept in healthcare is concierge-level health care. This is being pioneered by a firm in Baltimore, Pinnacle Care International. Essentially, they are a membership organization that provides its members with in-depth research to match doctors, treatments and medical facilities with their specific health care needs. They serve as a patient advocate for each member, providing expedited access to chosen physicians and coordinate most, if not all, aspects of its members' care.

11

Concentrated Equity Strategies

Sometimes a wealthy individual or family will sell their company and receive stock or a combination of stock and cash. Sometimes this stock position can be an overwhelming part of you estate. As a result, the dominant investment strategy for the family is to handle the concentrated holding and ultimately diversify away from it. This process is sometimes a very quick one as some investors decide to immediately sell part or even all of their position in the acquiring firm. Others do not want to take the tax hit, so they may deal with the holding over several years.

Investors today have multiple options when managing a single stock position as they do not have to just decide on either holding or selling the position outright. In exhibit 11-A, we have segmented the alternative strategies into three categories, with specific techniques listed under each. In exhibit 11-E, we offer a description of each strategy along with the advantages and disadvantages of doing each.

In earlier chapters, we discussed the estate planning and charitable strategies so we will not go into any further explanation of those.

However, we will say a few words about some of the equity financial techniques.

EXHIBIT 11-A

SINGLE STOCK CONCENTRATIONS
POTENTIAL STRATEGIES

EQUITY FINANCIAL TECHNIQUES	ESTATE PLANNING TECHNIQUES	CHARITABLE TECHNIQUES
• Sales • Premium Equity Amortizing Contingent Sales • Put Option • Costless Collars • 1X2 Call Spread • Variable Pre Paid Forward Sales • Exchange funds	• Family Limited Partnerships (FLP) • Grantor Retained Annuity Trusts (GRAT) • Combining FLP's and GRATS – Minority Interest Grantor Retained Annuity Trusts (MIGRAT)	• Charitable Remainder trusts (CRT) • Net Income Make-Up Charitable Remainder Unitrust (NIMCRUT) • Charitable Family Limited Partnership • Private Family Foundation • Donor Advised Fund • Supporting Organization

1. **Sales-** You always have the ability to sell the stock at any time assuming the stock has adequate daily trading volume. By selling, you will then be subject to capital gains tax.

2. **Premium Sales-** Some brokerage/banking firms will offer programs whereby you can sell your stock over a period of time at a price above the present price level. For example, you will be given the right to sell a percentage of the shares daily at the fixed price so long as the stock is selling above a designated price. As an example, consider a stock whose current price is $40. You may enter a transaction with a firm whereby you agree to sell 200,000 shares over a one-year period under these circumstances. For every day that the stock closes above $37, you will sell 1,000 shares at a price of $50. If the stock closes below $37, the 1,000 shares are returned to you.

3. **Costless Collar-** This is a combined transaction where you purchase a put option with a strike price below the current

market price and, at the same time, sell a call option at a price above the current stock price. You essentially create a "collar" around the stock. You can structure these in a way that the cost of the put is offset by the funds received from the call, so the overall cost is zero. Exhibit 11-B illustrates a transaction. The current price is $50 and you purchased a put option with a strike price of $40. You also sold a call option at a strike price of $70. If the share price at expiration is below $40, you still get the $40 per share and the counter-party can pay you in cash if it has been structured that way. Otherwise, you can deliver your stock and get the $40 share price. At the same time, if the stock closes above $70, you will have the stock called at that price or you could pay the counter-party. Between the $40 and $70 price at expiration, nothing happens.

4. **1 x 2 Call Spread-** This transaction involves the purchase of a call option with a low strike price, and the sale of two call options at a high strike price. The premiums again offset each other so the transaction is costless. We assume the investor holds the stock as well. The leveraging comes in as the investor can earn twice the return on the stock between the low call price and the high call price. The return comes from holding the stock and earning the same return on the purchased call option. Above the high call price, no further appreciation is realized.

5. **Variable Pre-Paid Forward Sales-** With a costless collar, you have the ability to borrow against the hedged position. Regulations govern how much you can borrow. If you are borrowing to purchase margin stock, you can only borrow up to 50 percent of the value of your underlying value. However, if you are borrowing to invest in something other than margin stock, you can borrow up to 90 percent of the put stock price. There is another way to monetize your position and not be subject to any reinvestment restrictions. This is through a pre-paid forward sale with a financial intermediary. Here you agree to sell your stock

forward, let's say three or five years from now. You can receive up-front proceeds at a percentage of the floor price and agree to deliver a variable number of shares at expiration based on the share price at expiration. Accordingly, you can still retain some of the upside in the stock up to a predetermined ceiling price.

6. **Exchange Funds-** This strategy involves contributing your stock to a partnership which consists of other like investors who have contributed their stocks. You generally need to maintain your investment in the partnership for at least seven years to receive the full intended benefits. Sometimes you can pull out early, but you would only get your own stock back and it could be valued according to the net asset value of the exchange fund at the time of withdrawal. When you withdraw after seven years, you then get a pro rata share of all the securities in the fund. Your cost basis on the stocks received will be at the same level as on the original contributed stock. You do not incur any capital gain until you sell the individual stocks received from the exchange fund itself.

7. **Tax Managed Index Portfolio-** This strategy involves establishing a separately managed index portfolio. As with any index consisting of many stocks, some will increase while others will decrease in any given year. Your manager could sell some of those that have incurred losses and replace those companies with other names or even buy ETFs for 31 days until he/she could then buy back the original stock. To offset the losses, the manager could then sell positions in the concentrated stock. This way, you could manage the trades so that you remain in a tax neutral position.

EXHIBIT 11-B

COSTLESS COLLAR ILLUSTRATION

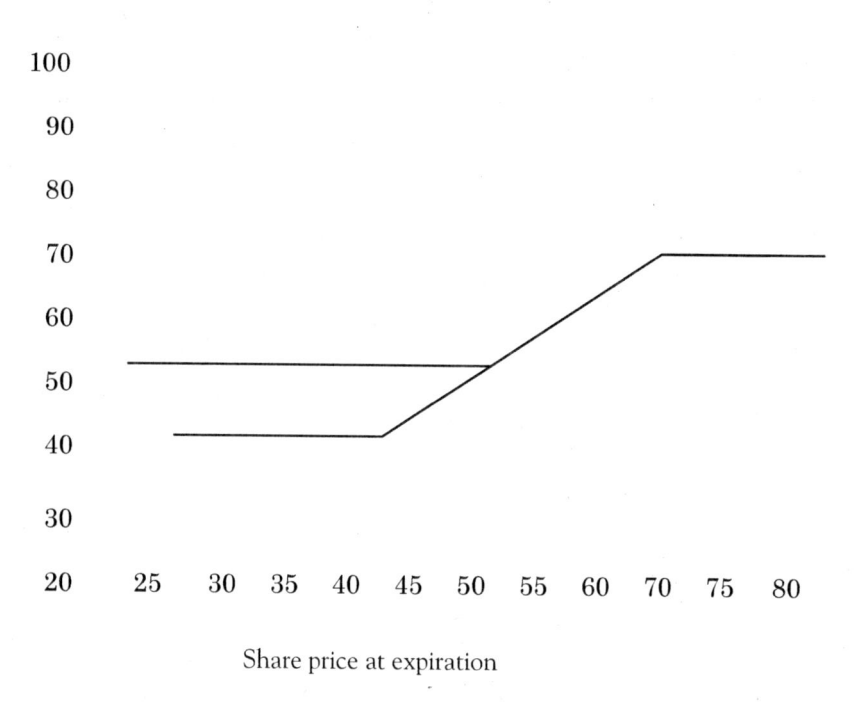

Share price at expiration

As you see, there are several different approaches to employ when trying to manage a concentrated position. Unless you are committed to sell a good part or all of the position at the start, you should always remain open to employing a range of strategies based on your objectives at the time. To help organize your approach, we have created a template consisting of several decision inputs. This is displayed in exhibit 11-C. We will now look at each of the inputs in this exhibit and suggest what strategies may work in each case. However, you always need to balance the range of decision factors as several could be important at any point in time.

EXHIBIT 11 – C

DIVERSIFICATION TEMPLATE

Decision inputs	Strategies
• Downside price risk • Upside price potential • Diversification • Tax deferral • Income / cash flow needs • Investment opportunities • Liquidity • Market perception • Charitable interests • Interest rate levels • Restricted Securities • Insider / affliliate • Age	• Sales • Private hedging • Hedging & monetization • Exchange funds • Charitable remainder trusts • NICRUT / NIMCRUT • Grantor retained annuity trusts • Charitable Lead trusts • Family limited partnerships integrated with trusts • 1 X 2 call spreads / GRAT

Downside Price Risk

If you want to protect the downside, you can always sell and you are then clear of that risk. However, if you wish to retain the stock, you can do a costless collar or just write a put option. The variable rate prepaid forward sale would also work.

Upside Price Potential

When you believe that the stock has decent upside potential, there are a couple of strategies to consider. First, this would be a good time to gift some of the stock to your heirs as they would presumably be getting the stock at a good value. Doing a GRAT or a CLAT may also work as you would be gifting the remainder interests at good values, leaving some room for upside appreciation. However, if you believe the stock is really undervalued, doing a 1x2 call spread may be appealing since you would be putting yourself in a position to leverage any expected upside.

Concentrated Equity Strategies

It may be useful to chart, in some way, the potential strategies based on your valuation of the stock. We attempt to do this in exhibit 11-D. The shaded areas show when each of the strategies would work.

Diversification

Where diversification is your key objective, several strategies can accomplish that, in addition to an outright sale and reinvestment. A collar plus loan, a prepaid forward as well as the exchange fund will accomplish some degree of diversification. However, each of these strategies is different and other inputs will need to be considered.

Tax Deferral

Both the prepaid forward and the exchange fund are designed to provide tax deferral. Also, to an extent, the charitable remainder trusts will provide tax deferral as well.

EXHIBIT 11-D

SINGLE STOCK STRATEGIES

Strategy/ Stock Valuation	Out-right Sale	1X2 Call Spread	PUT Option	Costless Collars	Var. Prpd. Forward Sale	Ex-change Fund	Charitable Remainder Trusts	NICRUT/ NIMCRUT	FLP with Trusts
Under-valued		▓						▓	▓
Slightly under-valued		▓					▓	▓	▓
Fairly Valued				▓			▓		▓
Slightly over-valued			▓	▓		▓			
Over-valued	▓		▓		▓	▓			

Income/Cash Flows

Where your stock pays little or no dividend, several of the strategies will improve cash flow and income. The prepaid forward will accomplish this but the GRAT and charitable remainder trust will as well, assuming you sell the stock within those structures.

Investment Opportunities

Sometimes you will want to engage in a strategy because you have a good investment opportunity elsewhere. A collar plus loan would be attractive if the loan is for business investment. A prepaid forward will always work as well. Naturally, you could just sell the stock.

Liquidity

Sales, collar plus loan and the prepaid forward will provide instant liquidity.

Market Perception

Part of you decision as to strategy will be influenced by the market outlook for the stock. Favorable outlooks will encourage you to engage in strategies that retain the stock in the family, such as the GRAT and family limited partnership gifting. Negative outlooks may encourage you to pursue sale or derivative strategies.

Charitable Interests

Where charitable interests drive the process, you have a range of options.

Interest Rate Levels

Interest rate levels and the outlook for rates can have an important influence on the appeal of some of the alternative strategies. For example, at low rates, the GRAT and the CLAT are very attractive due to the lower valuation of the remainder interests. To the extent that the portfolio beats the Federal rate used for valuation, that differential will go to the beneficiaries free of estate and gift tax. On the other hand, during higher rates, it may be more appealing to do the charitable remainder trust as the remainder interest would be valued at a higher rate. Therefore, the tax deduction will be higher.

Restricted Securities/Insider/Affiliate

There are several securities laws and regulations that govern these transactions. We will not go into detail on these as you should consult your legal counsel and in many cases, the corporate counsel where these rules apply. Some of the applicable rules are:

- **Rule 144** deals with the sale of restricted securities by affiliates and control persons, as well as by holders of unregistered stock. There are limitations on the amount of stock that can sometimes be sold and it is based on quarterly volumes, holding periods and methods of sale.
- **Section 10(b)(5)** deals with insider trading issues. Executives are able to take advantage of rule 10(b)(5)-1 plans whereby they can sell a predetermined number of shares in the market during window periods. The plans need to be fairly rigid and not modified. This way, the executive does not need to worry about any trades that occur during periods of important corporate events since the plan was put into place either before or after any meaningful public information.

- **Section 16-** This section deals with some reporting requirements as well as additional restrictions placed on insiders and significant shareholders. Section 16(a) requires shareholders with greater than 10 percent of a class of equity in a company to report those holdings as well as any trades in the stock. The rule covers not only shares held but also any options and derivatives. Section 16(b) prohibits insiders from buying and selling or selling and buying the company stock within any six-month period. Any profits must be disgorged. This is known as the "short-swing" rule. Section 16 (c) prohibits insiders from engaging in short sale transactions in the stock.
- **Section 13 (d)-** This rule requires holders of more than 5 percent of the common stock of a public company to disclose that to the public.

Age

Finally, age is also a factor in deciding what strategy fits. For example, younger people may not be able to use a charitable remainder trust because it may not qualify for the 10 percent remainder interest or 5 percent probability tests referred to earlier. However, many of the other estate planning techniques are attractive for transferring stock to the younger generation. Some older parents are sometimes more willing to fund foundations with significant assets than are younger folks who may not be certain about their future needs and lifestyle interests.

Stock Grants and Options

While of a different form, stock options and grants are also ways that individuals have concentrated wealth. The techniques for dealing with this type of asset can also be complicated and may, at times, require advice from tax counsel. I refer the reader to a comprehensive text on

Concentrated Equity Strategies

the subject, *Consider Your Option,* by Kaye A. Thomas. The author thoroughly covers the types of options and grants along with many of their tax implications. Accordingly, we will just raise some of the issues one faces when holding stock options and grants.

Stock Grants

Simply put, a stock grant is stock that a company gives to its associates without having them pay for it. Some call it restricted or founders stock. There are three parameters one has to deal with when receiving this type of stock:

- What happens if the stock is vested when you receive it?
- What happens if the stock is not vested when you receive it?
- What happens if the stock is not vested when you receive it, and you file a special capital gains tax election?

Stock is Vested

If your stock grant is vested immediately, you must report the benefit as ordinary income that year. The income is the market value of the stock, less any amount you had to pay for it. If you paid nothing for it, the total market price on the day received is considered as income. Then, if you hold the stock for more than one year, any further gain is treated as capital gains when sold. Your basis is the amount you paid for the stock plus any income you had to report.

Stock Is Not Vested

If the stock is not vested, you do not need to report any income until it becomes vested. Then the tax treatment is the same as outlined above. However, you will receive dividends on the stock even if it has not yet vested. The dividend will be considered as ordinary compensation income and will be taxed at ordinary rates, not the 15 percent rate.

Special Election

With stock grants that are not yet vested, you have the ability to file a Section 83b election, which enables you to treat the stock as having vested immediately. You would proceed to claim compensation income in the current tax year and pay the tax. Why would you do this? For a couple of reasons:

1. Your capital gain holding period begins on the date you file the election.
2. You expect the stock to increase, and possibly over the near term. This way, you begin the capital gain measuring period earlier.
3. Dividends are taxed at the 15 percent rate.

To obtain this election, you must file for it within 30 days after receiving the grants.

Stock Options

There are two types of stock options, non-qualified and incentive.

Non-Qualified Options

This is the most prevalent option type. They generally expire after ten years. You are taxed at ordinary rates when you exercise the options. If you elect to hold the stock after exercising it, your capital gain holding period begins then. One of the interesting things you can do with these options is to gift them if the plan allows that. Additionally, one of the ways to transact the gift could be through a GRAT. When doing so, you may want to set the parameters so that the gift element or the remainder interest is close to zero, so you have little or no gift tax liability. You would do this when you believe the stock will appreciate over the next year or two.

Incentive Stock Options

These options have certain parameters in term of qualified recipients. First, the option price must be 100 percent of the fair market value at the date of the grant. It needs to be 110 percent of the price if the recipient owns more than 10 percent of the outstanding stock of the firm. Second, the option period cannot exceed ten years or five years if the recipient owns more than 10 percent of the firm. Third, the value of the options that can vest in any year cannot exceed $100,000.

These options have some unique tax benefits, but also carry some significant complexities. Among the benefits is the possibility of capital gains treatment. If you hold your stock for a period of time that is greater than one year from exercising it or two years from the grant date, the entire gain is considered as long-term capital gains. Otherwise, it is ordinary income. On the other hand, the complexity comes in with the Alternative Minimum Tax. The spread between the exercise and market price is considered to be AMT income. You would report AMT income when you exercise the stock. If you exercise and hold the stock, you then begin the capital gains holding period. However, you then have two tax basis points. One is the basis for calculating the regular tax. The other is the AMT basis. The AMT basis is the regular basis adjusted by the AMT adjustment. It is possible that the AMT paid could later be recovered as a credit depending on your income tax situation in subsequent years.

When to Exercise Options

One of the tricky aspects of holding stock options is to decide when to exercise them as you will need to do so before expiration. We will not go into the required detail necessary to provide a thorough analysis of this important topic, but here are some concepts and processes to consider:

- You need to engage your financial advisor to run an analytical model for you that effectively values each of your options.
- Options have two basic value points. Their *intrinsic* value is simply the difference between the exercise price and the current market value. The *time value* is the valuation that incorporates the time left to expiration.
- A formula, called the Black–Scholes formula, has been developed to value options. The component factors going into this formula are: the current stock price, exercise price, interest rates, volatility factor (e.g. standard deviation of the stock price), time to expiration and dividend yield.
- Generally, the time value is highest when the exercise and market prices are equal. As the market price goes higher than the exercise price, the time value decreases. The time value could also be high if the market price is below the exercise price so long as there is considerable time to expiration.

EXHIBIT 11-E

LIQUIDITY STRATEGIES – SALES

Alternatives	Description	Advantages	Disadvantages	When to Employ
Outright Stock Sale	• Open market transaction. • Market or Spot Secondary offering • Block Sales	• Receive immediate liquidity. • Benefit of marketing effort by investment banker • Easy to execute. • Protected against price declines	• Taxable sale • May impact market and subject to discounts. • No future price appreciation in shares sold.	• When you believe stock is over-valued. • Need for immediate liquidity.

LIQUIDITY STRATEGIES – SALES

Alternatives	Description	Advantages	Disadvantages	When to Employ
Premium Sales	• Investors can sell a pre-determined number of shares over an extended period of time for a value above today's market price. • It is an amortizing structure whereby a percentage of the total shares are sold each trading day at the forward delivery price or returned to the investor. • Trade is executed so long as the stock price closes above a fixed level. If it closes below the fixed level, the daily shares are returned to the investor.	• Receive a premium over today's price. • Establishes a disciplined sales strategy over an extended period of time.	• No downside protection on shares returned. • No upside above premium price initially agreed upon.	• When investor believes the stock is slightly undervalued or fully valued with some upside potential but not much downside risk. • When investor seeks diversification over an extended time period.

LIQUIDITY STRATEGIES – DERIVATIVES

Alternatives	Description	Advantages	Disadvantages	When to Employ
1 X 2 Call Spread	• Involves the purchase of an in-the-money call option (low call strike price) offset by the sale of two out-of-the money call options (high call strike	• Investor is positioned to increase appreciation potential within a predetermined range. • Appreciation on	• No downside hedge. • Above the high call stock price, the investor does not participate in further appreciation. • Transaction	• When the investor believes the stock has moderate upside appreciation. • Investor is not that concerned about the downside. • Investor does not

	price). • The transaction is structured so that the premium received from the sale of the two out-of-the money options is equal to the premium paid on the purchase of the in-the-money option.	the stock holding will double up to the high call strike price as the investor receives appreciation on the stock holding plus the option. • Investor retains ownership and voting rights as well as the dividend. • Can settle in cash so as to defer selling the stock position.	requires the seller of the option to be able to borrow the stock and maintain a short position in the stock.	want to sell the position at this time.

LIQUIDITY STRATEGIES – HEDGING

Alternatives	Description	Advantages	Disadvantages	When to Employ
Purchase of a Protective Put Option	• Gives purchaser the right to sell the underlying stock at a predetermined price at some future date. • Generally able to purchase puts up to 5 times daily trading volume.	• Full downside protection on stock below Put Stock Price. • Ownership, dividends and voting rights maintained. • Investor retains full upside potential. • Cash settlement of option can defer sale of position.	• Out-of-pocket cost for option.	• When investor believes stock is overvalued and has significant downside risk.

LIQUIDITY STRATEGIES – HEDGING

Alternatives	Description	Advantages	Disadvantages	When to Employ
Costless Collar	• Purchase of a put option with a strike price at or below the current price, combined with the sale of a call option with a strike price above the current price. • Both have same maturity. • Premium from sale of call offsets purchase price of put. • Can collar up to 5 times daily volume. • Maturities range from 1 to 5 years.	• Full down-side protection below Put Stock Price. • Upside participa-tion to the Call Stock Price. • Retain voting rights and dividends. • Cash settlement defers sale of position. • No out-of-pocket expense. • Retention of voting rights and dividends.	• No upside beyond Call Stock Price. • Exposure to downside from current to Put Stock Price. • No liquidity generated unless a loan is obtained	• When you believe stock is slightly overvalued and wish to protect downside. • When you have a substantial overall position and want to protect a portion of it.

Concentrated Equity Strategies

Exchange Funds	• A limited partnership where participants contribute highly appreciated stock for a share of ownership. • Each fund has a predetermined termination date. • At least 20% of the fund to be in qualified, less liquid, investments such as preferred operating units of real estate operating partnerships (affiliated with publicly traded REIT's). Funds may borrow to purchase these investments or require some cash contribution from participants.	• Immediate diversification. • Tax deferral • At end of term, distributions can be in original stock or basket of portfolio stocks. No tax event until securities are sold. • Attractive estate planning tool due to valuation discounts and estate freeze options.	• Investment Performance risk. • Illiquidity as many will run 7 years. • Tax liability on early redemption. • No control over portfolio management process.	• Strong desire for diversification. • Tax deferral. • No need to monetize. • No great alternative investment opportunities. • Believe stock is fairly valued.

LIQUIDITY STRATEGIES – ESTATE PLANNING

Alternatives	Description	Advantages	Disadvantages	When to Employ
Grantor Retained Annuity Trust (GRAT)	• Grantor (investor) establishes an irrevocable trust and contributes assets to it. • Grantor receives an annuity for the term of the trust. • The remainder passes to another individual, usually children. • The present value of the remainder interest is a taxable gift. • Appreciation over the taxable gift amount passes to the remainder beneficiary, estate tax free. • If grantor dies before term expires, assets brought back to his or her estate.	• Attractive in low interest rate environment. • Can be funded with restricted stock. • Can be paid back with in-kind assets. • Grantor pays tax on income earned within GRAT.	• Must outlive the term of the GRAT or asset flows back to the estate. • If performance is less than the federal AFR, you paid gift taxes for nothing, unless it was a zeroed-out GRAT.	• When investor wishes to transfer property to children in a tax efficient way. • If investor believes the assets will appreciate at a rate greater than the Federal AFR at the time the GRAT was established. The Federal AFR is the rate used to value the growth of the trust and the expected remainder gift interest.

LIQUIDITY STRATEGIES – ESTATE PLANNING

Alternatives	Description	Advantages	Disadvantages	When to Employ
Minority Interest Grantor Retained Annuity Trust (MIGRAT)	• Combines a family limited partnership with a grantor retained annuity trust. • Limited partnership assets (discounted) are first transferred to a GRAT for a fixed number of years. • Investor then receives a fixed annual annuity for the term of the trust. The annuity can be in cash or kind (stock). • At expiration of the GRAT, the remaining assets pass to a designated beneficiary.	• Can be very tax efficient if stock rises • FLP units are at discount-ed values. • Grantor (investor) retains control over the FLP through its GP holding.	• If stock does not appreciate, no real benefit accrues. • Legal costs to set up. • Costs to maintain.	• As part of a wealth transfer plan • When investor believes stock is under-valued.

LIQUIDITY STRATEGIES – CHARITABLE

Alternatives	Description	Advantages	Disadvantages	When to Employ
Charitable Remainder Unitrust ("CRT")	• Irrev trust where grantor places appreciated assets. • At least 10% of initial property value must go to qualified charity upon the trust's termination. • Investor receives an annual payout at a fixed % of the fair market value of the trust. • Taxes are paid on this annual payout, based on the source of funds–income, capital gains or return of principal.	• Ability to diversify position without incurring an immediate taxable event. • Tax deduction on the present value of the charitable remainder interest. • Annual cash flow return. • Trust not taxed on sale of the assets or on income.	• Irrevocable transfer. • Legal costs to establish.	• Desire steady annual cash flow. • Believe stock is at least fully valued. • Want a diversified portfolio. • Desire income and estate tax benefits associated with this technique. • Philanthropic intent.

Concentrated Equity Strategies

LIQUIDITY STRATEGIES – CHARITABLE

Alternatives	Description	Advantages	Disadvantages	When to Employ
Net Income Make-Up Charitable Remainder Unitrust (NIMCRUT)	• Is an off-shoot of the CRT. • Investor receives the lesser of the stated unitrust % or the actual net income. • In the future, prior year shortfall can be made up to the extent that the present year income exceeds the unitrust %.	• Can place lower yielding assets into the trust at inception, sell the assets later and then reinvest to generate more income. • Other benefits same as for a CRT.	• Irrevocable transfer of assets. • Costs to establish and administer • May not successfully make up past income shortfalls.	• When investor wishes to retain part or all of the stock (or other assets) and then sell it in the future. • When current income needs are not great. • When you wish to contribute other assets such as real estate which may be sold in the future.

LIQUIDITY STRATEGIES – HEDGING & MONETIZATION

Alternative	Description	Advantages	Disadvantages	When to Employ
Variable Share Prepaid Forward Sale	• Here you sell stock forward, subject to a variable share delivery formula. • Counter-party sets a floor and cap price. • You receive upfront funds based on a % of floor price. • You then deliver stock at maturity, based on final price at expiration. • Final maturity ranges from 1 to 5 years. • A variation of the forward sale is a participating forward sale. Here the investor retains full upside potential on a limited number of shares, but the investor receives smaller upfront funds than with a standard transaction.	• Defer taxable sale. • Hedge downside exposure while retaining upside appreciation up to the Cap Price. With a participat-ing sale, upside participation is full on a % of the shares. • Ability to monetize well over 50% and investor faces no restriction on reinvesting the funds. • Retain voting rights and dividends. • Cash settlement can further defer sale of position.	• Limited participation above cap price. • Imbedded financing cost. • Investor exposed down to floor price. • Dividend increases paid to counterparty	• When you expect stock to continue to rise and you wish to retain some upside appreciation. • You wish to immediately diversify while deferring taxes.

12

Financial Governance

We are now ready to look at the process of family wealth governance. By this, we mean the legal structures through which you would manage your financial affairs. One has several options when structuring a family's financial holdings and it takes careful consideration of sometimes competing factors before arriving at a decision. To that end, we will examine the following:

- The role of trusts
- Family partnerships
- Asset protection trusts
- Family dynasty trusts
- Private trust companies
- Offshore trusts

The Role of Trusts

We have discussed the tax and estate savings that families can achieve through various trust forms. At the same time, there are some important non-tax benefits in using trusts, particularly trust established during your lifetime. Here are some advantages of managing some of your assets through a revocable living trust:

- The trustee can take over management of your assets in the event you are incapacitated.
- You can avoid or minimize probate expenses as everything would be handled through the trust.
- The trust could serve as the entity that receives some of your assets at death. In other words, you could have a pour over provision in your will to have your assets go to the trust.
- You can generally be the trustee

When establishing trusts, particularly those that will be managed after your death, one of your most important decisions will be the selection of trustees. A further decision is whether you will include corporate trustees. We will look at these issues below:

Factors When Selecting Individual Trustees

Where you select individuals to act as trustees, you may wish to consider the following:

- Technical skills in overseeing the legal and investment aspects of the trust. If you appoint a family member that does not have these skills, then you should at least appoint a co-trustee, such as your attorney, who will be able to deal effectively with those issues.
- Knowledge of the beneficiaries. At least one of the trustees should have good knowledge of the family and be able to deal with family issues that may arise.
- Limited conflict of interest. You may want to make sure there is no potential conflict of interest that the trustee could have. For

example, if your brother is named trustee and he is a stockbroker, there could be a tendency to run a lot of business through his firm. It may be in the best interests of the beneficiaries if the business is not with one firm.
- The term of the trust. If the trust is expected to last for a long time, you should provide for successor trustees, particularly if your first selection is older.

Should You Have A Corporate Trustee?

This has always been an age old question. The reasons against appointing a corporate trustee are that some have reputations for being inflexible and their services add an additional layer of fees, although you generally have to pay individual trustees today. Also, some trustees require you to use their proprietary products exclusively. There is another side to the discussion as there can be some good reasons to include a corporate trustee in your plans.

1. They have built-in successors. If your trust officer leaves the firm or retires, the company can appoint someone else. You do not need to go about finding a replacement as you would if an individual resigned.
2. They can do all of the reporting as they have systems well suited to keeping the appropriate records.
3. They know the tax laws and regulations and can keep the individual family members out of trouble.
4. They can serve as a buffer to prevent or dissuade other trustees or beneficiaries from suggesting and implementing ill-suited investments.
5. Many, today, have open architectures for handling investments. You do not need to just use the trustee's investment products.

Financial Governance

There are some compromise solutions to this issue:

- You can appoint a corporate trustee as the successor to an individual currently serving.
- You could engage the corporate trustee as a co-trustee.
- You could have a corporate trustee but also have a trust protector, who would monitor and evaluate the trustees and have the power to change them when appropriate. Generally, the trust protector would be able to remove the trustee quickly and without court approval.

Family Partnerships

Some families use the FLP or LLC structure to govern their financial holdings. This way, changes can be adopted more quickly than under a trust arrangement. An alternative is to use both. In this case, the family has the trust's own units in the family partnerships, but the investment decisions are then made and implemented through the partnerships.

Asset Protection Trusts

Throughout our discussion, we frequently pointed to the asset and creditor protection aspects of trusts and partnerships. While there are certainly features of these entities that can protect the assets, many investors still seek additional layers of protection. This became more popular as some states began to enact anti-creditor or asset protection legislation. The three states that have such laws are Delaware, Alaska and Nevada. As a result, individuals have established domestic asset protection trusts in these jurisdictions. Additionally, if you establish a dynasty trust in these jurisdictions and give the trustee the power to direct distributions, you further diminish the rights of the creditors.

Looking at Delaware as an example, there are a couple of benefits in locating a dynasty trust there:

- There is no state income tax on non-residents, so income can build up without being subject to state income taxes.
- There are also no personal property taxes.
- Delaware has eliminated its rule against perpetuities, meaning trusts can go on forever.

One must also be careful in believing that these trusts are foolproof. The asset protection legislation has not been severely tested yet. Also, there would unlikely be no protection against fraudulent conveyance.

Offshore Trusts

Some families have adopted the offshore trust as a haven for asset protection. They have also combined limited partnership structures with offshore trusts. For example, you could establish an FLP with a subchapter S corporation as its general partner. You then establish an offshore trust and either transfer or sell limited partnership interests to the trust. Another structural option is to establish an offshore corporation, which is then owned by a trust. The asset protection advantage is that it will be difficult to bring about litigation and enforce judgments in many foreign jurisdictions. There are many more details and regulations, but they are beyond the scope of this book. It is important to note that most trusts are grantor trusts, where all income is taxed to the U.S. individual.

Private Trust Companies

Some wealthy families will go the route of setting up their own trust companies to oversee and administer their family wealth. Today, there may be several dozen of these family trust companies but many more are probably considering it. A family might consider doing this for some of the following reasons:

- The family trusts may have very significant concentrations in the form of public equities or closely held company stock. Their current corporate trusts may not want the liability of holding these assets.
- Alternatively, family members may be the trustees and either do not want the continued liability or do not want to absorb the high cost of personal liability insurance.
- A trust company can afford the family the ability to establish pooled or collective family funds.
- The company may be attractive for distant relatives to join and thus defray some of the operating costs.
- It can provide the family with a form of governance and serve as the central entity from which to coordinate family financial activities as well as train the younger generation.

There are some issues when establishing a private trust company and one must consider those as well:

- It will cost money to operate, perhaps as much or more than you are now paying for financial services.
- You will likely need to have a minimum capital investment in most states.
- You would be subject to banking regulations and governmental audits.
- You will need insurance.

Generally, when families set up private trust companies, they will still outsource much of the custody and professional investment management so as to continue to avail themselves of the industry's top talent.

Included as exhibit 12-A is a template for visualizing the structure of a family trust complex. Like other documents contained in the book, it is offered as a sample to help you organize your records.

EXHIBIT 12-A

SMITH FAMILY ENTITIES

Trust – T/U/W Charles Smith
Term – 21 years after death of surviving child of Joseph Sr.
Dispositive Provisions – <u>As to income</u>: 1) Directly to Joseph Smith Sr. during lifetime. 2) After death, directly to trust for children. <u>As to principal</u>: 1) Children have testamentary powers of appointment among issue of Joseph Smith. 2) Failure to exercise power: outright to issue.
Tax Status – 1) Estate & generation skipping tax-free. 2) Children's trusts pay tax on ordinary income distributed to them. 3) Trust taxed on capital gains.
Fiduciaries - Current: Thomas Kline (attorney) and ABC Bank
Discretionary Powers of Trustees – Invade principal for health, welfare & education of beneficiaries.
Investment Objectives – 1) Long-term growth. 2) Trust must distribute all income and income is not currently an objective. Can be all equity portfolio.
3) Low yielding stocks and real estate are acceptable.

Trust – Trust for children Dated April 23, 1975
Term – 21 years after death of issue alive on 4/23/75.

Dispositive Provisions – 1) Income at discretion of trustees. 2) Testamentary power of appointment among issue of Joseph Smith. 3) If unexercised, outright to issue.

Tax Status – 1) Estate and generation skipping tax free. 2) Children pay tax on ordinary income distributed. 3) Trust taxed on accumulated income and on capital gains.

Fiduciaries - <u>Current:</u> Mrs. Joseph Smith <u>Successors:</u> ABC Bank and child for own trust.

Discretionary Powers of Trustees – 1) To accumulate or distribute income. 2) To invade principal for children

Investment Objectives – 1) Capital growth. 2) No need to distribute income currently. 3) Fixed income to be tax free.

Trust - Smith Grandchildren's Trusts. Separate trust for each grandchild. Additions can be specified for each person or if not specified, will be divided equally.

Term - For each grandchild, until he or she attains the age of 35 or at their death.

Dispositive Provisions - <u>As to income</u>: 1) Prior to age 21, income paid at discretion of trustees. 2) After age 21, all net income paid to beneficiary
<u>As to principal</u>: 1) When beneficiary attains age of 25, one third of principal is distributed. 2) When beneficiary attains age of 30, one half of existing balance is distributed. 3) When beneficiary attains the age of 35, remaining principal is distributed. 4) If beneficiary dies prior to age 35, trust terminates and distributes per child's will.

Tax Status – 1) Distributed income taxed to beneficiary. 2) Trust pays tax on accumulated income and capital gains. 3) Trust is part of grandchild's estate.

Fiduciaries – 1) Joseph Smith's children for each grandchild's trust. 2) If unable to serve, Joseph Smith may appoint additional trustees. 3) If no individual trustees appointed, ABC Bank is successor.

Discretionary Powers of Trustees – 1) Invade principal for child's health, education, support and maintenance 2) Broad discretionary powers for any other worthwhile purpose. 3) Spendthrift provision prevents an assignment of interest to another party. 4) Independent trustee has right to terminate trust if continuation is inadvisable for any reason.

Investment Objectives - Invest for growth. Fixed income invested based on marginal tax bracket of taxpayer.

Trust – Smith Family Descendants Irrevocable Trust

Term – Upon death of both Mr. & Mrs. Joseph Smith, Sr.

Dispositive Provisions – As to income and principal: 1) Trustees can pay principal and income to any of settler's descendants for health, education, maintenance and support. Upon death of Mr. & Mrs. Joseph Smith Sr. 1) Trustee distributes assets per power of appointment of surviving spouse.

2) Assets not distributed per power of appointment to be distributed to Smith Family Foundation.

Tax Status – 1) Income taxed to settlor 2) Property not part of settlor or settlers wife's estate.

Fiduciaries – 1) Mrs. Joseph Smith and Thomas Kline (attorney). 2) If both of above are unable to serve: ABC Bank.

Discretionary Powers of trustees: 1) Trustees may pay out equal or unequal amounts to any of the descendants. 2) The independent (non-family) trustee may terminate the trust.

Investment Objective – 1) No requirement to produce current income. 2) Assets can include real estate and private equity.

Trust - T/U/W Joseph Smith, Sr. fbo Mrs. Joseph Smith, Sr. (Marital trust to be funded at death of Joseph Smith, Sr.)

Term – Lifetime of Mrs. Joseph Smith

Financial Governance

Dispositive Provisions – As to income: 1) Mrs. Smith to receive all net income. As to principal: 1) Trustee to pay Mrs. Smith principal for health, maintenance and support. 2) Independent trustee is able to pay Mrs. Smith additional amounts for any other purpose. Upon Mrs. Smith's death: 1) Trustee to pay estate taxes caused by inclusion of Marital Trust in her estate. Mrs. Smith has power or appointment of principal balance.

Tax Status – 1) PR can exercise QTIP election. 2) Income taxed to Mrs. Smith. 3) Trust pays capital gains tax. 4) Property taxed in Mrs. Smith's estate. 5) Property can be allocated among GST exempt and non-exempt portions.

Fiduciaries – Current: Thomas Kline (attorney) and Mrs. Smith Successor to Thomas Kline: ABC Bank

Discretionary Powers of Trustees – 1) QTIP election. 2) Distribute funds to Mrs. Smith for non-health & support reasons.

Investment Objectives – Balance growth and income so that Mrs. Smith's income needs are met.

Trust - Charitable Lead Annuity Trust (funded at death of both Mr. & Mrs. Smith, Sr.

Term – Approx. 20 years

Dispositive Provisions – 1) At termination of CLAT, divided equally among children and issue. 2) Each child permitted to sell their remainder interest to the family dynasty trust. 3) Provide annuity to family's donor advised fund at community Foundation.

Tax Status – 1) Charitable estate tax deduction. 2) Each child's estate is taxed on remainder interest. 3) Sale of remainder interest to dynasty trust not a taxable event.

Fiduciaries – ABC Bank

Discretionary Powers of Trustees – Permit sale of remainder interest to family dynasty trust.

Investment Objectives – 1) Balance growth & income. 2) Target 70% equity and 30% fixed income.

Trust – Smith Family Delaware Trust
Term – In perpetuity
Dispositive Provisions – 1) Separate trusts established for each child and their issue. 2) Income to trust beneficiaries at trustees discretion. 3) Trustees can add charitable beneficiary until death of settlers.
Tax Status – 1) Estate and generation skipping tax free. 2) Settlors taxed on ordinary income and capital gains. 3) After death of settlers, trust pays tax on ordinary income not distributed and on capital gains.
Fiduciaries – Current: Children and Thomas Kline (attorney). Successor: Upon death or incapacity of all children, ABS Bank
Discretionary Powers of Trustees – 1) To accumulate or distribute income. 2) To invade principal. 3) Add charitable beneficiary until settlers death. 4) Can allow each child to sell their respective CLAT remainder interest to trust.
Investment Objectives – 1) Long term growth. 2) Alternative investments encouraged. 3) Income distribution not encouraged.

Trust – GRAT's children. Established September 1998
Term – 21 years after death of survivor of issue alive in September 1998
Dispositive Provisions – 1) Before 2008, fixed percentage annuity is paid to grantor, Joseph Smith, Sr. Income in excess of annuity can be distributed if available. 2) After 2008, separate trusts for each child with: a) All income distributed annually. b) Testamentary powers of appointment. c) Failure to exercise the power will result in outright distribution to issue.

Tax Status – 1) Estate tax free if grantor (Joseph Smith, Sr.) Outlives term. 2) Grantor pays tax on income before 2008; child pays tax on ordinary income after 2008. 3) Trust pays tax on capital gains. 4) Remainder interest is gift of future interest so is subject to gift tax.

Fiduciaries – <u>Current</u>: Mr. & Mrs. Joseph Smith <u>Successor</u>: ABC Bank

Discretionary Powers of Trustees _ 1) Invade principal for Beneficiaries. 2) Terminate trust.

Investment Objectives – 1) growth 2) Predominately invest in equities.

13

Establishing a Technology Plan

Despite the enormous advances in computer technology, finding a way to organize your investment reporting can be quite a task. While we cannot offer any silver bullet solution, we can offer you a framework for working through the issues. First, exhibit 13-A provides a template for organizing your approach. For example, when formulating the plan, you might want to consider these points:

1. How much detail do you need on investment performance?
2. Do you want a system that can consolidate across multiple custodians and brokers or do you want a single custodian?
3. How complex is you tax reporting?
4. Do you need to have complete balance sheet and income reporting? If you have a variety of debt, this may be necessary.
5. What is your budget and at what point is the value received for more detailed reporting not worth the incremental cost?
6. How much manual processing are you willing to absorb? Sometimes, it may be easier to still do things manually than to create difficult to maintain computer routines.

When building a technology base for your family office, we offer the template shown in Exhibit 13-B. Each of these components can have a meaningful impact on how your reporting structure is set up and how efficiently it will run. We will look at each one in turn.

EXHIBIT 13-A
ESTABLISHING A TECHNOLOGY PLAN

Objectives / Needs	Considerations	Solutions
• Investment positions	• Cost	• Aggregation
• Transaction sorting	• Willingness to pay	• Pool fund accounting
• Tax reporting	• Compatibility of systems	• General ledger systems
• Investment performance	• Complexity	• Performance measurement packages
• Performance analytics	• Information overload	
• Consolidate reporting	• Manual processes	
• Executive summaries	• Investing style	
• Integration		
• Funds transfer		
• Liquidity management		
• Balance sheet reporting		

Master Trust and Custody- Your decision on where to custody your assets will have a direct bearing on how easy it will be to get timely information and how customized your repots can be. If you custody all of your assets in one place and you choose a provider with a high degree of technology, you will find it convenient to get online, real time reporting. Also, you will have one source to tap when you need transaction histories. On the other hand, you may not always be able to custody all of your investments in one place. With some investment consulting platforms, you need to have the trading and securities settlement done on the host platform of the firm providing the investment program.

Performance Measurement- Sometimes you can acquire performance measurement services from your primary custodian, but generally you will rely on your primary investment consultant or advisor to prepare it. To effectively get this information, you will need to work out a process for transmitting data from all of the custodians to the performance measurement organization.

EXHIBIT 13-B

THE BUILDING BLOCKS OF TECHNOLOGY

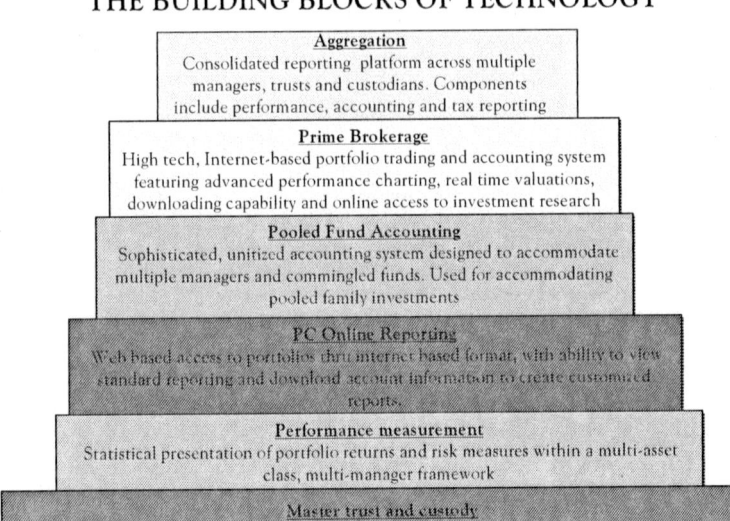

Aggregation
Consolidated reporting platform across multiple managers, trusts and custodians. Components include performance, accounting and tax reporting

Prime Brokerage
High tech, Internet-based portfolio trading and accounting system featuring advanced performance charting, real time valuations, downloading capability and online access to investment research

Pooled Fund Accounting
Sophisticated, unitized accounting system designed to accommodate multiple managers and commingled funds. Used for accommodating pooled family investments

PC Online Reporting
Web based access to portfolios thru internet based format, with ability to view standard reporting and download account information to create customized reports.

Performance measurement
Statistical presentation of portfolio returns and risk measures within a multi-asset class, multi-manager framework

Master trust and custody
Asset safekeeping, reporting and transaction processing

On-Line Access- Most custodians now have direct online access to your portfolios. You will want to make sure that the securities pricing is at least from the night before and that you have some downloading capability so that you can create some customized reports. Many of the better systems will enable you to view securities positions across managers, gain a snapshot of the asset allocation, view year-to-date capital gains/losses and see your transaction histories back to a certain date.

Unitized Accounting- Sungard Systems provides, through its subscriber bank and trust companies, a unitized portfolio accounting system. This enables clients to establish pooled funds that can combine family funds from various trusts, partnerships and other portfolios into common vehicles for investing. It is like setting up family mutual funds. Other systems of interest to family offices are partnership accounting systems that can feed into general ledger systems. Sungard, as well as a firm called SS&C, provide such programs. Another well-recognized general ledger package is Microsoft's Solomon Great Plains System.

Prime Brokerage- In an early chapter, we spoke about the role of prime brokers. One of their trademarks is a very sophisticated, internet-based reporting platform that features performance measurement, real time valuations, access to investment research, and downloading capabilities.

Aggregation- Suppose you have to work through multiple custodial and brokerage systems and have no feasible way to get a consolidated statement across all of the platforms. Through such firms as Advent Software, you can obtain a reporting structure that can aggregate all of the portfolio information from each of the custodians and brokers. Producing this report does not require that you have all of your assets custodied in one central place.

Much still needs to be developed in the field of consolidated investment portfolio reporting. Moreover, we still need to develop advances in getting systems to import and export data more efficiently. Nevertheless, we have seen some positive advances over the past few years.

14

The Family's 100-Year Plan

A hundred years is a long time. It is especially long in an age of the Internet, cell phones and Blackberrys. Society is also very much focused on instant results. Nevertheless, planning for the next 100 years is one of the most critical tasks a family faces today. With this 100-year plan, a family sets in motion a culture and philosophy that can guide future generations to perpetuate the family's financial and intellectual capital. To a great extent, the 100-year plan can help family members better understand how and why their parents and grandparents arrived at some of these decisions on the disposition of their wealth:

- The distribution of wealth between family and charity, and the distribution among family members.
- When both family members and charitable organizations will receive their designated funds.
- The form in which each will receive their funds.
- How any trust and charitable entities will be governed

The best way to illustrate a 100-year plan is to show an example and we did that in a sample document at the end of this chapter. At the same time, we will discuss some of the background thinking that goes into constructing a document of this nature. Accordingly, consider these key concepts:

1. **The Real Levels of Investments-**When looking at the ways families invest, one should look at it in three levels:

    - *Investments in Assets* through the traditional allocation of wealth into a range of financial asset classes, real property, private businesses, real assets and collectibles.
    - *Investments in Community*, through charitable giving, charitable trusts and a private family foundation.
    - *Investments in Family*, by using wealth to support family members in their business and personal endeavors. The objective here is to not only look at wealth in financial terms. Instead, it is also important to use your wealth to build a family "intellect" and to enable its members to contribute to each other and to the greater community. A wealthy family is not just one that has a substantial amount of money or real property. A wealthy family is also one that has produced leading doctors, social workers, professors, schoolteachers, musicians and scientists. Sometimes it is the availability of family wealth that may encourage or enable a member to pursue a profession that is very worthwhile but may not pay much.

2. **The Founders Attitude Toward Wealth-**Perhaps one of the key attributes of the document is how the founding patriarch and matriarch view their family's wealth and how they would like to see it employed over the generations. They will usually speak about how they would like future generations to be entrepreneurial, and how they would not want money to divide the family. They will also discuss the importance of education

and the importance of work over consumption. Most family leaders will also express their desire to see future heirs become leaders in their communities and perpetuate the family's good name.

3. **Managing Risks-**Most plans will deal with the issue of risks, as the overriding concern of most families is the loss of their wealth. Risk is present in different ways, depending on the specific family. This is where you address the issue of equity concentrations. In particular, you would convey your attitude toward retaining significant positions and diversifying away from those concentrations. Additionally, you may discuss the range of asset classes you believe the family should invest in along with the way they should handle risk in those asset classes. Another risk area you may comment on is the role insurance should play in protecting family wealth.

4. **The Family Business-**Where a family business still exists, it becomes an important part of this plan, with the following issues generally covered:

    - Desire to see the company always retained in the family, or a willingness to see it positioned to sell at an opportune time.
    - Guidelines for selling the stock, particularly to non-family members.
    - The allocation of stock among family members, particularly where some family members are not involved with the company.
    - The makeup of the board of directors, among family members as well as among family and non-family.
    - Succession plans.

5. **The Role of Philanthropy**-Nearly all wealthy families give something back to the communities where they made their fortunes. Accordingly, a 100-year plan will undoubtedly address how the founder would like to see the family spend its charitable dollars. In this section, you will likely see some of these issues covered:

- The extent of the estate going to charity.
- The preferred charitable structure, such as charitable remainder or lead trusts, donor advised funds at a community foundation or a private family foundation.
- If a private foundation is a chosen option, you may comment on the preferred governance structure including the makeup of the board of directors. You will also specify the role each of your children should play in the foundation. Some families allow each child to designate a portion of the charitable beneficiaries while others want each child to have a seat on the board and to act collectively. Finally, you would certainly comment on the foundation's mission.

6. **Wealth Transfer**-At the heart of the 100-year plan is how the family's wealth will be subsequently transferred to succeeding generations. This answers the questions of who, how much and when. There are a range of issues but here are some of the most prevalent ones:

- Who the specific heirs are
- How much is transferred at death and how much during lifetime
- The lifetime gifting strategy
- Dealing with disabled or elderly family members

- Attitude toward minimizing estate taxes versus retaining ownership and control of assets
- The use of trusts, including a family dynasty trust
- If trusts are established, should they be "pot" trusts or individual trusts
- The principal distribution guidelines for each trust
- Trust termination provisions
- Who the trustees should be. Also, should there be a corporate trustee
- The process for replacing trustees
- The need for a trust "protector"
- How advisors should be evaluated

7. **The Family Bank**-Critical to the process of expanding the family wealth is to create and implement a process for funding business and entrepreneurial opportunities. Even though an individual may be part of a wealthy family, that does not insure that any commercial bank will finance a business venture that he or she will present to it. Accordingly, the concept of a "Family Bank" may resonate well with certain family leaders. Here is how it works. Structurally, you do not need to form an actual bank. Instead, it could operate within the context of a revocable trust, limited liability company, or ultimately, a family dynasty trust. The dynasty trust could last in perpetuity and could engage in some of the following activities:

- *Investment Capital-* Here you provide equity capital for a family member's business. This would be an investment that is converted back to cash upon sale or redemption. You would generally invest alongside family members.
- *Loans-* Here you actually lend funds to family members, requiring many of the same conditions as do commercial

banks. You would expect the funds to be paid back so the family bank could re-lend capital to someone else. The idea is to have a perpetual source of debt capital for family members, encouraging them to seek out productive investment opportunities. This concept is patterned after the model introduced by the Rothchilds a couple of centuries ago.

- *Loan Guarantees-* Instead of directly lending money, you could offer loan guarantees to a commercial bank that would grant a loan to a family member. The idea is to encourage family members to deal directly with financial institutions and be on the line to service the debt.
- *Real Estate Partnerships-* This is a common investment for families and having a family bank invest alongside family members would be an appropriate activity. Also, as real estate has proven to be a productive investment over the long term, this is a prudent deployment of capital to earn higher returns.
- *Social Ventures-* Earlier, we discussed the importance of using some of the family's wealth to support its members in the pursuit of their life's work or interests. In some cases, a family member may wish to devote his or her livelihood to social-like ventures. Examples could include the purchase of a summer camp, day care center or a theatre. While these may not be great moneymakers, they could enable the particular family member to develop an important niche in his or her life. At the same time, they help to build the family's legacy in the community and add to the family's "intellect."
- *Education-* While this would be an outright distribution, one can view it as a long-term investment in the "family." This is always a productive way to give money

to the next generations. Education should also be looked at beyond the college degrees. Encouraging and supporting family members to attend seminars and specialized training is also productive. This expenditure could even be extended to include such activities as musical instruments and instruction and overseas study for grandchildren.

8. **Philanthropy**-Allocating wealth between family and community is always a tough decision. As expressed earlier, there are several ways to transfer wealth to charities, educational institutions and health care facilities. Some of these techniques may also actually facilitate the wealth transfer plans to your heirs. For example, you could establish a private family foundation now and fund it over a number of years. One funding mechanism could be a charitable lead trust where annual payments go to the foundation with the remainder going to your heirs. It is generally attractive to set these up during periods of low interest rates since the value of the remainder interest (which, in turn, determines the gift value) would be lower than in periods of higher rates. You may also elect to fund your foundation through various testamentary provisions under your will. This funding could be outright or via charitable remainder trusts. This again provides for your heirs as well as your foundation. Nevertheless, regardless of your preferred funding mechanism, you may want to address the governance of this entity within the context of a 100-year plan. To this end, there are a couple of governance alternatives you may want to consider:

- You could adopt the traditional approach where your children would be board members and can therefore oversee the distribution of grants.

- You could also broaden their direct involvement by enabling each child to nominate grantees up to a certain amount.
- Alternatively, you could actually establish separate charitable pools for each child's family group, giving that group discretion over the grants. There could also be a common pool where all members participate as directors. When families adopt this format, they sometimes establish a family advisory board consisting of family members, professional advisors and community leaders. The purpose of the Board is to insure that all grants and operations are compliant with tax regulations and the foundation's bylaws.

9. **Challenge Trusts-** With some families, the concept of incentive trusts is popular. Here you would have the family trust match the earnings of children. It could work along the following lines:

- The trust matches the earnings of each designated family member on the basis of $1 per $1 earned up to a maximum of, for example, $100,000.
- To further help family members who want to pursue very worthy but lower paid professions such as teaching, you could offer $2 per $1 earned with the same maximum dollar figure of $100,000. This way, each child could get the same maximum but those who make less money could get their match faster and at a lower threshold.

Results

To summarize, a family may craft a 100-year plan, or something like it, in an effort to articulate some of the following thoughts:

- Encourage business enterprise within the family
- Perpetuate a family culture of "doing and accomplishing things"
- Encourage "work" over "consumption"
- Promote philanthropy and active community involvement
- Continually build the family "intellect." This would happen as a result of encouraging both business as well as social type investments. You ultimately end up with a family that offers society a number of talents and where the members are also in a unique position to support each other.

Example

Next is a sample of what a 100 year plan document may look like. There is generally no set format as it will largely depend on the style of the family when it comes to documenting its governance policies.

GEORGE AND BARBARA SMITH
FAMILY WEALTH PHILOSOPHY
THE 100-YEAR PLAN

OVERVIEW & PURPOSE

Realizing that times and circumstances will change many times over the next 100 years or so, we nevertheless believe it would be useful to share our views and provide guidance on how future generations might manage the family's wealth. We are leaving our children and their successor heirs with the daunting task of stewardship over a large, extend financial and business fortune. Our four children have taken advantage of the many educational opportunities we provided to them. We have trained two of our children to handle various aspects of our business and investments. Our daughter has become a leader in the philanthropic community in her role as president of our family foundation. Our youngest son, a doctor, has now been overseas for nearly 12 years, helping AIDS victims and war refugees in Africa. We intend to spare no effort in preparing our children, and perhaps some of our grandchildren, to become proper stewards of the family wealth.

HOW WE SHOULD USE OUR WEALTH

Managing our wealth is more than how we select investment managers, buy a shopping center or find a glamorous hedge fund. Our heirs should approach wealth management by first focusing on its three overarching levels:

> A) Investment in Assets – Naturally, we want our heirs to be good investors and entrepreneurs. Accordingly, investing productively is essential to maintain future lifestyles and to capitalize on business opportunities. These investments cover financial assets,

real estate and private businesses. We encourage our heirs to be sound risk takers but to also be highly disciplined investors.

B) Investment in Community – We want future generations to perpetuate our charitable giving culture, whether they do it through our family foundation, charitable trusts or direct giving. More importantly, we want our heirs to make effective "charitable investments," selecting worthwhile causes and programs while demanding results.

C) Investment in Family – We would like to see our wealth employed productively to support family members in their business and personal endeavors. The objective here is to not only build family financial wealth but to continually expand its "intellect" and to enable its members to contribute to each other and to the greater community. We would like to see a future family filled with social workers, doctors, clergy, teachers, entrepreneurs, business executives and engineers. Our family's wealth should always be deployed in ways to perpetuate a culture of accomplishment.

GUIDING PRINCIPLES

As parents and grandparents, our greatest wish for our children and grandchildren is to become happy, healthy productive members of our society. This goal is a significant aspect of our intended wealth transfer plan. Before discussing our wealth transfer plans, let us offer some guiding principles on inheritance and the role it should play in the lives of our children and their heirs:

1. For the most part, we intend to divide equally among our children that portion of our wealth that passes to them. This is the only way to promote equality and fairness.
2. We do not want our family to be wanting of basic family needs, but we also never want money to be a corrupting influence. More

importantly, we never want to see money become the focus of conflict among family members.
3. Wealth should be used to give future generations the means to become successful in whatever they choose to do, and should never be looked as a reason not to work.
4. We hope that future generations will look for ways to rejuvenate the family wealth through the creation of new businesses that result in new fortunes.
5. It is important that family members be encouraged to establish their own identities. We do not believe everyone needs to be in business and family members should not be judged by how much money they earn.
6. We encourage social enterprises and ventures where family members have an interest.
7. Use our family's wealth to do as much as possible to maintain a family culture and its values. For example, we want our heirs to always favor "work" and "savings" over "consumption." Our wealth should not be used to support generations of "trust beneficiaries."
8. Finally, we hope that individual family units remain strong. Hopefully our wealth will enable current and future parents to devote adequate time to care for children and support their activities. Parents should make the time to attend their children's sporting events, dance recitals and concerts.

ROLE OF EDUCATION

A core operating philosophy of our family must always be able to encourage education and learning. We will be making adequate provisions in our trusts to insure that funds are available for college education for all of our heirs.

While a traditional college education is certainly the core learning mode, we also encourage future trustees to approve funds for a range of specialized education and training programs. For example, if a family member wants to learn carpentry, photography or culinary science, we should look favorably on it and provide funds. Many of these non-traditional programs will just require the good judgment of the trustees but they should be guided by the principal that education is not strictly confined to degrees at colleges and universities.

Financial education, in whatever form appropriate, should be a focus of all future generations. We must be a family that remains informed and educated on financial and investment matters. While we may hire external professionals to actually manage some of our assets, it is incumbent upon us to understand what they are doing.

FINANCIAL OBJECTIVES

We are a family that likes to set goals. Moreover, we sometimes establish stretch goals and enjoy striving to achieve them. In the financial area, goals are especially important so we would like to share our philosophy on establishing and managing to achieve them.

- A) **Investment Performance**
  Performance goals are much more than just beating the S&P 500 or Dow Jones. There are many factors to consider before establishing performance expectations. We will first discuss these factors:

  - How much income or cash flow does the family and its individual members need and want?
  - What is the level of "lifestyle" that we would like to maintain? This includes homes, watercraft, aircraft, etc.

- How much do we expect or need the "corpus" of our asset base to grow, net of outflows, keeping in mind the already significant reductions for taxes, management fees and living expenses.
- How do we project the family to grow over the next 10, 25 and 50 years? Will this growth outstrip our ability to generate net returns after distributions?

Accordingly we offer our heirs the following thoughts on setting performance goals:

- Keep overall distributions to less than 3 percent per annum.

  Strive for a net total return from all investments of 5 to 8 percent. This range is after taxes and management fees. Management fees include all services related to achieving investment results, including but not limited to, investment managers, attorneys, accountants and any family office staff.

  Equity and fixed income managers should collectively outperform market and peer group benchmarks over a market cycle. We encourage our overseers to not just chase the top performers in each asset class, but to include out-of-favor asset classes and managers where appropriate.
- Judiciously employ absolute return and other hedge fund strategies in an effort to diversify the portfolio and achieve the absolute target returns referred to earlier.
- Real estate and private equity are part of our family business and we will address them later.

B) **Use of Debt**

Needless to say, we would never want our family members to live beyond their means and incur debt to do so. On the other hand, debt can be a useful tool in managing family wealth and we encourage our advisors to employ it in the right circumstances. Here are some examples:

- Take advantage of the current mortgage interest deduction allowed on primary residences. During periods of low interest rates, it may be prudent to borrow and invest our capital.
- If investment opportunities should arise and it is not a good time to liquidate existing portfolio investments, borrowing against the portfolio may be wise so long as the investment opportunity is not speculative.
- Maintaining a line of credit for temporary cash flow needs, such as estimated tax payments, can be sound financial management so long as you have near term cash inflows to extinguish the debt.

C) **Managing Personal & Family Risks**

The family has always believed in the judicious deployment of insurance to transfer certain personal, family and business risks. In particular, we encourage future generations to properly evaluate the need for life insurance to cover estate taxes and to provide for buyouts in buy/sell agreements. We also encourage our heirs to properly insure tangible family assets, in particular, our valuable collections.

D) **Managing Equity Concentrations**

The family has equity concentrations in two forms. First, we still retain a substantial position in ABC Manufacturing Company, which we received for the sale of our family enterprise. We also retain positions in three New York Stock Exchange companies which my father accumulated over the year. Our investment posture toward these concentrated positions is as follows:

- In general, we strongly encourage the family to diversify away from each position over time, much as we have done to date.
- We have no allegiance to any of our concentrated positions. If we are completely liquidated of each holding in ten years, we will be fine with that.
- We have employed a range of strategies to diversify away our positions, including estate planning and charitable techniques as well as financial hedging programs. We will continue to add additional programs at opportune times.
- In addition to the above strategies, we invested in a separately managed index portfolio for some of our core equity funds. In certain years, we will have our managers sell positions with losses and offset them with sales of the concentrated stocks.

E) **Entrepreneurial Investments**

Key to the future viability of our family's financial empire will be the creation of new sources of entrepreneurial wealth. Later, we will cover how we hope to encourage continued wealth creation.

As we mentioned in the introduction, investing does not just include financial assets. It should also cover investing in human or family assets. Accordingly, we encourage using family wealth to also support social enterprises favored by family members. These could include investing, for example, in day care centers, summer camps or other areas of interest that a family member may have.

SOCIAL RESPONSIBILITY

We currently have a $50 million family foundation and we expect to fund it with an additional $50 million over time and at our deaths. We have established the following governance structure for the foundation, but the board of directors may alter it as circumstances change:

- The foundation board of directors consists of light members including:
    - George Smith (Chairman)
    - Barbara Smith (Vice Chair)
    - Sally Smith (President)
    - Thomas Smith
    - Daniel Smith
    - Harry Smith
    - Charles Perkins (Legal Counsel)
    - Fred Watts (CPA)
- Each of our children, via their Will, should name a successor to their board position. The foundation bylaws require that each family member must name a direct heir or the remaining family members shall elect a family member in his/her place.
- The attorney and CPA positions represent community board positions. The bylaws only specify that the existing board shall nominate and elect at least two non-family board members.

The foundation's mission is broad by design. We always want its board of directors to be able to adapt to the needs of the community. Regarding community needs, we have mandated that 75 percent of the grants must be within the metropolitan area of our home city. The "home city" definition includes cities where each of the family board members reside.

There is a 10 percent carve out for each family board member. This means that each child board member may designate up to 10 percent of the total grants (to a combined 40 percent)

In addition to employing a family foundation to support the community, we will also support it through the career choices of our family members. We will describe this program more fully in the last section on wealth transfer.

FAMILY BUSINESS

Our family presently owns and operates a real estate business consisting of residential apartments, shopping centers, suburban office buildings and resort properties. We also have a controlling interest in two operating businesses. Attached to this statement is a chart delineating the companies and the entities that own them. Regarding the ownership of our business, we and our four children and grandchildren are the shareholders. Everyone participates in the ownership through their interest in the various partnerships and trusts. Additionally, our two sons (Daniel and Thomas) who work in the business, along with Barbara and I, own units directly in the businesses. We believe that family members who work directly in the business should have some direct ownership in addition to their beneficial ownership through trusts.

To govern the family business ventures we have established a family board of directors. The board is essentially a holding company board which oversees all of the family businesses.

The present directors include:

- George Smith (Chairman)
- Barbara Smith
- Thomas Smith (President of Smith Family Investment, LTD)

- Daniel Smith
- Charles Perkins (Counsel)
- John Friedman (EVP of Smith Family Investments, LTD)
- Charles Jones (CEO of local company)
- Brandon Watkins (Retired real estate broker)
- Susan Fallston (President of local college)

We will not mandate any future board composition but do have these thoughts on board composition and their responsibilities

- We would like to see active family involvement but do not believe that all family members need to be represented. We favor including only those who are actively engaged in operating the business.
- We encourage including non-family board members. In particular, we should always try to have some local business executives and community leaders on our board of directors.
- We encourage the board to always challenge management to perform while at the same time insure that the companies practice fiscal soundness and always play by the rules.

Retention of Business

Our partnership agreements do not permit the transfer of ownership units to non-family members and there are certain restrictions on the transfer of stock held independently. While we permit non-family members to hold stock ownership interests and even encourage it for senior non-family managers, we would always want the family to maintain controlling ownership.

While we hope that the family will always maintain a business of some kind, we realize that opportunities could develop where it is in our best interest to sell. We would not be against that action.

Family Succession Plans

While we would like to see the family retain ownership control, we do not feel the same way with management responsibilities. The shareholders elect the board and the board will select the executive team. We are perfectly fine if, someday, our board selects a chief executive from outside the ranks of the family. It is more important that the business thrives and prospers than to keep family members employed. We look at the family business as we do any another investment. We should have the most qualified executives run the company, whether family members or not.

WEALTH TRANSFER

We have given careful consideration into how we should transfer our estate. Among the issues we considered are who will receive our estate and when will they receive it? Also, how would it be received–outright, in trust or through a foundation? Furthermore, for what purposes can the recipient or beneficiary use it and who will have the responsibility to manage the disposition of our estate and its subsequent assets? Here are the important elements of our wealth transfer plan:

Wealth Recipients

Globally, we intend to leave our wealth as follows:

To our children:	70%
To our grandchildren:	10%
To charity:	20%
Total	100%

Timing

We have already transferred significant amounts of our wealth to our children and grandchildren and will continue to do so over the years. We have also established a family foundation with significant funding. Going forward, we plan to continue gifting units of our family limited partnership and will establish additional GRATs and CLATs as appropriate. However, a significant part of our estate will still pass at the second death of Barbara and George.

Many years ago, we established separate trusts for our children and grandchildren. We intended to have these trusts terminate at some point in the future when each child attained a specified age. The following distribution schedule pertains to both the children and grandchildren's trusts:

- 33% of the trust value at age 35
- 50% of the then trust value at age 45
- The remaining value at age 55

Family Limited Partnership / Limited Liability Company

We established FLPs and LLCs as the core governing structure for our wealth. Much of our wealth transfer will occur via the gifting of units in these entities. To insure that we comply with the spirit as well as the letter of the tax law, we have included real estate and private business interests in these entities. This way, no one can challenge their business purpose.

Grantor Retained Annuity Trusts

We also established a series of GRATs which, in turn, own units of our family limited partnerships. This enables us to get a further discount when gifting our wealth. The GRAT is also employed to transfer down our large stock concentrations. Our intent with the GRATs is to structure them so that little remainder interest is left at inception.

Charitable Lead Annuity Trusts

At opportune times in the market, we have established CLATs to move funds to our foundation and at the same time to position the remainder interest for transfer to our children. We have particularly taken advantage of low interest rates and favorable prospects for some of our concentrated stocks when establishing CLATs.

Family Dynasty Trust

Several years ago we established a Delaware Dynasty trust. With this trust, we hope to provide our family with the means to perpetuate its wealth for generations to come

A key activity of this trust is to therefore serve as a "Family Bank," where we can leverage our wealth to facilitate business opportunities for our heirs. In many instances, family members would not be able to obtain commercial loans for these purposes and if they could, it may not be on very favorable terms. As a result, obtaining a loan or capital from the family may be the only way a member can take advantage of an opportunity and make it work.

We envision our family bank would engage in the following activities:

1) **Provide Direct Investment Capital** – Our family bank will directly invest in projects with the expectation that if the investment is successful and ultimately sold, the family bank's share would revert back to the "bank" so that we have capital to re-invest in other enterprises.

2) **Directly Lend Funds** – Our bank would lend money to family members with the expectation it will be paid back and re-lent to others.

3) **Guarantee Loans** – Our family bank could also provide guarantees so that family members can obtain traditional bank credit. There is an advantage in having family members go through the formal process of applying for, servicing and then repaying a commercial loan.

4) **Create Investment Partnerships** – A common way to encourage family members to invest together is to have our family bank invest alongside with them. We would expect our family bank to provide funding for real estate deals as well as other partnership ventures.

5) **Invest in Social Enterprises** – We specifically want our family bank to invest in or provide credit for social ventures. For example, we should support family members if they want to buy and operate a summer camp, a theatre or a day care center. Profit shouldn't be the only motive in these cases. Instead we want to be in a position to support a family member's mission in life so long as there is a reasonable chance the invested capital can be recovered in the future.

The family dynasty trust is also mandated to fund the flowing activities:

1) **Invest in Education** – If no other trust or funds are available, the family bank (through the dynasty trust) should provide monies for education.

2) **Fund Challenge Trusts** – To demonstrate our commitment to "work and accomplishment," we have provided for challenge grants to our grandchildren and their direct heirs after our passing. The terms of these challenge grants are as follows:
   - The dynasty trust will match the earnings of our direct heirs (beginning with our grandchildren) on the basis of $1 per $1 earned, up to maximum of $100,000.
   - To support our heirs who wish to pursue lower paid but socially-noble professions, the trust will pay $2 per $1 earned up to a total payment of $100,000. The professions that qualify include but are not limited to the following:
     - Public and private school teaching
     - Social worker
     - Peace corps or similar position
     - Working for non-profit organizations that serve hunger, homelessness and medical causes.

We will leave it to our trustees and trust protector to establish the ground rules for the acceptable professions so as to accomplish our intent.

Life Insurance

We are employing life insurance primarily to help our children cover estate taxes on assets that we have not transferred prior to our deaths. To accomplish this in a tax efficient manner, we established an irrevocable life insurance trust to own the policy. We purchased a survivor–life (or second-to-die) policy for this purpose.

Governance

To oversee our trusts after our deaths, we have put in place the following structure:

- First, the executor of our estate will be our attorney, Charles Perkins and the Main Street Trust Company.
- Each of our trusts will have a designated family trustee along with a corporate trustee. We believe that a corporate trustee can add balance to the decision-making required in trusts today.
- Additionally, we are adding an additional layer of governance with an overall trust protector. Our trust protector's role is to oversee the governance of all of our trusts and to regularly evaluate the performance of the trustees. The trust protector has the power to remove any of the trustees and to select a successor in accordance with the provisions of the respective trust. The trust protector is appointed by and can be removed by a majority of the adult current income and adult remainder beneficiaries of each trust. Our family's legal counsel at the second death of George and Barbara will be the first trust protector.

Tax Policy

Even though we are patriotic citizens, we, like most families, want to minimize the taxes we pay. However, our wealth transfer plan will efficiently balance tax mitigation with control of assets. We do not intend to transfer all of our assets just to reduce taxes. Moreover, it has always been our family philosophy to play by the rules and we will not engage in strategies that test the limits of the tax regulations.

George and Barbara Smith
September 30, 2004

SMITH FAMILY BUSINESS STRUCTURE

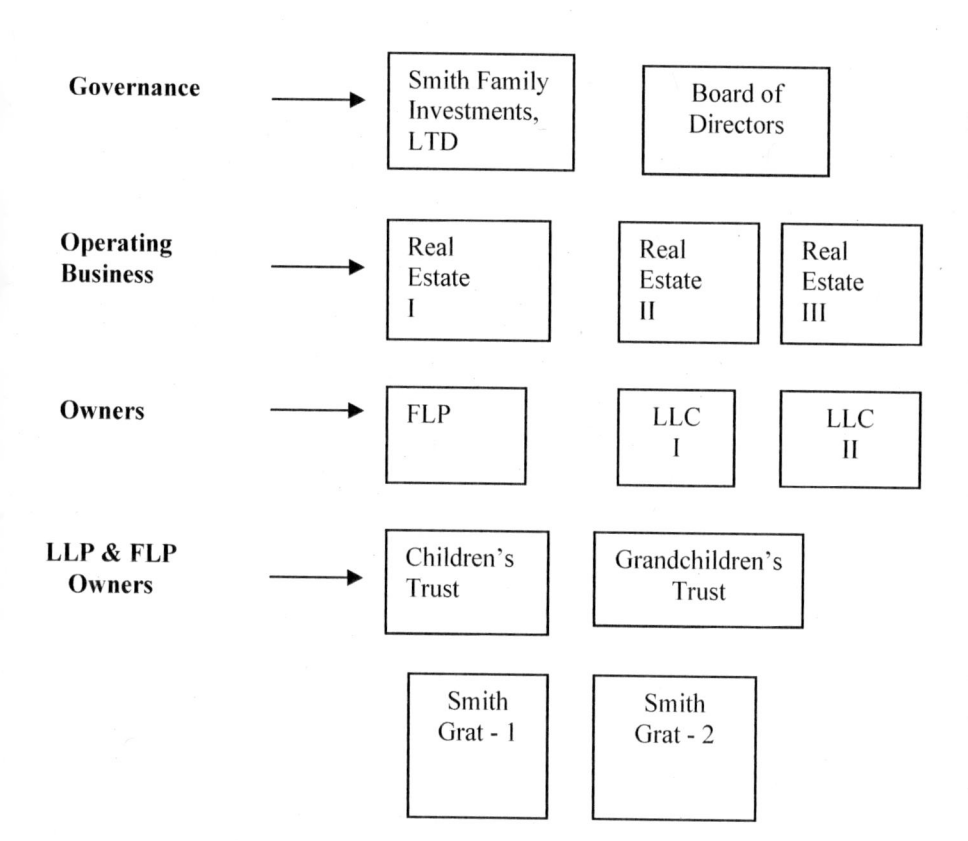

Governance → Smith Family Investments, LTD | Board of Directors

Operating Business → Real Estate I | Real Estate II | Real Estate III

Owners → FLP | LLC I | LLC II

LLP & FLP Owners → Children's Trust | Grandchildren's Trust

Smith Grat - 1 | Smith Grat - 2

Bibliography

Adams, Roy M. Contemporary Estate Planning: A Definitive Guide to Planning and Practice. New York: Cannon Financial Institute, Inc, 2000.

Anderson, Brett. "Making Meaning of Wealth Across Generations." Robb Report- Worth Dec. 2003: 60-82.

Bodie, Zvi , Alex Kane, and Alan J. Marcus. Investments. 4th ed. Boston: Irwin/McGraw-Hill, 1999.

Cass, Dwight. "Private Equity." Robb Report- Worth Apr. 2004: 53-54.

Doyle, Jr, Robert J., and Stephan R. Leimberg. The Tools and Techniques of Life Insurance Planning. 2nd ed. Cincinnati: The National Underwriter Co, 1999.

Evensky, Harold R. Wealth Management- The Financial Advisor's Guide To Investing and Managing Client Assets. New York: McGraw-Hill, 1997.

Fabozzi, Frank J. Fixed Income Analysis. New Hope, PA: Frank J Fabozzi Associates, 2000.

Gibson, Roger C. Asset Allocation- Balancing Financial Risk. Homewood, Illinois: Richard D Irwin, Inc, 1990.

Giordani, J.D., Leslie C., and Amy P. Jetel, J.D.. "Investing in Hedge Funds Through Private Placement Life Insurance." The Journal of Investment Consulting 6.2 (2004): 77-87.

Gunn, Eileen P. "A House of Cards." Robb Report- Worth Apr. 2004: 57-62.

Hedge Funds- Definitive Strategies and Techniques. Ed. Kenneth S. Phillips, and Ronald J. Surz. Hoboken, NJ: John Wiley & Sons, Inc, 2003.

Jaeger, Lars. Managing Risk in Alternative Investment Strategies- Successful Investing in Hedge Funds and Managed Futures. London: Prentice Hall, 2002.

Jaeger, Robert A. All About Hedge Funds. New York: McGraw-Hill, 2003.

Kochis, S T. Wealth Management- A Concise Guide to Financial Planning and Investment Managment for Wealthy Clients. Chicago: CCH Incorporated, 2003.

Leimberg, Stephan R., et al. The Tools and Techniques of Charitable Planning. Cincinnati: The National Underwriter Co, 2001.

Leimberg, Stephan R., et al. The Tools and Techniques of Estate Planning. 12th ed. Cincinnati: The National Underwriter Co, 2001.

Nicholas, Joseph G. Hedge Fund of Funds Investing. Princeton: Bloomberg P, 2004.

Paulson, Bruce L. "Integration of Hedge Funds and Wealth Transfer Structures: Where Should They Be and Why?" The Monitor 18.6 (2003): 19-24.

Shein, Jay L. "What Consultants Must Know About Exchange Traded Funds." Journal of Investment Consulting 3.1 (2000): 31-38.

Shenkman, Martin M. The Complete Book of Trusts. 3rd ed. New York: John Wiley & Sons, Inc, 2002.

The Handbook of Fixed Income Securities. Ed. T D. Fabozzi, and Frank J. Fabozzi. 4th ed. Chicago: Irwin Professional, 1995.

The Handbook of Managed Futures. Ed. Carl Peters, and Ben Warwick. 2nd ed. Chicago: Irwin Professional, 1997.

Thomas, Kaye A. Consider Your Options. 2004 ed. Lisle, Illinois: Fairmark P, INC, 2003.

Weiss, Howard M. The Philanthropic Executive. N.p.: Aspatore, Inc, 2003.

Welch, Scott. "Comparing Financial and Charitable Techniques for Disposing of Low Basis Stock." The Journal of Wealth Management (2002): 37-46.

APPENDICES

Appendix I: 376
The Smith Family Request for Proposal Services for Family Offices

Appendix II: 417
Smith Family Investments – Investment Policy Statement

Appendix III: 446
Investment Policy Statement – Municipal Bond Portfolio

Appendix IV: 449
Investment Policy Guidelines – Cash Management

Appendix V: 451
Statement of Investment Policy – Foundation

APPENDIX I

THE SMITH FAMILY

REQUEST FOR PROPOSAL

SERVICES FOR FAMILY OFFICES

Firm Submitting: _____

   Name

   _____
   Address

   _____
   Client Contact

   _____
   Phone Number

The Smith Family
Request for Proposal

Contents:

Subject Area	Section
Company profile	I
Investment management	II
Investment consulting	III
Custody services	IV
Trust services	V
Credit services	VI
Concentrated Equity Strategies	VII
Fees	VIII

Section I

Company Profile

- *General company information*

- *Professional Staff*

- *Management & Personnel Backgrounds*

- *Assets under management*

- *Asset class composition*

- *Client servicing & personnel practices*

- *General questions*

General Company Information

Company: _____

Address: _____

City: _____ State: _____ Zip Code: _____

Contact Person: _____

Year Founded: _____

Ownership: _____

Parent or Affiliated Firm:
_____

Professional Investment Staff

Personnel Summary Professional Staff Turnover
As of December 31, 2003   Year   Turnover %

Portfolio Managers _____ 1998 _____

Research Analysts _____ 1999 _____

Traders _____ 2000 _____

Economists & Strategists ____ 2001 _____

Marketing _____ 2002 _____

Administrative _____ 2003 _____

Total Investment Employees _____

Management & Personnel Backgrounds

1. List your firm's principals or the executives in charge of your investment business along with their professional backgrounds.

2. Provide a list of the staff that would be assigned to our relationship along with their bios.

Assets under Management

Total Assets under Management

        1995 _____   1998 _____   2001 _____
        1996 _____   1999 _____   2002 _____
        1997 _____   2000 _____   2003 _____

Latest Year End # of Accounts Dollar Amount

Employee Benefit Funds

    Corporate _____ _
    Union / Taft Hartley   _____ ____
    Public Funds   _____ ____
    Total Employee Benefit   _____ ____

Endowment Funds/Foundations _____ _

Individuals - Private Portfolios,
Trusts   _____   _____

Mutual Funds (retail only)   _____ ____

Other   _____ _____

Total Assets   _____ _____

Asset Class Composition

Cash Equivalents   Market Value

$ _____

Fixed Income
Domestic fixed income – taxable _____
Domestic fixed income – municipal
tax free   _____
International fixed income _____
High yield bonds   _____
Guaranteed investment contracts _____

Equities
Large cap equities _____
Mid cap equities   _____
Small cap equities _____
International equities _____
Emerging market equities _____
Convertible securities _____

Alternative Accounts
Real Estate   _____
Timber   _____
Farm & Ranchland   _____
Oil & Gas   _____
Hedge funds   _____
Private equity   _____
Venture capital   _____

Total Assets $ _____

Client Servicing & Personnel Practices

1. What would the account manager / team structure look like for our relationship?

2. What is the average number of client relationships handled by the lead relationship manager and portfolio manager?

3. Describe, to the extent you are permitted, your firm's compensation structure for key investment and client relations staff. Are they incented for new clients and are they penalized for lost clients?

4. Describe your company's philosophy toward continuing education and credentialing of your staff.

5. Explain your approach to servicing the multi-generational, taxable client. How do you manage the role of taxes when handling their investment portfolios? Do you have any tax-advantaged products? If so, describe.

6. Do you offer any supporting services to investment clients (e.g., estate & tax planning, insurance)? If so, please describe.

General Questions

1. Do you have errors and omission insurance?

2. Do you have fiduciary liability insurance?

3. Is there any litigation, governmental investigations or administrative proceedings pending against your firm?

4. Have there been any judgements against your firm or any member of your firm in the past 10 years?

5. Is your firm registered with the SEC under the Investment Advisors Act of 1940? If so, submit a copy of your form ADV, Parts I and II.

6. Describe how your firm or the investment business of your company is structured. An organization chart will suffice.

7. Do you propose to use the services of an affiliated broker / dealer? If so, explain the types of transactions or services that would be channeled through it.

8. Describe any conflict of interest policies your firm has.

9. Briefly describe your internal and external audit procedures as it relates to client portfolios. What controls exist on your trading desk to prevent or immediately detect "rogue" traders.

10. If you are an independent, private firm, do you have a business succession plan? If so, please describe

Section II

Investment Management

- *Investment product inventory*

- *Asset allocation process*

- *Fixed income methodology*

- *Equity investment methodology*

- *Portfolio decision making process*

- *Alternative investment program*

- *Performance*

Investment Product Inventory

1. Please indicate which products you offer to clients and how you deliver them. Place an "x" under the appropriate column. You can mark more than one column:

<u>Asset Class</u>   <u>Proprietary</u>   <u>Third Party</u>   <u>Do Not Offer</u>

<u>Cash Equivalents</u>
- Money Market Mutual Funds
- Individual management

<u>Fixed Income</u>
- Domestic fixed income – taxable
- Domestic fixed income – municipal tax free
- International fixed income
- High yield

<u>Equities</u>
- Large cap core
- Large cap growth
- Large cap value
- Mid cap core
- Mid cap growth
- Mid cap value
- Small cap core
- Small cap growth
- Small cap value
- International core
- International growth
- International value
- Emerging markets
- Convertible securities

Alternative Investments
- Real estate
- Hedge funds
- Private equity
- Venture capital
- Timber
- Oil & gas
- Commodities

2. List your line-up of mutual funds, indicating where you will also offer separate account management as well (either through a third party or proprietary).

3. Briefly describe any alternative investment programs that your company offers or sponsors. Later, we will ask for more specifics on the investment approach and operating controls.

Asset Allocation Process

1. Describe the role of asset allocation in managing individual portfolios.

2. Do you employ quantitative techniques? Please describe.

3. What is the range of asset classes included in your model? Include a sample output.

4. Describe your process for monitoring asset allocation and rebalancing portfolios.

5. Explain your firm's decision - making process as it pertains to arriving at asset allocation guidelines for the firm's discretionary accounts.

Fixed Income Methodology

1. Describe the resources devoted to fixed income management and trading.

2. List the various types of fixed income securities employed in managing discretionary portfolios.

3. Describe your approach to duration management.

4. What are your quality parameters for discretionary portfolios?

5. What is the size of your municipal bond operation? Describe the resources specifically devoted to this asset class.

6. Do you use derivatives to control interest rate risk? Please describe.

7. Do you use derivatives to enhance return? Please describe.

8. Do you actively conduct or suggest bond swap transactions? If so, describe your approach.

Equity Investment Methodology

Portfolio Structure

For each of the questions below, you have the option of submitting answers by specific equity style.

1. What is the role of and approximately how much of your total return is attributed to:

    - Market timing
    - Sector / industry emphasis
    - Stock selection

2. Over a market cycle, what could your cash reserve level be in an all equity-managed portfolio?

    - Up to 100%
    - Up to 75%
    - Up to 50%
    - Up to 25%
    - Up to 10%
    - Fully invested at no more than 10%

3. If cash levels are raised to high levels, is the decision based on:

    - Subjective analysis
    - Quantitative analysis
    - Valuation analysis
    - Technical analysis

4. To what degree do your sector weightings match the S&P 500 or other index benchmarks?

- Precisely
- Moderately
- Differ substantially (by design)
- Do not relate at all (e.g., do not pay attention to sector weightings)

5. Describe in detail your approach to sector / industry weightings.

6. List the various equity styles you manage internally.

7. What is the average P/E ratio of each of the styles?

8. What is the average turnover in your individual, taxable portfolios?

9. How many stocks are in your typical portfolio?

10. What is the maximum percentage of a portfolio that you will invest in any one stock?

11. Do you control the aggregate ownership of the outstanding shares of a company? How do you accomplish that?

12. Do you offer quantitative products, particularly tax-enhanced index management? If so, describe your approach, indicating minimum portfolio size and fees. Also, indicate what index you are able to track.

Research

1. Describe the functional organization of your research department.
2. Are your analysts generalists or industry specific?

3. Do you have an approved stock list and how many securities are on it?

4. Describe the top down and bottom up stock selection discipline, commenting on the relative importance of value verses growth factors.

5. Do you have a ranking or stock rating system? If so, please describe it.

6. Do you visit companies?

7. Describe your sell disciplines.

8. Do you utilize technical analysis? Comment only if you did not cover this in the above questions.

Portfolio Decision Making Process

1. Describe your firm's equity portfolio decision making process. Do you have formal committees or is the process reliant upon a key individual?

2. Describe the discretion allowed to individual portfolio managers.

3. What is your internal process for reviewing individual portfolios?

4. How do you practice risk management, particularly in dealing with portfolios that deviate from the firm's guidelines?

Alternative Investment Programs

1. List the specific asset classes where you provide clients with alternative investments, indicating how you deliver those products. Where you use external managers / advisors, indicate who those advisors are.

2. Where you offer a multi-strategy hedge fund of funds, please provide the following:

   - Portfolio advisor and background.
   - Specific strategies employed and percentage allocation to each strategy.
   - Overall number of funds and list of those funds.
   - Process for monitoring not only performance but the execution of a funds investment approach.
   - Process for selecting a new fund and for terminating a fund.
   - Investment terms such as liquidity, minimum investments, etc.
   - Fee arrangements

3. Do you offer both low volatility (or market neutral) as well as directional hedge funds?

4. For private equity and venture capital fund of funds, provide the following:
   - Portfolio performance of sponsor fund or, if relatively new, performance of advisor or previous funds of the sponsor.
   - Industry diversification if available
   - Terms of investment such as minimum period, liquidity, schedule of distributions, etc.
   - Description of fund types
   - Approximate number of individual funds and total number of companies
   - Fee structure
   - Capital commitment by your firm and / or partners
   - Investment decision process

Performance

1. List your flagship managed disciplines for which you wish to submit performance numbers on separate accounts (individual securities).

2. For each discipline describe the composite of accounts and include the following in your response:

    - Is it AIMR complaint?
    - Number of accounts and total size of asset pool
    - Percentage of firm's assets for this discipline

3. Provide performance numbers in the following format:

    - 1,2,3,4, and 5 years annualized
    - Performance for each of last five calendar years
    - Performance since inception or last 10 years.
    - Quarterly performance for past five years

4. Indicate approximate degree of performance depression among individually managed portfolios.

5. Can you provide performance after-tax and net of fees?

6. Highlight your historical performance in up markets versus down markets. Explain the methodology used.

Appendices

Section III

Investment Consulting

- *Business profile*

- *Investment infrastructure & process*

- *Reporting & controls*

- *Client servicing*

Business Profile

1. How long has your firm been in the investment consulting business?

2. Through what organizational structure is this service delivered if you are part of a multi-faceted banking and brokerage firm?

3. Provide a breakdown of your client base accordingly:

Client Type	# of Relationships	Asset Value
Private individuals/trusts		
Private & public foundations		
University/school endowments		
Corporate retirement funds		
Public funds		
Taft Hartley funds		
Other		
Total	_____	_____

4. Indicate the specific types of consulting services your firm provides, including but not limited to: investment policy development, manager search & selection and performance measurement.

5. Can you act as a trustee?

6. Can your platform accommodate managers outside of your data base? Are you willing to follow those managers that we may wish to retain?

Investment Infrastructure and Process

1. Describe your approach to asset allocation. Specifically cover inputs to your model, range of asset classes covered and philosophy on rebalancing. Provide a sample of your output.

2. Describe your manager data base encompassing the following:

   - Number of managers in universe
   - Name of data base if provided by a third party
   - Asset classes and styles covered

3. Fully describe your process for selecting / recommending investment managers. Comment on both the quantitative as well as qualitative measures you employ.

4. Comment on why and when you would terminate an investment manager. On average, how many managers might you terminate in a given year?

5. How many managers are on your "highly recommended" list?

6. Describe the type and number of professional resources allocated to the investment consulting business. Provide their functional responsibilities.

7. Do you conduct on-site visits to investment managers? How often do you visit managers you are presently engaging?

Reporting and Controls

1. Provide a sample of your client reports.

2. Do you provide clients with on-line access to their portfolios?

3. How often do you provide full performance reports?

4. How often do you perform due diligence on your managers and describe the process?

5. Do you provide written summaries, for clients, on each of your recommended managers?

6. Describe your conflict of interest policies. Does your firm maintain other business relationships with its investment managers beyond the consulting field? If so, please describe fully.

7. Describe your process for portfolio rebalancing as it pertains to investment managers.

Client Servicing

1. How frequently do you conduct face-to-face review meetings with clients?

2. Describe the relationship team that would service this relationship from an investment consulting standpoint only. Provide bios on each member.

3. How many clients would a lead relationship manager cover?

4. Does your firm have experts in tax planning and trust management? If not, how does your firm handle some of the tax & wealth transfer issues that may arise in large, multi-generational relationships that operate through trusts?

Section IV

Custody

- *Business profile*

- *Transaction processing*

- *Accounting system*

- *Performance evaluation*

- *Other services*

Business Profile

1. How many custody assets does your firm handle? These would be assets over which you have no investment responsibilities.

2. What is the breakdown by client type:

Client Type	Assets
Individuals & trusts	
Endowments	
Corporate retirement	
Public entities	
Taft Hartley funds	
Other	
Total	_____

3. Who would be servicing the relationship? Provide a bio

4. How many relationships do you have over:

- 50 million
- 120 million
- 250 million
- 500 million

Transaction Processing

1. Are purchases and sales charged or credited on the contractual settlement date, the actual settlement date or some other date?

2. Are dividends and interest credited on the payable date, date of receipt or some other date?

3. Describe your cash sweep mechanism in terms of when cash is invested and into what vehicles?

Accounting System

1. Do you operate a proprietary (in house) accounting system. If not, what system do you use?

2. Provide sample asset statements and transaction reports.

3. When are your month-end statements available for clients?

4. Does your system enable one to create consolidated statements for entire relationships or groupings of accounts?

5. Can you offer unitized accounting?

6. Do you provide income and principal accounting, for trust accounts? Do you have a full scale master trustee platform?

7. Do you provide year-end annual statements to assist in tax return preparation?

8. Do clients have on-line access to your system? If so, describe the capabilities of this system, including but not limited to the following:

    - Is it internet-based?
    - What standard screens or reports are available?
    - Do clients have the ability to download information and create customized reports?
    - What PC system configuration must the client have?
    - How current is the pricing of securities?
    - Can clients access realized gain & loss information?

Performance Evaluation

1. Is your system proprietary or do you access a third party platform? If you utilize an external system, what is it?

2. Does your system provide summary asset allocation data by:
    - Asset class
    - Manager
    - Product type

3. Can you provide returns over designated time periods for:
    - total portfolio
    - each asset class
    - each manager
    - each asset class within a manager

4. Does your system provide comparisons to relevant market indices? If so, what indices are available within your system?

5. Provide a sample performance report with all supporting schedules. If this report contains answers to questions 6 through 8, you do not need to respond below.

6. Does your report provide sector / industry charts comparing the portfolio to market indices?

7. Do you provide attribution analysis by manager?

8. For fixed income managers, do you provide:

    - Quality analysis
    - Maturity schedules
    - Sector percentages
    - Coupon percentages

9. Can you show non-marketable assets if clients provide pricing information?

10. Is performance data available on line and can it be downloaded into excel or other spreadsheet software?

11. How soon after the end of a period are performance reports available?

12. Can you provide performance aggregation reporting on assets you do not directly custody? If not, are you able to work through a third party "aggregator?"

Other Services

1. Do you provide global custody?

2. Is your system proprietary or do clients access it though a third party? If through a third party, who is it?

3. Does this system integrate into your domestic accounting system? Do you also provide performance measurement?

4. Is the global custody system available on-line?

5. Provide asample account statement?

6. Do you offer securities lending?

7. Do you provide options and future accounting?

8. Do you provide fiduciary, foundation and individual tax preparations?

9. Do you have a prime brokerage platform and what services are offered through it?

Section V

Trust Service

- *Company profile*

- *Product & service inventory*

- *Client servicing structure*

- *Operations support*

Company Profile

1. Is your firm a bank, brokerage firm or private (independently owned) trust company?

2. What are your firm's personal trust assets and number of accounts?

3. What are your firm's private foundation and charitable trust assets?

4. How long has your firm offered trust services?

5. How does the trust function fit within your organizational structure? Describe the functional structure of your trust business.

6. Does your firm operate under a state or national charter?

7. In which states do you have physical offices to service this business?

8. In which additional states, where you do not have offices, are you authorized to do business?

9. Where you do not have a physical presence in a particular state, describe how you service and support that business.

Product and Service Inventory

1. Listed below are a variety of trust products. For each, indicate whether you presently offer and administer them and then estimate what percentage each is of your total trust business:

Type   Offered (Y or N)   % of Business

Living Trusts
- Revocable living trusts
- Grantor retained annuity (GRAT)
- Grantor retained unitrusts (GRUT)
- Dynasty trusts
- Intentionally defective grantor trust
- Family limited partnership vehicles
- Limited liability companies
- Trust for minors (e.g. Sections 2503-c and 2503b)
- Rabbi and secular trusts
- IRAs
- Irrevocable living trusts
- Qualified personal residence trusts
- Standby trusts
- Offshore trusts for nonresidents
- Irrevocable like insurance trusts

Charitable Trusts
- Charitable remainder unitrusts (CRUT)
- Charitable remainder annuity trusts (CRAT)
- Charitable lead unitrusts (CLUT)
- Charitable lead annuity trusts (CLAT)
- Private foundations
- Community foundation trusts

- Supporting organization trusts

Testamentary Trusts
- Marital power of appointment trust
- Residuary/Credit shelter/By-Pass trusts
- QTIP trusts
- Estate trusts
- Qualified domestic trusts
- Pour over trusts

2. Which of the following services do you offer and which are performed internally vs. those that are outsourced? Also, are they centralized or decentralized?

Function	Offered? (Y or N)	Internal or Outsourced? (I or O)	Centralized or Decentralized? (C or D)

- Administration
- Operations
- Tax Preparation
- Investment Management
- Small/closely held business evaluations
- Bill paying
- Estate settlement
- Real estate management
- Oil, gas and mineral mgt
- Financial planning
- Any other services provided by outside vendor

3. What types of investment options do you offer? Also, please rank in order of most frequently selected, 1 being the most frequently selected.

Investment	Offered? (Y or N)	Rank

- Internal individual portfolio management
- Internally managed common trust funds
- External individual portfolio management
- External portfolio management
- Mutual funds
- Pooled income funds
- Alternative investments

4. Are there specialty units for the following services?

Function	Yes or No (Y or N)

- Philanthropic unit
- Family offices
- Private banking
- Closely held / small businesses

Section V

Client Servicing Structure

1. Do you have specialized fiduciary officers? How many trust officers does your firm employ?

2. Provide biographies of the senior trust officers of your firm. Also, if you have multiple offices, provide biographies of the local officer(s) that will service our relationship.

3. How many relationship would a typical fiduciary officer handle and does this vary by size and complexity?

4. Are fiduciary relationships tiered where small accounts are handled in separate units? Please describe.

5. What types of access do clients have to their accounts?

Access Method	High Net Worth	Average Sized Clients	Small Clients

- Face-to-face

- Dedicated, assigned contact

- Client service center/ 800 line

- Internet access

- PC Dial up Wireless/PDA

Operations Support

1. Do you operate an in-house trust accounting system or is it outsourced? If outsourced, who is your provider? What specific <u>systems</u> and software are utilized across your business?

2. Describe your operations organization by functionality.

3. Do you prepare fiduciary tax returns in house or do you outsource them? If outsourced, who is your provider?

4. Describe, more fully your capabilities to handle these assets:

    - Real estate including commercial properties
    - Closely held businesses
    - Farm and ranchland
    - Timber properties
    - Oil and gas properties

Section VI

Banking and Credit Services

1. Do you provide the following banking services:

   - Credit cards with increased limits for high net worth clients?
   - Credit cards with dividend miles? Which airlines do you cover?
   - Foreign exchange services? Also, in which major international cities do you have offices?
   - Online bill paying services?
   - Wire transfers?

2. Do you have a consumer website that enables clients to access their accounts, pay bills and view balances at other institutions?

3. Does your website offer access to your brokerage platform? Describe these features.

4. Do you offer the following credit programs?

   - Mortgages
   - Home equity lines
   - Loans to purchase private aircraft
   - Loans to purchase yachts
   - Loans to purchase fine art
   - Stock option financing
   - Generational asset transfer funding

5. Does your firm provide interest rate management programs via swaps, caps and collars? Please describe.

Section VII

Concentrated Equity Strategies

1. Does your firm advise clients on strategies for hedging and monetizing significant equity positions? Describe the scope of your capabilities.

2. For each of the strategies listed below, indicate whether your firm has the capability to execute the transaction on your firm's trading desk or whether you outsource it to a third party.

<u>Strategy</u>   <u>In House</u>   <u>Third Party</u>

- Put & call options
- Costless collars
- Participating collars
- Costless put spread collars
- Variable share pre-paid forwards
- Premium equity amortizing contingent sales

3. Fully describe your firm's capabilities to advise clients on restricted stock sales. In particular, cover your firm's expertise to advise clients on the legal, reporting and tax issues surrounding restricted stock.

4. Provide data on the size of your equity risk management business and the length of time you have offered these services.

5. Do you offer exchange funds? If so, describe the features and benefits of your program. At this stage, please provide highlights only.

Section VIII

Fees

1. Provide a full schedule of fees for each service line.

2. Do you offer rebates on internally-managed mutual funds where you also charge an investment management fee on the portfolio?

3. Do you offer bundled as well as unbundled pricing?

APPENDIX II

SMITH FAMILY INVESTMENTS

INVESTMENT POLICY STATEMENT

I. INTRODUCTION

This Statement of Investment Policy governs the investment management of the assets for the Smith Family (hereinafter referred to as the "investor"). The statement outlines the macro-level process of allocating assets to a broad group of asset classes and securities. The policies and objectives provided below apply directly to the assets to be managed and advised under the direction of Main Street Investment Advisors (hereinafter referred to as the "advisor"). The Statement will provide realistic risk guidelines to help establish asset allocations and asset class strategies as well as to direct the selection of investment managers. This Statement has also been written to document procedures in monitoring and evaluating the Family's Investment Portfolios through establishing investment restrictions to be placed upon the managers and will outline procedures for policy and performance review.

This Investment Policy Statement (IPS) is not a contract, but serves as a Letter of Understanding (LOU) between all directly involved and interested parties. Legal counsel has not reviewed this investment policy statement. The Advisor and the Investor use it at their own discretion. This IPS is intended to be a summary of an investment philosophy and the procedures that provide guidance for the Investor, Advisor and Investment Managers. The investment policies described in this IPS should be dynamic, and the IPS should be reviewed for validity on an annual basis as a minimum maintenance measure. These policies should reflect the Investor's current status and philosophy regarding the investment of the Portfolio. These policies will be reviewed and revised periodically to ensure they adequately reflect any changes related to the Portfolio, to the Investor or to the capital markets.

It is understood that there can be no guarantee about the attainment of the goals or investment objectives outlined herein.

This investment policy statement covers the following portfolios with approximate market values as of June 30, 2004:

Smith Family Investments L.P.	$30 million
RWS Unitrust #1	10 million
RWS Unitrust #2	5 million
Smith Family Holdings, LLC	3 million
Grantor Retained Annuity Trust	2 million
T/U/W Charles A. Smith	27 million
Smith Children's Trust	7 million

Additionally, the family maintains a substantial position in Smith Corporation stock along with significant real estate, including farm and ranchland.

PURPOSE OF STATEMENT

In general, the purpose of this Statement is to articulate the goals and objectives of the portfolios and to direct the investment management of the assets toward desired results. Specifically this Statement will cover the following:

- Establishing overall investment objectives encompassing expected return, risk levels, and income.
- Articulating attitudes toward investment portfolio risk.

- Developing guidelines and constraints including tax efficiency, marketability, liquidity, time horizon, legal issues and any other unique circumstances.

- Establishing a framework for portfolio construction, addressing such issues as diversification strategies, asset class preferences, asset allocation alternatives and guidelines.

- Broadly discussing the strategic options for managing the Smith stock position.

- Stating the broad criteria for selecting and terminating investment managers.

- Establishing performance benchmarks for individual investment managers along with operating restrictions.

- Discussing the process for performance evaluation and rebalancing the portfolios.

- Articulating the responsibilities of the investor, advisor, investment managers and custodian.

INVESTMENT OBJECTIVES

1. <u>Overall Portfolio Return Objective</u>

    The primary objective of the Portfolios is to attain an average annual total return (net of investment fees) of 4.0% to 6.0% (pre-tax) above the risk-free rate of return over a full market cycle (defined as five years). The risk-free rate of return will be measured by the returns of 90-Day U.S. Treasury Bills. This representation of the risk-free rate of return will serve as a proxy for inflation. It is recognized that the real return objectives may be difficult to obtain in any five-year period, but should be attainable over a series of five-year periods. This performance objective assumes economic and capital market conditions that are consistent with historical norms.

2. <u>Individual Portfolio Return & Risk Goals</u>

The Advisor will, from time to time, present asset allocation alternatives depicting various points along the "efficient frontier". For each point, there is a set of statistical measures including expected return, expected risk and a sharp ratio (return per unit of risk). These numbers are largely based on historical performance and correlation among the asset classes. The present portfolios display the following characteristics:

	Expected Return	*Standard Deviation*	*Sharpe Ratio*
Smith Family Investments L.P.	8.2	8.7	0.94
RWS Unitrust #1	8.8	9.2	0.96
RWS Unitrust #2	9.0	9.6	0.94
Smith Family Holding, LLC	6.0	4.5	1.33
GRAT	8.0	8.2	0.98
T/U/W Charles A. Smith	7.0	7.6	0.92
Smith Childrens Trust	8.0	9.2	0.87

3. Asset Class Return Objectives

Continuing on, there will also be general objectives for each asset class. The following represent guideline objectives for each:

Total Portfolio   T-Bills + 5.0%
Large Cap Equity   T-Bills + 6.0%
Mid Cap Equity   T-Bills + 6.5%
Small Cap Equity   T-Bills + 7.0%
International Equity T-Bills + 6.0%
Fixed Income   T-Bills + 2.0%

4. Income / Distribution Objectives

Income from the portfolios will be largely derived from fixed income securities and the Smith stock dividend. However, the portfolios are largely invested according to a "total return" approach, producing both interest and dividend income as well as capital gains. Each portfolio will have its own distribution requirements which will be funded from the total return. The distributions may be needed for lifestyle, savings or investments. For each portfolio, the following represents the distribution goals, realizing that in any given year, the total return goals may not be achieved.

Smith Family Investments L.P.	4%
RWS Unitrust #1 -	5%
RWS Unitrust #2 -	5%
Smith Family Holdings, LLC -	4%
GRAT -	5%
T/U/W Charles A. Smith -	6%
Smith Children's Trust -	3%

RISK TOLERANCE

1. Statement on Risk Measurement

    Risk may be defined in several different ways. Risk may be measured as a loss of value of a security, of an asset class, or of the aggregate portfolio. Risk may be measured as the volatility in the return of an asset, sector, or the entire portfolio. Risk of failing to achieve the Portfolio's stated objectives may be the most pressing concern to an investor. The risk of allocating to out-of-favor asset classes may also concern the investor. Regarding investment managers, there is a risk of underperforming the benchmark. All of these represent issues the investor needs to deal with.

2. Elements of Risk

    When determining your risk profile, we consider the relative importance of each of these factors:

    - Preservation of principal
    - Willingness to tolerate principal fluctuations
    - Willingness to tolerate an overall portfolio loss in a given year
    - Need for liquidity
    - Willingness to stay with an out-of favor style and manager

3. Smith Family Risk Attitudes

    - The family is generally willing to sacrifice some opportunities for gain during rising markets in order to avoid large losses during declining markets.

- However, they subscribe to the theory that equities, while they carry higher risk than fixed income, will provide higher returns over the long term.

- Accordingly, the family is willing to accept market risk with it traditional equity and fixed income mangers. However, it is adverse to firm – specific risk associated with companies whose survival is in question.

- The family is willing to invest in and stay with out-of-favor or contrarian managers so long as the manger sticks to its style and performs well against its peer groups.

GUIDELINES

1. <u>Tax Efficiency</u>

   While taxes cannot totally drive the investment strategy, the family does expect its advisors to practice efficient tax management wherever possible. Among the issues to consider are:

   - Short-term verses long-term realized capital gains
   - Low turnover portfolio management
   - Use of separate accounts or partnerships verses mutual funds where possible.
   - Loss harvesting in equity portfolios
   - Tax loss swaps in bond portfolio
   - Yield suppression in certain portfolios
   - Estate & wealth transfer structures
   - Use of tax loss carry forwards

2. Liquidity and Marketability

   There are no substantial immediate liquidity needs. Given the total return objectives for the Family Portfolios, it is anticipated that the fixed income allocations of the above mentioned portfolios may not produce sufficient interest income to meet the full annual income or cash flow requirement. To generate the full income requirement, securities may be sold to harvest capital gains to supplement the interest income from municipal bonds

   Additionally, there will be a need to rebalance the portfolios from time to time. Therefore, the Investor has determined that all assets under this Investment Policy that are managed by traditional managers should be considered "marketable" or liquid relative to comparable assets in the same asset class and style.

   The Investor will have discretion to determine the suitability and applicability of recommended "illiquid", long-term investments over the life of the portfolio. Such investments may include, but shall not be limited to: deferred annuities, private real estate investment trusts, hedge funds, limited partnerships and; bank certificates of deposit with extended maturities.

3. Time Horizon

   These portfolios are to be invested over a long-term time horizon, defined as a full market cycle or five years. This period shall be long enough to withstand short-term fluctuations in the value of the overall portfolio.

4. Legal Requirements

   The significant legal issues include the following:

- Mr. Smith is subject to SEC insider rules (144) on the sale of his Stock.

- The Unitrusts are subject to IRS rules on charitable trusts as they pertain to annual distributions, tax reporting and remainder interests.

- The Portfolio shall be invested in compliance with the Prudent Investor Rule (or Prudent Expert Rule), under which fiduciaries must adhere to the fundamental fiduciary duties of loyalty, impartiality, and prudence. Fiduciaries must strive to maintain overall portfolio risk at a reasonable level. Risk and return objectives must be reasonable and suitable to the Family's needs; provide for the reasonable diversification of portfolio assets; act with prudence in deciding whether and how to delegate authority to experts and; be cost conscious when investing.

II. PORTFOLIO COMPOSITION

DIVERSIFICATION

The advisor will employ a range of diversification techniques as the means for managing risk within each of the portfolios. Among those techniques are the following:

1. Appropriately diversify the portfolios among the major asset categories of cash, stocks and bonds.

2. Within each major asset class, further diversify among various sub asset classes. Exhibit A displays the range of sub asset classes.

3. Select within each asset class, various style managers such as value, growth or core.

4. Finally, within each individual portfolio, establish diversification guidelines as to single- issue concentration, sector exposure, etc.

5. Employ correlation analysis when constructing the portfolios. Favor asset classes that may offer unique correlation type benefits.

6. Insure that the portfolios contain an adequate number of investment managers that have historically displayed attractive down-market performance.

7. Put together a group of managers that fit well together, by asset class and style.

ASSET ALLOCATION

Strategic Asset Allocation is the guiding philosophy for the family portfolios. Simply stated, assets are allocated to multiple asset classes and given target weights for each class. A band, or range, for each asset class is developed. The initial allocations are set at the target weights. Market forces, appreciation or depreciation of assets, as well as income production will change the relative weights of the asset classes in the aggregate portfolio. When the weight of an asset moves beyond its target range, the portfolio is re-balanced back to the target allocation (usually either quarterly or annually). Strategic Asset Allocation is a disciplined approach, making no timing bets on investing in specific asset classes. This discipline involves selling asset classes that appreciate, while purchasing those that are depressed. While it may be difficult to adhere to this "contrarian" philosophy, over long periods of time such strategic asset allocation ensures sufficient diversification by maintaining static weights to specific asset classes.

For each portfolio, the advisor has suggested asset allocation targets. These are depicted in Exhibits B through H. To arrive at these suggested allocations, the Advisor employed quantitative programs employing historical asset class returns, standard deviations and correlation coefficients.

ASSET MANAGER GUIDELINES

1. <u>Equity Managers</u>

    a. Each portfolio should be invested primarily in equities (common stocks and convertible securities). However, the manager is authorized to use cash equivalents and fixed income investments to the extent dictated by current economic and market conditions. Performance, however, will always be measured against equity industry benchmarks.

    b. When utilized, fixed income securities should be limited to publicly issued instruments rated BBB or better by both Standard & Poor and Moody's.

    c. Funds should generally be diversified. No more than 10% of each portfolio at cost or 15% at market shall be invested in any one company.

    d. Long puts and calls are permitted as well as covered puts and calls.

    e. The following investments are prohibited.

        1. Short (uncovered) puts
        2. Short (uncovered) calls
        3. Short sales or trading on margin
        4. Commodities

5. Currency speculation other than hedging against pre-established positions.
6. Leveraged transactions

f. Cashless collars, pre-paid forward sale transactions and other equity derivative hedges are permitted but only with approval of the family.

g. Assets will be broadly diversified according to economic sector, industry, number of holdings, and other investment characteristics. Investment managers will be selected and monitored to insure that their investment strategies will not produce an excessive concentration of risk in any individual security or industry.

h. With the exception of designated alternative investment vehicles, it is expected that assets will be listed and traded regularly on a United States securities exchange, over-the-counter (and reported on the National Association of Securities Dealers Automated Quotation System-NASDAQ), or on a primary securities exchange in a foreign market.

i. Investment in foreign securities by a domestic equity manager including ADRs/ADS/GDRs, should not exceed 20% of the market value of a manger's assets.

j. The cash equivalent portion should not exceed 10% of the market value of the manager's assets. Cash generation (from income or other) will be utilized to meet income requirements, for reinvestment purposes, or to restore the portfolios to their target allocations.

2. Fixed Income Managers

   a. There is no limit on the U.S. Government or Agency obligations.
   b. Corporate bonds shall be limited to publicly issued instruments rated BBB or better by both Standard & Poor and Moody's.

   c. No single industry group, as defined by Standard & Poor, shall constitute more than 30% of the bond portfolio and no single company shall constitute more than 10% of the total portfolio.

   d. The fixed income mangers may use money market instruments, as well as bonds, but equities are prohibited. Fixed income managers may at their discretion hold cash reserves, but with the understanding that they will be measured against an all-bond index.

   e. As the portfolio is taxable, securities should be purchased based on the best available after-tax return.

   f. The domicile of the beneficiaries should also be factored.
   g. Municipal bonds shall carry a BBB or better rating.

   h. No more than 20% of the portfolio may be in BBB rated securities. The average portfolio rating should be AA.

   i. Manager should use proper judgement in exposure to any one state.

   j. Manager may employ interest rate derivatives but only to hedge an existing position.

3. International Equity Mangers

   a. International equities are subject to most of the applicable domestic equity guidelines. This investment will consist primarily of large capitalization stocks of companies domiciled in both developed and emerging markets.

   b. International assets are to be held in commingled funds or institutional mutual funds. This provides the typical high-net-worth client more flexibility in meeting account minimums and more liquidity than investing in separate account vehicles.

4. Alternative Asset Managers

   a. Managers are hired for specific alternative strategies such as private equity, venture capital, hedge funds, real estate, etc.

   b. Within each strategy, managers are selected to operate under a set of disciplines and are expected to adhere to them.

   c. With hedge funds, the family will understand the specific macro-strategies it is exposed to and the appropriate allocation to each. Deviations must be reported.

   d. Managers will be required to articulate the due diligence and control processes in place. Again, they must report any changes in process to the family.

II. SMITH STOCK STRATEGY

BACKGROUND

The Investor has decided to begin a structured sale of its Smith Stock holdings over an extended period of time. As Mr. Smith is subject to Rule 144, he will accomplish this sales strategy through a 10(b)5-1 plan.

ALTERNATIVE STRATEGIES

Over time, the Investor may manage the Smith Stock by utilizing a wide range of strategies beyond outright sales. These strategies include but are not limited to:

- Put and call options
- Costless collars
- Variable Share pre-Paid Forwards
- 1 X 2 Call Spread
- Exchange Funds
- Tax-Managed Index Portfolio
- Gifting through FLPs, GRATs and similar techniques
- Charitable techniques such as charitable lead and remainder trusts as well as foundations alternatives.

III. INVESTMENT MANAGER IMPLEMENTATION

A. MANAGER SELECTION PROCESS

A key role of the Advisor is to recommend and monitor a variety of separate account managers to implement this investment policy and strategy. The process is quite involved and is summarized in an attached slide, titled "Manager Selection Process." Generally, when selecting investment managers, the Advisor and Investor will be guided by some of the following considerations:

1. A minimum 5-year risk-adjusted performance against appropriate benchmarks.

2. Rolling period analysis and up / down market analysis.

3. Consistency of that performance against the benchmarks.

4. Peer universe comparisons.

5. Evaluation of a firm's resources, operations and business model.

6. Experience of staff and length of service of key executives or partners.

7. Purity of investment style / attribution analysis.

8. Growth of assets under management and, if a small independent firm, its willingness to close portfolios to new investors when appropriate.

9. Relationships per investment manager.

10. Investment decision process and reliance upon a key individual verses a team.

B. MANAGER TERMINATION

While the Investor and Advisor reserve the right to terminate any investment manager relationship at any time, it would generally do so under the following circumstances:

a) Investment performance is significantly below established benchmarks and peer groups, and has been for an extended time period. Moreover, the reasons for underperformance are not convincing.

b) Failure of a manager to follow his or her prescribed style

c) Violation of investment guidelines

d) Significant departures from the organization

e) Change in ownership of the organization where the change is not acceptable to the Investor or Advisor.

f) Significant business growth or loss of clients.

C. PERFORMANCE OBJECTIVES

Performance goals will be established for each investment manager. These objectives will be stated in terms of achieving market related benchmarks as well as exceeding peer group rankings. These manager objectives are delineated in exhibit K. Managers would be expected to perform as follows against these benchmarks:

- Against the market benchmarks, managers must outperform over a full market cycle or over five year periods. Managers should also demonstrate some consistency in achieving these benchmarks and this will be measured by 3-year rolling period analysis.

- Against its peer groups, managers should place in the top quartile over a full market cycle or five years and in the top half over three year periods.

Additionally, each manager will also be judged in terms of achieving the following two risk related benchmarks:

- Placing in the northwest quadrant of the Risk / Return matrix.
- Achieving a favorable up market / down market capture ratio compared to its respective market benchmarks.

D. PERFORMANCE REPORTING

The advisor will prepare quarterly performance reports that could include the following features:

- Current asset allocation
- Changes in market value
- Growth of account over time periods
- Performance verses market benchmark
- Risk / Return analysis
- Equity sector allocations
- Top 10 equity holdings
- Up / down market returns
- Peer group universe comparisons

E. PORTFOLIO REBALANCING

The Investor and Advisor will generally rebalance the portfolio under the following circumstances:

- Major asset classes (stocks, bonds, cash and alternatives) exceed maximum ranges
- Sub asset classes exceed maximum ranges
- Tax loss harvesting opportunities

- Desire to add new asset class(es)
- Altered family circumstances
- Reaction to changing market conditions

V RESPONSIBILITIES OF PARTIES

Each party to this Investment Policy Statement has certain general responsibilities to insure its proper implementation. Listed below are some of the major responsibilities of each:

A. ADVISOR

Main Street Investment Advisors acts as the present advisor to the Smith family. As such its duties include:

1. Assisting in the development and periodic review of investment policy, objectives, guidelines, and constraints, including establishing, updating and monitoring asset allocation targets and parameters for the Portfolio.

2. Recommending the selection and termination of investment managers, as well as conducting investment managers searches when requested by the Family. Managers may be terminated or replaced whenever the Family and the investment advisor deem that it is in the best interests of the Family Portfolio.

3. Monitoring the performance of the investment managers to provide the Family with the information to determine the progress toward achieving the investment objectives.

4. Communicating matters of policy, manager research, and manager performance to the clients. The investment advisor shall be responsible for providing general investment advice and assistance. In addition, the investment advisor is responsible for recommending action plans for investment related projects, when appropriate.

5. Keeping the investor apprised of current trends and developments in the capital markets, as appropriate.

6. Being available to meet with the investor to discuss investment issues, as needed.

B. CUSTODIAN

The custodian, First National Bank and Trust, shall be responsible for maintaining possession of securities owned by the Smith Family, collecting dividend and interest payments, redeeming maturing securities, accurately reflecting changes form corporate actions, and effecting receipt and delivery following purchases and sales. The custodian will also perform regular accounting of assets owned, purchased, or sold, as well as movement of assets into and out of the Smith Family accounts.

C. INVESTMENT MANAGERS

Each investment manager will have full discretion to make all investment decisions for the assets placed under its jurisdiction, while observing and operating within all policies, guidelines, constraints, and philosophies as outlined in this Statement. Specific responsibilities of the investment manager(s) also include:

1. Discretionary investment management including decisions to buy, sell, or hold individual securities in accordance with the Portfolio's guidelines and objectives.

2. Adhering to the investment management style for which they were hired.

3. Reporting on a timely basis, monthly investment performance results to the Investment Advisor.

4. Communicating (to the client and the investment consultant) any major changes to economic outlook, investment strategy, or any other factors which effect implementation of investment process, or the progress of the Portfolio's investment management toward stated objectives.

5. Informing the investment advisor and the Family regarding any qualitative changes to the investment management organization, providing quarterly detail on the following: material changes in the organization such as changes in philosophy or personnel, growth of assets, results versus expectations, key decisions made and portfolio structure with regard to market conditions.

6. Voting proxies on behalf of the Portfolio (if applicable) in the best interest of the clients. If proxy-voting guidelines are distributed, the manager must do so in accordance with the stated guidelines.

7. Consistent with their respective investment styles and philosophies, investment managers should make reasonable efforts to preserve capital, understanding that losses may occur from time to time, in individual securities. Individual managers should not experience capital losses greatly outside

of the range experienced by their appropriate and respective benchmarks and relevant peer group over similar periods.

D. INVESTOR

The Investor will provide guidance and direction in the following manner:

1. Review, revise and approve the Investment Policy Statement.

2. Define the investment objectives and risk parameters.

3. Approve asset allocation structure and manager line-up.

4. Approve/direct rebalancing of the portfolios when necessary.

5. Provide the Advisor with all relevant financial information as it impacts the design and implementation of this investment policy.

EXHIBIT A

ASSET CLASS RANGES

FIXED INCOME

- Domestic Taxable Bonds
- Domestic Municipal Bonds
- International Bonds
- Cash Equivalents

EQUITIES

- Large Cap Stocks
- Mid Cap Stocks
- Small Cap Stocks
- Convertible Securities

ALTERNATIVE INVESTMENTS

- Real Estate
- Timber
- Farm & Ranchland
- Oil & Gas
- Hedge Funds
- Private Equity
- High Yield Bonds
- Emerging Markets

EXHIBIT B

SMITH FAMILY INVESTMENTS LP

ASSET ALLOCATION

Asset Class	Minimum %	Target %	Maximum %
Large Cap Growth	5	10	20
Large Cap Value	5	10	20
Mid Cap Growth	2	5	10
Mid Cap Value	2	5	10
Small Cap Growth	2	5	10
Small Cap Value	2	5	10
Fixed Income	30	40	55
Hedge Funds – Absolute Ret	0	5	10
Hedge Funds – Directional	0	5	10
Private Equity	0	5	10
Real Estate	0	5	10

EXHIBIT C

RWS CHARITABLE UNITRUST #1

ASSET ALLOCATION

Asset Class	Minimum %	Target %	Maximum %
Large Cap Growth	15	20	25
Large Cap Value	15	20	25
Mid Cap Value	7	10	15
Small Cap Growth	10	15	20
Small Cap Value	10	15	20
Fixed Income	15	20	25

EXHIBIT D

RWS CHARITABLE UNITRUST #2

ASSET ALLOCATION

Asset Class	Minimum %	Target %	Maximum %
Large Cap Growth	15	20	25
Large Cap Value	15	20	25
Mid Cap Value	10	5	20
Small Cap Growth	10	15	20
Small Cap Value	10	15	20
Fixed Income	10	15	20

EXHIBIT E

SMITH FAMILY HOLDINGS, LLC

ASSET ALLOCATION

Asset Class	Minimum %	Target %	Maximum %
Fixed Income	100	100	100

EXHIBIT F

GRANTOR RETAINED ANNUITY

ASSET ALLOCAITON

Asset Class	Minimum %	Target %	Maximum %
Large Cap Growth	10	15	25
Large Cap Value	10	15	25
Mid Cap Growth	5	10	15
Mid Cap Value	5	10	15
Small Cap Value	5	10	15
Fixed Income	30	40	55

EXHIBIT G

TRUST UNDER WILL OF CHARLES A. SMITH

ASSET ALLOCATION

Asset Class	Minimum %	Target %	Maximum %
Large Cap Growth	5	10	15
Large Cap Value	5	10	15
Mid Cap Value	2	5	10
Small Cap Value	2	5	10
International	2	5	10
Hedge Funds	2	5	10
Fixed Income	30	40	55
Hedge Funds – Absolute Return	0	5	10
Hedge Funds – Direct'l	0	5	10
Real Estate	0	10	15

EXHIBIT H

SMITH CHILDREN'S TRUST

ASSET ALLOCATION

Asset Class	Minimum %	Target %	Maximum %
Large Cap Growth	5	10	15
Large Cap Value	5	10	15
Mid Cap Value	2	5	10
Small Cap Value	2	5	10
International	2	5	10
Hedge Funds	2	5	10
Fixed Income	25	35	50
Hedge Funds – Absolute Rt.	2	5	10
Hedge Funds – Directional	5	10	15
Private Equity	0	5	10
Real Estate	0	5	10

EXHIBIT I

INVESTMENT MANAGER PERFORMANCE OBJECTIVES

Manager	Asset Class	Market Benchmark	Peer Group Benchmark
Manager A	Large Cap Value	S&P 500 Barra	Large Cap Value
Manager B	Large Cap Growth	S&P 500 Barra	Large Cap Growth
Manager C	Mid Cap Value	Russell	Mid Cap Value
Manager D	Mid Cap Growth	Russell	Mid Cap Growth
Manager E	Small Cap Value	Russell 2000	Value
Manager F	Small Cap Growth	Russell 2000	Growth
Manager G	Municipal Bonds	Lehman Index	Fixed Income

APPENDIX III

INVESTMENT POLICY STATEMENT

MUNICIPAL BOND PORTFOLIO

Purpose & Objectives

- Provide an increasing stream of tax-free income to family members.
- Long-term goal of 5.0% income return but will accept progress toward that goal in stages. Initial stage is to achieve 3.0% with new purchases. Investment commitments will increase as yields approach 4.0% with a long-term permanent portfolio in place at 5.0 %.
- Portfolio represents "safe money" with no tolerance for real loss of principal.

Investment Vehicles

- Municipal Notes
- Municipal Bonds
- Tax-Free Money Market Funds

Sector Allocation and Guidelines

Sectors as defined below will be managed to insure minimum and maximum exposures. These guidelines are not mutually exclusive and they will overlap. However, the portfolio in aggregate should pass each test.

Sector	Minimum Exposure (%)	Maximum Exposure (%)
Par Bonds (at 101 or below at purchase)	65	100
Pre-Refunded	0	100
General Obligation	45	75
Insured Revenue	0	50
Infrastructure (to be defined)	0	35

Maturities

- Intermediate term weighted average (3 to 8 years) depending upon yields available and required to meet income return objective (see above).
- Maximum maturity of any one issue is 15 years from date of purchase.

Credit Quality Parameters

- Average AA quality for portfolio.
- Size AA issues permitted by aggregate portfolio of A securities may be no greater than 20%.
- Short-term paper to be rated A-1, P-1 by Standard & Poors and Moody's.

Issuer Guidelines

- Single Issue 5%
- Individual Issuers 15%
- Individual Municipality 25%
- Individual State 35%

Service Delivery

- Actively managed portfolio

Portfolio Review

- Perform regular review of credits, particularly revenue bonds
- Review spreads among sectors, suggesting opportunities for re-positioning portfolio.
- Review for measurable bond swaps including yield pick-up, quality, maturity, etc.
- Review for tax loss swaps during rising interest rate environment.

Performance

- A highly specific benchmark may not exist for this portfolio
- Nevertheless, use a basket of market indices that display comparable duration and credit quality features. This would serve as a guideline.
- Measure income return separately against established objectives (e.g. progress toward goals of 3.0%, 4.0% and 5.0%)

APPENDIX IV

INVESTMENT POLICY GUIDELINES

CASH MANAGEMENT

Purpose & Objectives

- Arrange for an alternative to the traditional money market funds.
- Provide for extended cash management for funds not immediately needed.
- Investments must be of a high quality with virtually no principal credit risk.
- On the other hand, there could be slight interest rate risk as the average maturity would likely exceed those of traditional money market funds.

Investment Vehicles

Tax Exempt

- Municipal tax anticipation rates
- Municipal commercial paper
- Variable rate demand notes
- Municipal auction rate securities
- Tax exempt money market funds

Taxable (where tax equivalent yields surpass tax free instruments)

- U.S. Treasury Bills and Notes
- U.S. Agency Notes
- Commercial Paper
- Certificates of Deposit

- Eurodollar Deposits
- Short-Term Corporate Notes
- Master Notes
- Strategic Cash Reserve Fund

Purchase Price

- Can purchase discount or par securities
- Prefer no premium securities

Maturities

- Between 0 and 2 year maturity on any one issue.
- Maximum cap of 30% on 2-year maturities
- Expect average maturity to be 6 months but range would generally be 30 days to 1 year
- Would target a minimum percentage of portfolio to mature within 30 days if desired.
- A daily liquidity target can also be maintained.

Credit Quality

- Commercial paper and short-term credits to be rated A-1, P-1 by Moody's and Standard & Poors.
- Municipal and corporate securities must have a AAA credit rating by the major rating agencies. The credit rating may be achieved through MBIA or AMBAC insurance.
- Limits on individual issues as follows:
    - Individual issue 5%
    - Individual issuer 20%
    - Individual municipality 35%
    - Individual state 50%
- No limit on U.S. Government securities.
- Limits do not cover investments within mutual funds

APPENDIX V

SMITH FAMILY FOUNDATION

STATEMENT OF INVESTMENT POLICY

July 1, 2003

Table of Contents

Topic	Page
Overview	1
General Operating Guidelines	3
Establishing Risk Profiles	5
Articulating Investment Objectives	6
Statement on Mission-Related Investments	7
Determining Asset Classes and Allocations	9
Defining Asset Class Strategies	10
Selecting Investment Managers	11
Establishing Manager Objectives & Guidelines	12
Tracking Investment Performance	12
Terminating Investment Managers	14
Rebalancing the Portfolio	14
Responsibility of the Parties	15

Statement of Investment Policy

Smith Family Foundation

Overview

The scope of this document is to delineate the general operating guidelines, investment objectives, specific asset class strategies and the process for selecting and monitoring investment managers for the Smith Family Foundation. This process involves the following steps, each of which we will cover in detail below:

1. General Operating Guidelines
2. Establishing Risk Profiles
3. Articulating Investment Objectives
4. Statement on Mission – Related Investments
5. Determining Asset Classes and Allocations
6. Defining Asset Class Strategies
7. Selecting Investment Managers
8. Establishing Manager Objectives & Guidelines
9. Tracking Investment Performance
10. Terminating Investment Managers
11. Re-Balancing Portfolios
12. Responsibilities of the Parties

I. General Operating Guidelines

A. The Investment Committee of the Foundation is charged with governing the investments of the Foundation's assets.

B. Specifically, it is responsible for overseeing the allocation of fund assets and selecting and monitoring the individual investment managers.

C. To assist it in executing these duties, the Investment Committee may hire a professional investment consulting organization. At the present time, the Committee is engaging Bank of America to serve as its investment advisor.

D. The Investment Advisor shall submit quarterly performance reports to the Investment Committee. Additionally, individual managers will appear before the Investment Committee of the Foundation as requested by the Committee from time to time.

E. Subject to restrictions listed in these guidelines and objectives, investment managers shall have full discretion in their investment decisions.

F. As an overriding policy, no manager may make an investment which would be considered a "jeopardizing investment" under section 4944 of the Internal Revenue Code.

G. The Foundation will not permit investments that could be subject to the Unrelated Business Income Tax (Section 501-A) or the tax on Excess Business Holdings (Section 4943) without appropriate legal review.

H. When funds are needed by the Foundation to pay grants, they will be taken on a pro rata basis from each manager.

II. Establishing Risk Profiles

A. Risk can be approached in a number of ways and there is not necessarily one correct way to fit all situations. Determining risk is as much an "art" as it is a "science." To therefore arrive at a statement of investment risk for the portfolio, we consider the relative importance of each of these factors.

- Desire for high total return.
- Desire for long-term capital growth.
- Need for high level of income.
- Ability to tolerate principal fluctuations.
- Ability to suffer a loss in any single year.
- Need for liquidity.

B. The primary risk factors for the foundation are: maintaining sufficient liquidity for annual distributions, achieving a total return that will allow the Foundation's assets to grow net of distributions and inflation, and diversifying the investments to minimize the fluctuations of the principal value.

C. The Foundation also maintains certain attitudes toward the assumption of risk. These attitudes, as expressed below, will provide guidance to the Investment Advisor and Managers alike:

- The Foundation is willing to sacrifice some opportunities for gain during rising markets in order to avoid large potential losses during declining markets
- The Foundation is willing to accept market risk with its traditional equity and fixed income managers. The foundation is adverse to the firm-specific risk associated with companies whose survival is in question. Non-investment grade-rated securities and equity investments in such companies are not encouraged by traditional equity and fixed income managers.

- The Investment Committee adheres to the capital market theory which maintains that over the very long term, the risk of owning equities should be rewarded with a somewhat greater return than available from fixed income investments. Consequently, the asset allocation policy allows a higher concentration in equity securities as a means of enhancing portfolio returns over the long term.
- Notwithstanding the above statements, the Investment Committee may allocate a percentage of its asset into alternative investments (e.g. private equity, hedge funds and real estate) if it feels that the impact would be meaningful to future returns and the portfolio's risk profile. It realizes that alternative investment managers would not be subject to some of the same guidelines as the traditional managers.
- The Investment Committee will manager its overall risk through asset allocation and investment manager styles.

III. Articulating Investment Objectives

A. Using the risk profile as a basis, we then establish general investment objectives for the Foundation. These objectives address the relative importance of distributions, income, preservation of principal, capital growth, and liquidity.

B. Over a five-year period, the Foundation desires to achieve a real rate of return in excess of its Spending Policy. In today's environment, the Spending Policy is as follows:

Annual payout-	5.00%
Administrative expenses-	0.25%

Inflation-	2.50%
Real growth-	1.50%
Target return-	9.25%

    C. The Committee wants to achieve this return at the optimal level of risk. Accordingly, the target risk levels (as measured by the standard deviation) should range from 9 to 12%.

IV. Statement on Mission – Related Investments

    A. The Foundation's investment managers will exclude from the investment portfolio all stocks and bonds of companies engaged in the manufacture of tobacco, alcohol and small hand guns.

    B. The Foundation Trustees may elect to allocate some of its assets into program related investments as part of its philanthropic strategy.

V. Determining Asset Classes and Allocations

    A. Tempering the investment objectives with the Foundation's risk profile, we derived the general asset classes we wish to employ to implement the investment program. Providing background for these decisions, we employed a quantitative evaluation of alternative portfolio allocations taking into account an asset class's projected return, its projected volatility and correlation with other asset classes. The major asset classes are equities, fixed income and cash equivalents as well as alternative investments encompassing private equity, real estate and hedge funds.

B. Through this optimization process, the Foundation arrived at the following overall target allocation on a consolidated basis:

	Minimum	Target	Maximum
Cash Equivalents	0	1	5
Fixed Income	20	25	40
Equities	40	55	65
Real Estate	6	7	10
Alternative Invest.	0	12	15

C. Drilling down further, we have established general consolidated guidelines for the sub-asset classes as well:

	Minimum	Target	Maximum
Cash	0	1	5
Fixed Income			
- Preferred	0	3	5
- Investment Grade (Corp / Gov.)	15	20	30
- Municipal	0	0	15
- Convertible	0	2	5

	Minimum	Target	Maximum
Equities			
- Large Cap	25	33	45
- Mid Cap	0	8	10
- Small Cap	0	5	8
- International	0	10	15
- Emerging Markets	0	2	4
Alternative Investments			
- Hedge Funds	0	6	10

- Private Equity	0	1	8
High Yield	0	2	5
Real Estate			
- REITS	6	7	10

VI. **Defining Asset Class Strategies**

Within each asset class, there is a specific strategy as delineated below:

Equities

1. There are two major segments to the equity portion—core and specialty.

2. The core segment encompasses the large cap components and is further segmented between value and growth styles. Managers will be hired to focus on a specific style. Alternatively, the Foundation could hire a core large cap manager that follows a blended style.

3. The specialty segment encompasses the following asset classes:
    a. Small cap equity
    b. Mid cap equity
    c. International equity
    d. Emerging markets
    e. Focused equity

Managers could be hired in each of these categories to follow a growth, value or blended style.

4. For each asset class, we may elect to hire individual managers, participate in a limited partnership, or purchase mutual funds.

Fixed Income

1. The purpose of fixed income is to provide current income and preserve principal value. As well, it should keep down the volatility or risk of the portfolios. Therefore, it should be managed to achieve an optimal level of current income as opposed to "total return."

2. The fixed income segment can be delivered through the following asset classes:
   a. Investment Grade Bonds (Taxable Corporate & U.S. Government)
   b. Preferred Stock
   c. Convertible Bonds
   d. Municipal Bonds (specialty)

Cash Equivalents

1. The liquidity would be maintained in a money market mutual fund.

2. Where cash balances become large, our strategy is to invest out on the yield curve up to two years.

3. We should take advantage of opportunities to invest in commercial paper, variable rate demand notes, corporate put bonds and dutch auction rate securities.

Alternative Investments

1. The alternative investment asset classes the Foundation will invest in are:

    a. Hedge Funds
    b. Private Equity
    c. Hi-Yield Bonds
    d. Real Estate

2. The purpose of alternative investments is to promote diversification by combining low correlated assets to the portfolio. Alternative investments, depending on the unique characteristics of each class, can lower risk, increase expected return, and generate income.

3. For hedge funds and private equity, the Committee will generally favor a fund of funds approach so as to achieve adequate diversification among investment types as well as among investment managers.

VII. **Selecting Investment Managers**

A. Managers would be hired by asset class and specific style. We expect them to always adhere to their specific style.

B. When selecting managers the Investment Committee will consider both performance and qualitative factors. The performance factors could include but not be limited to:

- Five-year track record
- Rolling period analysis

- Risk adjusted returns
- Downside analysis
- Style analysis & consistency
- Index & peer group benchmark comparisons

C. The qualitative factors beyond performance could include:

- Firm's ownership structure
- Key personnel
- Investment philosophy & process
- Asset growth rate
- Business model
- Administrative resources & client servicing capabilities
- Attribution analysis

VIII. Establishing Manager Objectives & Guidelines

A. **Traditional Equity Managers**

1. Outperform the specified, relevant market benchmark over a full market cycle or five years. Also, managers will be compared to peer groups and will be expected to perform at certain levels.

2. The funds shall be diversified. Permitted securities may include common stocks, preferred stocks, convertible debentures, corporate bonds, commercial paper, U.S. Treasury and federal agency obligations and short-term money market funds.

3. However, each portfolio should be invested primarily in equities. The manager is authorized to use cash

equivalents and fixed income investments; however, the entire portfolio performance will be measured against a relevant equity benchmark.

4. No more than 10% of each portfolio at cost, or 15% at market, shall be invested in any one company.

5. While we are not mandating any specific sector or industry weightings, the Committee requests that the managers exercise prudence in the degree to which they will overweight a particular sector or industry relative to its measured benchmark.

6. Managers (handling separate accounts) are not permitted to invest in mutual funds where they are acting as an advisor unless those assets are excluded from the standard management fee or the mutual fund advisory fee is rebated.

7. Managers should not invest in mutual funds that require front or back-end loads.

8. Managers are not permitted to conduct the following activities:

    - Trading in naked options
    - Short sales or trading on margin
    - Purchase of commodities
    - Currency speculation

B. **Fixed Income Managers**

1. Achieve a total rate of return that exceeds the specified benchmark. Secondary objectives include preserving capital, maintaining a high degree of liquidity, and maximizing income. Additionally, managers may be compared to peer groups.

2. Corporate bonds at the time of purchase shall be limited to investment grade instruments rated BBB-/Baa3 or better by both Standard & Poor and Moody's. Rule 144a securities are permissible but shall be limited to no more than 10% of the portfolio.

3. There is no limit on the use of U.S. Government or Agency obligations.

4. No single company shall constitute more than 10% of the total fund at time of purchase.

5. Commercial paper should be rated A-1, P-1 by Standard & Poor or Moody's.

6. Certificates of Deposit shall be limited to banks whose senior debt rating is A or above

7. Futures contracts and exchange traded options on futures are permitted ONLY for the purpose of hedging interest rate exposure, managing volatility exposure, managing term structure exposure, managing sector exposure, and reducing transaction costs.

8. Managers should not invest in mutual funds where they are acting as an advisor unless those assets are excluded from the standard management fee or the mutual fund advisory fee is rebated.

9. Managers should not invest in mutual funds that require a front or back end load.

10. Managers are not permitted to engage in the following activities:

    - Trading in naked options
    - Short sales or trading on margin
    - Purchase of commodities
    - Currency speculation

C. **Alternative Investment Managers**

1. Hedge funds are expected to provide some stability to the annual returns due to their low cross correlation to each other and to the traditional financial assets in the portfolio. Each manager must adhere to the style for which it was selected.

2. Market neutral or absolute return hedge funds are expected to achieve a spread return above Treasury Bills. Additionally, their expected risk (standard deviation) should be low.

3. Multi-strategy or directional hedge funds are expected to achieve equity-like returns, exceeding the appropriate equity index over a market cycle.

4. Real estate, venture capital and private equity investments should exceed a benchmark of peer group investments in the marketplace.

IX. Tracking Investment Performance

A. Investment Advisor to prepare quarterly reports.

B. Investment Advisor to conduct on-going due diligence of managers.

C. The investment time horizon for each manager is either a full market cycle or five years, with the recent three-year performance also being important.

D. Investment Advisor to review manager attribution analysis and risk adjusted returns.

E. Investment Advisor to also measure rolling three year returns.

X. Terminating Investment Managers

While the foundation reserves the right to terminate any investment manager relationship at any time, it would generally do so under the following circumstances:

A. Investment performance is significantly below established benchmarks and has been for an extended time period. Moreover, the reasons for underperformance are not convincing.

    B. Failure of a manager to follow his or her prescribed style

    C. Violation of investment guidelines

    D. Significant personnel departures from the organization

    E. Change in ownership of the organization

    F. Significant changes in the foundation's investment strategy

XI.   **Rebalancing the Portfolio**

    A. When maximum asset allocation targets are exceeded, the portfolios will generally be rebalanced.

    B. Some re-balancing may also take place for liquidity and tactical considerations to take advantage of changing market conditions.

    C. Generally, this Investment Policy Statement and the Foundation's asset allocation structure will be thoroughly reviewed annually.

    D. From time to time, the Trustees and Advisor may even re-evaluate the overall strategic allocation and target ranges.

XII.   **Responsibilities of the Parties**

    Each party to this Investment Policy Statement has certain general responsibilities to insure its proper implementation. Listed below are some of the major responsibilities of each:

A. Investment Advisor

The Investment Advisor essentially oversees all of the individual managers and investments with specific duties that include:

1. Assisting in the development and periodic review of investment policy, objectives, guidelines, and constraints, including establishing, updating and monitoring asset allocation targets and parameters for the Portfolio.

2. Recommending the selection and termination of investment managers, as well as conducting investment managers searches when requested by the Foundation. Managers may be terminated or replaced whenever the Foundation and investment advisor deem that it is in the best interest of the Portfolio.

3. Monitoring the performance of the investment managers to provide the Foundation with the information to determine the progress toward achieving the investment objectives.

4. Communicating matters of policy, manager research, and manager performance to the Foundation Trustees. The investment advisor shall be responsible for providing general investment advice and assistance. In addition, the investment advisor is responsible for recommending action plans for investment related projects, when appropriate.

5. Keeping the investor apprised of current trends and developments in the capital markets, as appropriate.

6. Being available to meet with the investor to discuss investment issues, as needed.

B. **Custodian**

The custodian shall be responsible for maintaining possession of securities owned by the Foundation, collecting dividend and interest payments, redeeming maturing securities, accurately reflecting changes from corporate actions, and effecting receipt and delivery following purchases and sales. The custodian will also perform regular accounting of assets owned, purchased or sold, as well as movement of assets into and out of the Foundation accounts.

C. **Investment Managers**

Each investment manager will have full discretion to make all investment decisions for the assets placed under its jurisdiction, while observing and operating within all policies, guidelines, constraints, and philosophies as outlined in this Statement. Specific responsibilities of the investment manager(s) also include:

1. Discretionary investment management including decisions to buy, sell, or hold individual securities in accordance with the Portfolio's guidelines and objectives.

2. Adhering to the investment management style for which they were hired.

3. Reporting on a timely basis, monthly investment performance results to the Investment Advisor.

4. Communicating (to the investor and the investment advisor) any major changes to economic outlook, investment strategy, or any other factors which effect implementation of the investment process, or the progress of the Portfolio's investment management toward stated objectives.

5. Informing the investment advisor and the Foundation regarding any qualitative changes to the investment management organization, providing quarterly detail on the following: material changes in the organization such as changes in philosophy or personnel, growth of assets, results versus expectations, key decisions made and portfolio structure with regard to market conditions.

6. Voting proxies on behalf of the Portfolio (if applicable) in the best interest of the clients. If proxy-voting guidelines are distributed, the manager must do so in accordance with the stated guidelines.

7. Consistent with their respective investment styles and philosophies, investment managers should make reasonable efforts to preserve capital, understanding that losses may occur from time to time, in individual securities. Individual managers should not experience capital losses greatly outside of the range experienced by their appropriate and respective

benchmarks and relevant peer group over similar periods.

D. Investor Foundation

The investor (Foundation) will provide guidance and direction in the following manner:

1. Review, revise and approve the Investment Policy Statement

2. Define the investment objectives and risk parameters.

3. Approve asset allocation structure and manager line-up.

4. Approve/direct rebalancing of the portfolios when necessary.

5. Provide the Advisor with all relevant financial information as it impacts the design and implementation of this investment policy.

About the Author

Howard Weiss is a Senior Vice President and Wealth Management Consultant at Bank of America, specializing in the family office and private foundation markets. He advises clients on how to establish and run family offices and also provides strategic advice to wealthy families in the areas of investment policy, concentrated equity strategies, fiduciary structures, risk management, wealth transfer, and philanthropic management. In the area of private foundations, he assists clients with governance, investment policies and grant-making.

Mr. Weiss has been with Bank of America and its predecessors nearly 20 years. Joining Maryland National Bank's Trust Division in 1985, Weiss served as its Chief Investment Officer and later as its Head of Personal Asset Management and Fiduciary Services, overseeing operations in both Baltimore and Washington, D. C. When NationsBank purchased Maryland National in 1993, Mr. Weiss became head of Personal Trust and later Private Banking for the greater Baltimore market. In that position, he led an integrated trust, investment management and credit business. He also spearheaded the effort to establish a private banking office for Bank of America in Philadelphia as well as a Delaware Trust Company in Wilmington.

Prior to joining Bank of America, Mr. Weiss was with Equibank in Pittsburgh, where he served as the Chief Investment Officer and Manager of the Trust Division over a five year period. He also served in the International Banking Division for six years, working in a variety of positions, including Head of International Operations, Director of Correspondent Banking, and Comptroller & Operations Manager of the Luxembourg Branch.

Mr. Weiss has also held a number of leadership positions in the Baltimore and Washington, D. C. communities. For three years, he was Chairman of the Board of LifeBridge Health, a multi-hospital health care system. He is presently Chairman of LifeBridge's Planning Committee and still a member of the system's executive committee. He has also served on the boards of the National Aquarium in Baltimore, the B & O Railroad Museum, the American Jewish Committee, the Lyric Foundation, and the Northwest Hospital Center. Within the foundation communities, he is a member of the investment committee of the Morris Goldseker Foundation of Maryland and is a director of the Mary and Daniel Loughran Foundation of Washington, D. C. Additionally, Mr. Weiss served as Treasurer and a member of the Board of Directors of the Association of Baltimore Area Grantmakers.

Over the past two years, Mr. Weiss has been selected by Worth Magazine as one of the nation's 100 most exclusive wealth advisors. He is also the author of "The Philanthropic Executive", also published by Aspatore Books.

C-LEVEL QUARTERLY JOURNAL
What Every Executive Needs to Know

The Quarterly Journal Written by C-Level (CEO, CFO, CTO, CMO, Partner) Executives from the World's Top Companies

The objective of C-Level is to enable you to cover all your knowledge bases and be kept abreast of critical business information and strategies by the world's top executives. Each quarterly issue features articles on the core areas of which every executive must be aware, in order to stay one step ahead - including management, technology, marketing, finance, operations, ethics, law, hr and more. Over the course of the year, C-Level features the thinking of executives from over half the Global 500 and other leading companies of all types and sizes. While other business publications focus on the past, or current events, C-Level helps executives stay one step ahead of major business trends that are occurring 6 to 12 months from now.

Sample C-Level Executive Contributors/Subscribers Include:

Advanced Fibre Communications, Akin Gump Strauss Hauer & Feld, American Express, American Standard Companies, AmeriVest Properties, A.T. Kearney, AT&T Wireless, Bank of America, Barclays, BDO Seidman, BearingPoint (Formerly KPMG Consulting), BEA Systems, Bessemer Ventures, Best Buy, BMC Software, Boeing, Booz-Allen Hamilton, Boston Capital Ventures, Burson-Marsteller, Corning, Countrywide, Cravath, Swaine & Moore, Credit Suisse First Boston, Deutsche Bank, Dewey Ballantine, Duke Energy, Ernst & Young, FedEx, Fleishman-Hilliard, Ford Motor Co., General Electric, Hogan & Hartson, IBM, Interpublic Group, Jones, Day, Reavis & Pogue Ketchum, KPMG, LandAmerica, Leo Burnett, Mack-Cali Realty Corporation, Merrill Lynch, Micron Technology, Novell, Office Depot, Ogilvy & Mather, On Semiconductor, Oxford Health, PeopleSoft, Perot Systems, Prudential, Ropes & Gray, Saatchi & Saatchi, Salomon Smith Barney, Staples, TA Associates, Tellabs, The Coca-Cola Company, Unilever, Verizon, VoiceStream Wireless, Webster Financial Corporation, Weil, Gotshal & Manges, Yahoo!, Young & Rubicam

Subscribe & Become a Member of C-Level
Only $219.95/Year for 4 Quarterly Issues

Call 1-866-Aspatore or Visit www.Aspatore.com to Order

Management Best Sellers

Visit Your Local Bookseller Today or www.Aspatore.com for More Information

- Corporate Ethics - Making Sure You are in Compliance With Ethics Policies; How to Update/Develop an Ethics Plan for Your Team - $17.95

- 10 Technologies Every Executive Should Know - Executive Summaries of the 10 Most Important Technologies Shaping the Economy - $17.95

- The Board of the 21st Century - Board Members From Wal-Mart, Philip Morris, and More on Avoiding Liabilities and Achieving Success in the Boardroom - $27.95

- Inside the Minds: Leading CEOs - CEOs from Office Max, Duke Energy and More on Management, Leadership and Profiting in Any Economy - $27.95

- Deal Teams - Roles and Motivations of Management Team Members, Investment Bankers, Professional Services Firms, Lawyers and More in Doing Deals (Partnerships, M&A, Equity Investments) - $27.95

- The Governance Game - What Every Board Member and Corporate Director Should Know About What Went Wrong in Corporate America and What New Responsibilities They Are Faced With - $24.95

- Smart Business Growth - Leading CEOs on 12 Ways to Increase Revenues and Profits for Your Team/Company - $27.95

Buy All 7 Titles Above and
Save 40% - Only $114.95

Call 1-866-Aspatore or Visit *www.Aspatore.com* to Order

Other Best Sellers

Visit Your Local Bookseller Today or www.Aspatore.com for More Information

- Ninety-Six and Too Busy to Die - Life Beyond the Age of Dying - $24.95
- Technology Blueprints - Strategies for Optimizing and Aligning Technology Strategy and Business - $69.95
- The CEO's Guide to Information Availability - Why Keeping People and Information Connected is Every Leader's New Priority - $27.95
- Being There Without Going There - Managing Teams Across Time Zones, Locations and Corporate Boundaries - $24.95
- Profitable Customer Relationships - CEOs from Leading Software Companies on using Technology to Maximize Acquisition, Retention and Loyalty - $27.95
- The Entrepreneurial Problem Solver - Leading CEOs on How to Think Like an Entrepreneur and Solve Any Problem for Your Team/Company - $27.95
- The Philanthropic Executive - Establishing a Charitable Plan for Individuals and Businesses - $27.95
- The Golf Course Locator for Business Professionals - Organized by Closest to Largest 500 Companies, Cities and Airports - $12.95
- Living Longer Working Stronger - 7 Steps to Capitalizing on Better Health - $14.95
- Business Travel Bible - Must Have Phone Numbers, Business Resources, Maps and Emergency Info - $19.95
- ExecRecs - Executive Recommendations for the Best Business Products and Services Professionals Use to Excel - $14.95

Call 1-866-Aspatore or Visit www.Aspatore.com to Order

ASPATORE BOOKS